W9-AJC-423

101

HORSEMANSHIP EXERCISES

IDEAS FOR IMPROVING GROUNDWORK AND RIDDEN SKILLS

RIO BARRETT

D&C
David and Charles

This book is dedicated to all horses, especially Spirit.

A DAVID & CHARLES BOOK

Copyright © David & Charles Limited 2007

David & Charles is an F+W Publications Inc. company
4700 East Galbraith Road
Cincinnati, OH 45236

First published in the UK in 2007

Text copyright © Rio Barrett 2007
Illustrations on pages 44, 45, 170, 108, 146 and 147 by Dianne Breeze,
all other illustrations by Maggie Raynor copyright © David & Charles Limited 2007
Photograph on page 7 copyright © Andrys Basten 2007

ISBN-13: 978-0-7153-2672-5 hardback
ISBN-10: 0-7153-2672-4 hardback

Printed in China by Shenzhen Donnelley Printing Co., Ltd
for David & Charles
Brunel House   Newton Abbot   Devon

Commissioning Editor Jane Trollope
Assistant Editor Emily Rae
Designer Jodie Lystor
Production Controller Beverley Richardson

Visit our website at www.davidandcharles.co.uk

David & Charles books are available from all good bookshops; alternatively
you can contact our Orderline on 0870 9908222 or write to us at FREEPOST EX2 110,
D&C Direct, Newton Abbot, TQ12 4ZZ (no stamp required UK only);
US customers call 800-289-0963 and Canadian customers call 800-840-5220.

Acknowledgments

My eternal thanks go to my parents for providing me with an
enquiring mind and a childhood that revolved around horses.

Special thanks to my mother for always teaching me to be
'one think ahead of the horse', and for passing on her desire
for what Henry Wynmalen described as 'dressage on a silk
thread'.

Thanks also go to:

Anthony Paalman, whom I never met, but who's 'Natural
Training Method' shaped my ideas through his book *Training
Showjumpers* – the well-thumbed bible of my childhood.

Mary Wanless for hours of help with my riding, but mostly for
teaching me to think outside the box.

Pat Burgess for her inspiring energy and commitment to
training with love and respect for the horse.

Pat Parelli whose programme changed my life forever.

Ken Faulkner for filling in so many pieces in the jigsaw puzzle.

Andrew McLean for valuable scientific input, Maggie
Raynor for her wonderful illustrations and to Carina Parkes,
Kate Mably and Sue Gardner for their helpful photographic
contributions.

And the horses themselves – for their generosity and honest
feedback.

About the author

Auriol (Rio) Barrett began riding as a young girl. She was
brought up through the Pony Club and BHS exam system and
competed extensively in Dressage and Eventing. She worked
for several years with Mary Wanless, and then studied Parelli
Natural Horsemanship both in the UK and USA, becoming
an Instructor in 2001. She is a qualified Further Education
teacher, writer, accredited course developer and independent
horsemanship trainer.

www.riobarrett.com

Contents

Foreword

Rio Barrett's book makes fascinating reading and will prove invaluable to all equine enthusiasts. Every page is filled with common sense advice on firstly how to understand the horse and his behaviour and how he communicates and then gives a series of exercises to ensure there is a true understanding between horse and human.

So often one hears stories of people having difficulties with this noble and beautiful animal only to realize that it has been caused by mismanagement or misunderstanding of what the horse is trying to convey to the handler. *101 Horsemanship Exercises* sets out to broaden the knowledge of horse behaviour and in so doing this leads to better handling and ridden skills, which combine to increase basic welfare and safety skills.

The horse is often described as 'man's best friend' but if mistreated or handled incorrectly it can become a danger to all – just as much from overindulging as general ignorance or cruelty. Working through this book will guide the reader to a much wider comprehension of what makes the horse so special, or in most cases such a unique companion.

While it may not be necessary to work through all the exercises mentioned it is important to recognize the safety aspects when practising them. The reader will quickly come to recognize the benefits of 'working with' the horses and the power such communication engenders.

Most great partnerships between man and horse have been built on a combination of understanding, trust and communication; reading through and learning from the following pages should really help to set you on your way.

Good luck!

Jane Holderness-Roddam

Jane Holderness-Roddam was born in Catherston, near Charmouth, in Dorset. In 1968, she achieved sporting fame by winning Badminton on her horse 'Our Nobby', that was followed by her selection for the Olympics in Mexico the same year. There, she became the first British woman to compete in the Olympic three-day event and won a team gold medal. She has since ridden, judged, instructed and competed in many countries around the world and made a major contribution to equestrian sport and to the promotion of related education and training – including that concerned with improving the welfare of horses and ponies.

Her horses have included 'Warrior', which carried her to: victory at Burghley in 1976; the Team Gold at the European Championships at Burghley in 1977; and, to victory at Badminton in 1978. Following her retirement from 'event riding' in the mid-1990s, Jane remained involved as Chairman of British Eventing from 1999–2004.

Introduction

The primary intention of this book to provide practical suggestions on how to improve horsemanship skills through exercises that will create a greater understanding of how horses think and act and how to communicate better with them.

It is aimed at owners and riders who want to be safe and have fun with their horse and who care deeply about how the horse feels about it all. This book contains a set of exercises designed to improve the relationship between horse and human so that day-to-day interactions both on the ground and in the saddle run more smoothly, but more than that, it is an approach that will cause you to think about how to communicate with an animal whose actions are mostly guided by his need to survive.

There are five sections: the first is theory, which looks at what 'horsemanship' is and gives some insight into equine behaviour and horse–human interactions; the second is the process of training, fundamentals of movement and control of direction; the third contains the ground exercises; the fourth contains the ridden exercises; and the fifth deals with resolving specific problems.

THE TRUTH BEHIND THE TRAINING

'The biggest problem is that people like me learn how to compete before we learn how to ride, and we learn how to ride before we develop a language with horses.'
David O'Connor, Olympic gold medallist

Leisure riding on a wide scale is a phenomenon of the past 50 years or so and has given millions of people worldwide the opportunity to enjoy the many benefits of being with horses.

Previously it was only the very wealthy who were able to engage in horse sports, such as racing, hunting and polo. Other disciplines were seldom practised outside the military. The fact that people can now have access to these sports is a wonderful thing, but this new leisure explosion has its downside.

Horsemanship today is largely a forgotten art as, while more people ride for pleasure than ever before, few have been brought up around horses or people with generations of horse 'know how' and experience behind them, and the result is a lack of 'horse sense'. Add to this the fact that the horses we ride are more highly bred than ever before, because of the influence of the thoroughbred and the desire for the 'performance horse', and that they don't work anywhere near as hard as the horses of yesteryear and you have a volatile mixture, as is borne out by the high accident rate in horse sports.

Since the horse is no longer our servant as in days gone by, we have the opportunity to take a step back and look at things from the horse's point of view, to understand the fundamental reasons why they and we react and respond in the ways that we do.

It is our responsibility to approach our training with the utmost care and respect for this special animal whose unique qualities of strength and generosity have been integral to the spread of civilization and has also shaped the world as we know it today, and yet is innately sensitive and vulnerable to both misunderstanding and exploitation.

What is a horseman?

To me, a horseman is someone who understands the innate characteristics and behaviour of the horse and can work with a horse to cause him to think and act in certain ways. This is a person who can bring out the potential of a horse without taking away his dignity through force or mechanical means.

As a statistically dangerous sport, greater awareness and understanding would increase our safety and the welfare of our horses. It is also a highly rewarding way to spend one's leisure time. Whatever our chosen discipline, goals or motivation most of us crave a harmonious connection that is based on mutual trust and understanding. Horsemanship is a huge subject and there is a myriad of books, tapes, clinics and systems available often with apparently conflicting ideas on how to arrive at our goals.

Like many vocations, horsemanship at its best is an art and is made up of many factors, some of which are intangible. Describing an art in a book risks denaturing the very essence of what its about, and creating a systematic way of learning such an art can result in standardizing something that was originally innovative – rather like painting by numbers. Very often, the more information that is presented, the worse the problem becomes. Horsemanship is not prescriptive, it is creative and dynamic and each scenario is unique. *However*, science, theory, method, tools and techniques underpin and support the art, so having enough information is vital as a starting point.

To illustrate this, I use the concept of playing the piano. There are only eight fundamental notes, and yet the combinations on the keyboard are infinite. You may aspire to the artistic genius of a concert pianist but the first step you have to take is to understand the theory and learn to play scales. These are the tools in your tool kit. How and when you choose to apply them as your proficiency increases becomes the art. The better you get, the less you have to think and the more intuitive and creative you become. Learning your scales will not guarantee that you'll ever perform a concerto, but you certainly won't if you cannot master the most basic skills.

So the aim of this book is to add some tools to your tool kit and to give you some exercises to help you practise using them. It won't make you a horseman but it will help! The book is designed to help you develop a deeper understanding of training principles and offers many suggestions on ways to work with your horse to build a good foundation from which you can go on to any discipline. This is a map for your journey, not a book of definitive answers or some great new original truth. Everything here has been done and said before, passed down in many different ways through generations of good horsemen and what I offer are simply suggestions, possibilities, insights and techniques I have learned from a wide range of sources and that I personally have tried and tested over thousands of hours of teaching and training, on hundreds and hundreds of horses – it is not a system as such, though by following its natural sequence you will see how one skill builds from another. Through practise and

experience you will one day find yourself able to apply them creatively to the unique scenarios that will present themselves.

Learning is a lifelong process and this book is a distillation of everything I understand, at this point in my development, into its fundamental organizing principles – the elements from which everything else is composed. I encourage all readers of this book to explore a wide range of other ideas too (though getting a good grasp of one at a time will minimize confusion). By cross-referencing with other 'maps', a picture of the 'territory' will gradually emerge, like putting a jigsaw puzzle together. The insights and tools that are offered here should help fill in some of the pieces missing in the 'harmony with your horse' picture.

Sometimes your 'maps' will appear to contradict each other and inevitably the question will come up, 'But which is the *right* way?' Well, there is not necessarily a right way, just some ways that will work better than others for certain individuals and some ways that will have effects, desirable or undesirable. I strongly believe that

Control

We live in a world where control of just about everything becomes more widespread each day. Yet, as individuals, some of us are more comfortable with exerting control over our horses than others, and this I believe is a major factor that leads certain people to certain types of training. We naturally tend to look for a trainer whose style resonates with us because it fits with our belief system of what is best for us and (hopefully) our horse. Among the horse people you know, there may be some you regard as over controlling and some who are under controlling, but if we are to think about training, that's what it's actually for – control. The questions then arise, 'What type and how much is reasonable?' and 'How should we go about achieving it?'

Control of our horses is essential if we are to be safe around them, if they are to be safe in our world and if we want to do anything with them. Anyone who owns a horse controls it in some way – even if only to restrict its movement by keeping it in a field. I think this is an important point to consider and acknowledge. If we don't want to control our horses, we shouldn't keep them, as they will be a danger to us, themselves and other people who may have to deal with them, such as vets, farriers, horse transporters and so on.

Our job is to find a way to control our horse that is acceptable, and argument about that has raged for centuries. For each of us it comes down to personal choice but it may help to think that every way of doing things will have consequences, and its for you to decide (with some honest feedback from your horse) whether they are good, bad or indifferent. In this book, you will find some suggestions that will have consequences I think you will like, and your horses will benefit from and perhaps by learning to better understand our horses' behaviour, we will finally be inviting him to have a vote in the debate.

the important thing is to keep an open mind and know that understanding the cause of a problem will usually lead you to a solution.

If in doubt ask yourself, 'Am I doing this for and with my horse, or at him or to him?' Just asking the question and accepting the honest answer is the first step in the evolution of a horseman. If the answer matters to you, this book will help you take the next steps and give you some ideas on how to build confidence, responsiveness and control.

Leadership

We hear a lot about leadership and alpha dominance and often apply these concepts to the relationship we have with our horses as if we can replicate the position of an alpha horse in a herd. But are these lofty ideals really good descriptions of what is actually happening? If we opened all the gates and let the horses vote with their feet, we would get some pretty honest feedback about how much they see us as their leaders!

Much as we may wish for their devoted following, given the choice, few horses would rather be with humans than their own kind, except when they are motivated by something they think is in their interests. This is the key point. The trick to good training is knowing how to create this kind of motivation in our horses, so that they are willing to do the job we want them to do. Creating a robot with dead eyes is not the same. A horse that complies with the human out of total submission or with a sour attitude is not something to aspire to.

The dictionary definition of *dominate* is 'to have a commanding or controlling influence over'. We should not be bullies, seeking to rule our horses as dictators looking for total submission, instead we should assume a position of 'relative dominance' that aims for collaboration but where we retain the casting vote on any given situation and use it for the good of all concerned.

Just as horses establish a pecking order among themselves, we may have to set some firm boundaries to begin with, but after that the process can be remarkably subtle if we use the communication styles similar to those they use with each other to communicate, teach, guide and discipline.

It is when communication breaks down that the trouble starts. Behavioural 'problems' start to show up and we all too often place the blame on the horses, labelling them mean or bad, awkward or stupid. But there are no 'naughty' horses, only confused ones. Horses just do their best to survive and they adopt behavioural strategies to this end. The human sees the horses behaviour as a 'problem' rather than a barometer and such an attitude does not set us up well for resolving the issue. Sadly, the world is full of horses that have been misunderstood or dealt some injustice at some point in their lives. When events go wrong, it is often because the horse is mirroring our less endearing qualities back at us! Aggressive control is borne out of fear or frustration on the part of the human and the key to changing it is knowledge.

A dictionary definition of leading is 'to be someone's reason or motive for doing something'. A leader is defined as a 'person who commands a group', but it is important to remember that leadership does not mean we are superior – we must respect our horses for the amazing qualities that they have. Horses are stronger, bigger hearted, more forgiving and less judgemental than we are. They are extremely smart, highly evolved socially, predominantly passive, naturally tolerant and excellent teachers.

Perhaps we should follow their example in some aspects of our lives, and I think this may help to explain our enduring fascination with them – deep down perhaps we are looking to learn the lessons they can teach us.

It's easy to get hung up on semantics; however, no matter what words we use, as horsemen we should be aiming for a relationship where both human and horse sees the other as a resource that should be valued and respected.

This now leads us to examine what it is that horses value.

Motivation

A horse is a prey animal perfectly evolved for survival. Deeply suspicious with lightning-fast reactions, they have long legs for speed, acute hearing from antennae-like ears and almost 360 degree vision. Having eyes on the sides of their heads means their depth perception is reduced compared to that of a predator. Their eyes also have a different structure and they have to use their long necks and tilt their heads to adjust their focus for different distances.

Since they are constantly in fear of ending up as someone else's lunch, horses value safety above all.

The association between man and horse then is unlikely at best. Man, the ultimate predator, with his gripping claws and his intense focus on what he wants, is an unsettling influence on a horse. For man to get the best from the horse he has to adopt a different behaviour from what is natural to him, and that is partly what this book is about (and what makes horsemanship challenging!).

If you don't think that this sounds like you or people you know with horses, consider the scenario of the horse that doesn't want to be caught in the field. The human almost always adopts a plan of deception or stealth to capture his prey. The horse instantly wises up to the human with the halter and lead rope hidden behind his back, creeping up and looking suspicious and knows he has an ulterior motive!

It is not an instinctive reaction for a human to put pressure on a horse if he leaves and to take the pressure off the horse when he stops. Most people do the opposite such as standing in the middle of a field until the horse stops running away and then trying to grab hold of him at the first opportunity. People don't realize that they are discouraging the horse from being caught by applying pressure at the wrong time. This is because we think in opposites to the horse – we want to catch him, he wants to leave!

This underlying difference in instinctive behaviour is the root cause of most of the difficulties between humans and horses. For the slightest reason, they can go from calm to reactive because at that moment they simply don't feel safe around us. And it's quite a challenge to rethink how we interact with them, and especially to accept that we may be causing some of the behaviour we don't want. But if we could learn what it takes to motivate the horse to be happy to go along with our requests, to be a confident, trusting, responsive, willing partner, all the frustrations would dissolve.

Just think how much more enjoyable time with your horse would be if you were in harmony with each other, and how much safer if your horse would wait for your instructions when he lacked confidence because he trusted you – a horseman can create this.

Studying the behaviour of the horse (ethology) can really help the fear and frustration so common between horse and human become a thing of the past as we learn to approach our training with the horses' psychology in mind.

Comfort

Once they feel safe, most horses are happy to wander about doing very little. They like to have a full belly and to stand around with friends, interspersed with mutual grooming and the occasional burst of energetic play.

We can use these factors in our training to motivate our horses because they are specific to the species.

A horse can become highly motivated to do what you ask when he is confident you will deliver something he requires – for example, comfort – and you set it up so he understands how to get it. This is how you become a valauble resource to him. If you are consistent and can make his world more predictable, a trusting bond will form and the horse will willingly look for solutions to the puzzles you set him. If you are not, if you make him feel wrong or give no reward that makes sense to him, he will lose trust, stop trying and see you as someone to keep away from or to resist. He will start to develop various stress-induced strategies to this end, or may just shut down and hide from you that way – under these conditions an uneasy truce may exist, but it will never be a bond.

Comfort is a powerful motivator for a horse, but is sometimes hard for a human to understand. We find it difficult to release quickly enough, to leave our horses alone and to do nothing for long enough, but if you observe horses together you will see that they control each other's movements by pressure and release.

Hierarchy

In a herd of horses, whether they be wild or domesticated, there is a complex social structure in place that is constantly evaluated and renegotiated.

It is not the case that there can only be one lead horse at a time in a group. In a natural herd, family bonds and friendships have a strong bearing on relationship and roles of leaders and followers, and many behavioural scientists think that the 'pecking orders' we see are a more common feature in groups of domesticated horses who are less free to follow their own social preferences and have to compete for resources such as space, food and attention. Certainly we commonly see that some horses are more assertive than others and some will more readily defer.

When horses play with each other, like many other animals, it takes the form of play fighting, and is really a preparation for more serious encounters. It is usually (though not exclusively) males who engage in the most obvious play, as they prepare for reproductive rights, and the winner causes his opponent to submit. Whether

it is a 'game' or for real, the winner will be the one who controls the other and moves his own feet the least (see below).

It's pretty easy to recognize these games being played in the field as horses rear and plunge and chase each other around, but it also goes on at a very subtle level too and we scarcely notice it, particularly when they are doing it to us, which they do – all the time.

The feet are connected to the mind

Controlling footfall is the key to how one horse establishes dominance over another. This is what your horse does to you too. If he can move your feet, he will soon have you literally dancing to his tune.

If you think about it, all the riding disciplines focus on different ways to improve and test your control of your horse. That is what competitions

are about, the higher the level of competition the more exacting the degree of control required.

Successfully controlling a horse is more than just a physical factor however. The very best riders clearly have something more going on than just an ability to stop, start and steer at a given point. What they have is a connection with the horse's mind. Unity you could call it. This unity is the magic that gives a performance that is so beautiful it can bring a tear to your eye, and for me denotes the difference between a rider and a horseman (half horse, half man!). The horseman knows how to connect with his animal on every level, to become at one so they both think, feel and move together, and knows at which point they can unite to tackle a challenge or test together. Without this connection it is the relationship itself that becomes the challenge and horse and rider will be mostly working against each other – which is where accidents often happen.

The purpose of this book is to help you create that connection with your own horse, through exercises that will help you get through to your horse's mind and have him become your willing partner. You can control a horse mechanically but by far the safest, most reliable and most satisfying way is through his mind. If you can cause the horse to want to do your bidding, the need for mechanical devices is reduced and so is resistance. At this point, you can control your horse's body and mind as much as you can control your own!

Attitude, intention and the power of focus

On wildlife programmes we have seen the horses' cousin the zebra displaying his perception to intention as he judges whether or not it is safe to drink from a waterhole while a lion watches. The lion's body language belies his intention.

And so does ours to our horse. What we think and intend is given away in our body language, and horses are acutely attuned to this.

If you are short tempered with your horse (whether caused by an outside source or from frustration with him), he will be defensive. I believe that when we become frustrated or aggressive, the horse sees a difference in us that may be something like an aura or pheromone change, or perhaps he feels a different vibration from us. The same is true if we are nervous – the adrenaline in our system alters our body language in ways that can be very subtle.

Certainly, you can't fool them – they see straight through any subterfuge. In fact, that often alarms them too. They are aware of congruency – where your actions match up with your thoughts, or don't! Think of riding towards a big fence you don't really want to jump, your horse will most probably stop as your drop in confidence level will affect his. Or think of the pony that normally loads in the trailer OK at home, but on the day of the show he won't go anywhere near it. Why? He detects a different intention from you. The more you want him to load in the trailer, the more he perceives a trap; the more you try to look nonchalant, the more suspicious he finds you!

As a matter of survival, horses are highly perceptive and quick to learn what is in their best interests, which instinctively is usually the opposite of what the human wants. You could think of it as a culture clash and it is this that makes our interactions intriguing and also at times challenging. If you don't find it interesting or enjoy the challenge, you will find horses endlessly frustrating!

Our attitude is very important. We humans are quick to judge something that we don't understand. People are often to be heard calling their horses 'stupid'. The more that we understand our horse and learn to work with his nature, the less we are inclined to place the blame on him. Such frustration comes from our of lack of knowledge.

If we have a positive attitude, this will be transmitted, and if we focus, it will help us achieve the effect we want. Focusing is not just about where we look, it's where we direct our intention and our energy and is an extremely powerful tool. A concentrated focus will transmit your intention through your body and give your horse clear guidance as to what you are asking. It will also enable you to receive feedback from him and help you develop the feel, timing and balance of a horseman.

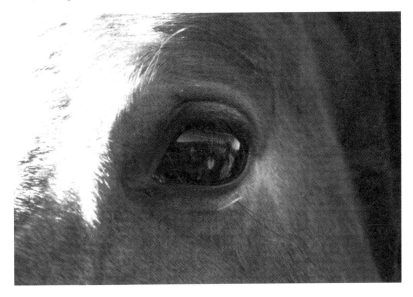

The way we use our eyes can convey our attitude very clearly (just as your mother or school teacher could you look at you and you'd instantly know if you were in trouble or not!). Bear this in mind when working with a horse. Looking at him doesn't have to mean you are putting pressure on him. It's the way you look at him that is important, and it works both ways – keeping your eyes (at least your peripheral vision) on your horse's body language conveys his attitude and intention to you in return. Accidents can and do happen when you lose concentration, so I strongly believe that when working with a horse you should keep your eyes on him at all times for safety but you should just be aware that there are different ways of looking at him.

Reading horses

We have looked at how horses read our body language, but it also helps if we can understand theirs. Just like us, their body language gives information about their intentions and emotions and this should have a bearing on how we approach our training.

You can roughly divide the type of body language exhibited into three basic emotions: confidence, fear and introversion.

Confidence is indicated by showing a number of the following: soft eyes, curiosity, soft ears, low head, soft ribs, still feet, even cadence, normal breathing, normal muscle tension, relaxation, blinking, thinking, responsiveness or accepting. Your horse may be confident but it doesn't necessarily mean he's doing what you've asked. In this case, you can approach more than retreat – pressure can motivate him to look for release (see page 21).

Fear may be displayed by a number of the following: fight, flight, freeze, tight lips, flared nostrils, high head, rigid and braced body, clamped tail, reactiveness, worried eyes, poor doer, shallow breathing, snorting, need to move feet or loose droppings. If your horse is fearful, you will need to do more retreat than approach, use low pressure and get subtle. Giving confidence is the priority, as without it you will have defensiveness and resistance and will never achieve relaxation.

Introverted horses are less obvious. It is a form of defence by which they shut down to insulate themselves from events. They may show a glazed eye with a far away look, appear very submissive yet look away when stroked avoiding eye contact, exhibit 'stable vices' (stress behaviours) or be on the outside of a group. These horses may also be in a kind of freeze mode; however, they can also snap out of this state in an explosive way – one minute seemingly calm and the next doing 'airs above the ground'. This makes them a bit like a ticking bomb. The key to these horses is to be aware and stay alert. Get creative, keep them interested and engage their curiosity. Use pressure with care.

Of course, these are generalizations and most individuals will display many of these to some degree at different times, but they may help you decide how to handle a situation at a given moment.

During your training sessions you will hopefully start to see more signs of confidence in your horse as you learn to communicate better with him and his trust in you grows. As this takes place, you will often notice that things are changing. When a horse learns something he will often lick and chew, as if mulling over an idea, or sometimes he will start yawning, not because he is bored or tired, but because he is relaxing and letting go of held in tensions or emotions.

These are important signs to look for, and are times to just allow the horse a moment to be with his thoughts.

Balance and biomechanics

In any kind of riding, there are underlying fundamentals that we cannot ignore. Among them are the scientific principles of biomechanics and balance. The horse was built to run, not to carry weight. In order to carry weight without damaging himself, his posture has to change so that he becomes light and manoeuvrable in front with the hindquarters well underneath to support him and his rider.

The horse's hind legs need to come well underneath him to take this weight, which is achieved by the use of his stomach muscles to tilt his pelvis under him and his back muscles to stretch and lift his back and allow the withers to be raised. As this happens, his front end lightens, his neck arches and his nose moves in more towards the vertical. His point of balance comes up and back to a central point about level with the rider's knee. When not contrived mechanically, it is beautiful, graceful, powerful and, above all, totally natural! If you watch horses playing in a field, they will have moments of this elegant, elevated self-carriage from which position of perfect balance they are poised to do anything.

Such collection with hindquarter engagement gives your horse strength and power and is very desirable in the right circumstances. But if he is opposed to your ideas, he may use this strength and power against you. So while you are learning how to get his heart and mind tuned to positive reflexes, we will first focus more on disengaging, which takes his power away. However, once he sees you as a valuable resource and is more 'on-side', it is beneficial to start paying attention to his posture so he can carry you without strain.

We tend to think of balance as being something physical but it is also in the mind.

If a horse is not balanced emotionally, he will not be balanced physically and vice versa. In the German scales of training (the bench mark of conventional training), the first requirement, from which everything else follows, is relaxation, that is, emotional balance. The opposite is tension, leading to resistance and stress, that is, emotional imbalance. Therefore you need to pay attention to both if you want to produce a 'happy athlete'.

By way of an example, let's look at impulsion. Our goal is that wonderful state where we have controlled energy – where our 'whoa' equals our 'go'.

Energy cannot be controlled unless you have balance. A horse cannot be balanced if he does not have a posture that takes more weight on the hindquarters and lifts the weight off the forehand (even with a balanced rider let alone under the influence of an unbalanced one).

An impulsive horse may get faster and faster because he is not balanced. Being out of balance is an unpleasant feeling that leads to anxiety, and this makes him move his feet more – so immediately there is a connection from the physical to the emotional that feeds back to the physical again.

You can address balance through the horse's mind or through his body and there are different situations where one approach might be more appropriate than another. This book provides exercises that work on both, but bear in mind that changing a horse's balance is a process and there is no quick fix. They naturally have their weight on the forehand because of their long neck and heavy head, and are inclined to travel without the best posture – just like we do. Improving his posture requires strength and suppleness that have to be developed and cannot be forced. Trying to make changes quickly will result in strain that is just as damaging as the poor posture.

Equipment

Buying the right equipment won't make you a horseman! Only investing your time and dedication in gaining knowledge and experience can do that, but having a tool that's designed for the job will make it easier.

Halter

For training I like to use a simple rope halter that doesn't have any leverage action on the poll and is light and comfortable for the horse to wear, but not very comfortable for him to lean on. Horses naturally push into pressure, and can get very heavy if given the opportunity. Leather and webbing halters do little to discourage this as they are wider than rope and therefore more comfortable to lean on.

Rope

I recommend a good quality 3.5 metre (12 foot) rope made out of yachting line. It is strong, non-fraying and washable, but most importantly it transmits energy impulses far better than cotton or normal nylon ropes. For more advanced work, you will need a longer communcation line, but the exercises in this book are all designed to work with a 3.5 metre rope. This may seem a bit of a handful at first, but you will soon come to love the feel it offers and its versatility. You can use the end as a tool for supporting your requests and the length means that if your horse is more lively than you would like, if offers you something important – distance! You won't be able to do many of the exercises in this book without one.

Stick

A stick is a very useful communication tool for groundwork because it gives you clarity and influence over a greater distance. It is even better if you get one you can add a string to. A stiff stick is great for training as timing is critical and whippy sticks don't stop at exactly the moment you want them to. They also sting even when used with minimal pressure. A rigid stick is more controllable and can be used quite firmly if necessary, without causing pain.

Please read the directions for the use of the stick in all the exercises very carefully. The idea of the stick is to make your communication clearer. You may need to tap your horse with it, but it can be just as effective to tap his bubble (the air around him). Use it as little as possible and only as much as necessary and *never* in anger. Once your horse understands your requests and responds at low degrees of pressure, use the stick less, using your body language and rope signals instead.

Rein positions and responsibilities

In this book, you will learn how to use specific rein positions to communicate different messages to your horse along with your intention focus and body language, both on the ground and when riding.

Each rein position performs a different function and 'speaks' to different parts of the horse's body, aiding clarity and helping to avoid the confusion that can result when reins and legs are used all together giving the horse blurred messages.

You may not have heard of the following terms before, and they are only one way to describe what is happening, but they can help demystify how to influence your horse's footfall.

❏ Neutral rein – the rein has feel or contact through it but is not asking for anything. Imagine it as being on standby – you've just made a connection with the horse (see Figure 1).
❏ Inside rein: indirect – the indirect rein talks to the outside hind leg in a turn. The fingernails are turned up through twisting the wrist, which brings the rein closer to the midline (yours and the horse's) (see Figure 2).
❏ Inside rein: direct – also called the lateral or open rein, the direct rein directs the front end and talks to the inside foreleg in a turn. The fingernails are turned down through twisting

1

Neutral rein

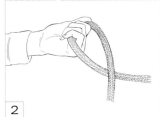

2

Indirect rein

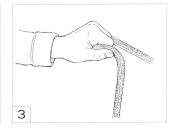

3

Direct rein

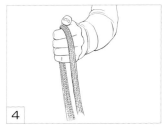

4

Supporting rein

the wrist, which takes the rein away from the midline (see Figure 3).

❑ Outside rein: supporting – the supporting rein talks to the outside foreleg in a turn. The wrist is not twisted and the rein comes against (but never across) the horse's neck. The stick is often used like a supporting rein to ask the forehand to yield (see Figure 4).

Problem solving

If something is not working, you might ask yourself whether it is because the horse doesn't understand or whether it is because he lacks motivation. Depending on the answer, you should alter your response (see 'Reading horses' page 14). If he doesn't understand, you need to find a way to be clearer. This may mean getting clear on something yourself. If you don't know what you're doing, what chance does your horse have? And it will usually mean breaking it down into simpler components and getting clarity on those before putting them together again.

When the horse doesn't understand, never apply greater pressure – this is like shouting at him in a foreign language.

If you think he understands but is not motivated to co-operate, it may mean you need to give him more incentive – more reward and comfort, or increasing the pressure to get him to put more energy into finding that comfort.

Either way, when an issue arises, try to work out how to be part of the solution, not part of the problem.

Move onto greater challenges

Many of the exercises suggest different ways of testing your skill levels with more difficult versions of the task. This is to help you have an idea of what could be done to raise the level of challenge and keep the work interesting once you have mastered the basic exercise. But watch out for that human tendency to try the most difficult first! The object of this book is to make it possible for you and your horse to make steady progress while maintaining confidence and softness and making lightness possible. If you ask too much too soon, you may find neither you nor your horse understand the exercise sufficiently to succeed at it or gain any value from it, and both of you will end up feeling wrong, confused and stressed.

The most difficult versions of the exercises are not dreams! They are perfectly possible for the average horse and rider to achieve given understanding, patience, empathy, methodology and lots of practise!

CHAPTER 2

FUNDAMENTALS

THE EXERCISES

In training there are essentially two objectives we need to achieve with our horses – desensitize them to the things they find scary and sensitize (or condition) them to respond to our commands/stimuli.

Horses are quick to form associations (good or bad) with actions or events, so how we time our communication through the application of pressure or release is critical for developing the response we desire.

You will sometimes come across scientific terms that make the process seem more complicated than it actually is (and it doesn't help that such terms are quite commonly used inaccurately). However, understanding some of the language used in learning theory is useful because it can help to explain, demystify and simplify training techniques.

Learning theory

Training an animal is primarily about establishing a series of conditioned responses to requests (or stimuli). Reinforcement is the name given to the way those responses are made more likely in the future. Reinforcement that is added after the desired response is given, such as food or comfort, is called positive reinforcement; reinforcement that is removed after the response is given, such as pressure, is called negative reinforcement. These scientific terms are used in the mathematical sense and are a bit confusing to the layperson who often misunderstands them thinking they mean that something positive (that is, good) or negative (that is, bad) is being done to the animal, which is not their meaning at all.

Horse training is said to be predominantly about negative reinforcement – that is, the removal of pressure following the desired response, such as yielding from your leg, or moving forwards from the halter. Although if comfort is the result of the release, there is an element of positive reinforcement too – indeed, some scientists argue that the difference is in fact indistinguishable.

Problems arise when pressure is applied but *not* removed (that is, not negative), as horses become resistant, dull to the stimulus, tense or chronically stressed. For example, if you use your leg but keep the pressure on after he yields, your horse will most likely become dull and cease to respond to it because yielding holds no benefit for him.

Both forms of reinforcement work together and complement each other by giving guidance, support and clarity to the animal. There will be times when it is appropriate to emphasize one over the other but training is less effective if they are not used in some combination.

It is the application of a stimulus, its reinforcement by some kind of pressure (be it physical or psychological) and its subsequent (and immediate) removal upon obtaining the desired response that creates understanding, acceptance and motivation in the trained horse. Good horsemen have applied these principles whether consciously or unconsciously for many centuries.

Desensitizing

The horse by its nature is alert to danger in all sorts of ways, and when that danger is perceived, every hair on his body tells him to move his feet. Sometimes he will freeze first, but generally, if he is able to move, he will. If he can't, he may fight to move his feet either in a struggle to get away or possibly to attack what is preventing him from leaving. It is rare that horses will continue to fight if they are given the opportunity to flee, unless they are extremely angry or in pain.

What people often fail to think about is how uncomfortable it must be for such an animal to live in a human's world. Not only is there potential danger from the human itself but also from other frightening factors such as equipment, noise, trailers, stables, plastic, barking dogs, crowds, traffic and so on. Many horses live in a perpetual state of anxiety, which can be detected by signs such as raised head carriage, wide eyes, flared nostrils,

twitchy ears, high tail, tension and a need to move their feet.

Therefore, for you to get the most from your horse and he from you, it would seem obvious that you should help him to overcome his fears. I say obvious, but it is common to see even highly trained horses spook at objects such as flags or flowers outside an arena. To give a top performance, a horse may need some adrenaline, but that is not the same as lacking confidence in his trainer, rider or surroundings.

In the German Scales of Training, the first requirement is relaxation. Without this there can be no learning and the horse will be defensively holding some tension somewhere in his body, and this will show as a resistance.

Confidence starts in his mind and shows itself in his body – and so does defensiveness. So the process of desensitizing your horse to as many different scary things as possible is a great idea, but how do you go about it?

There are a number of ways that you can do this. Which method you use will depend on the horse and the situation.

In simple terms, 'progressive desensitization' is the process by which you gradually build up the stimulus, allowing the horse time to accept each stage; 'flooding' is where you bombard the horse with a frightening stimulus until he becomes used to it.

Flooding can evoke a dramatic reaction from the horse and while it can be very effective when done expertly, it can be dangerous for both horse and handler and so it is not the primary method I am going to recommend here.

Progressive desensitization is looking for the 'threshold of tolerance'. It is the point at which the horse feels the need to move his feet in preparation for flight (to some degree or another). Consider for a moment what happens when the horse reaches that threshold in reaction to something – his head goes up, ears are pricked or laid back, eyes widen, nostrils flare, body stiffens, legs brace. Depending on the degree of alarm, he may display some or all of these actions. Our aim is to extend his threshold and we can only do this by exposing him to the things he finds scary. We are not trying to frighten him, but to help him overcome his fear and extend his comfort zone bit by bit – otherwise it may shrink. By hiding the stick from the showjumper, sedating the hunter for clipping or not riding the nervous horse out beyond the gate, we are not helping them become more confident – we are just avoiding the issue that in the future may work against us.

We need to understand that if we reach that threshold of tolerance and the horse needs to move, we must let him do so. This is most important for the horse and goes against the grain for the human, who usually wants to make the horse stand still (predators are programmed to catch things).

The key to sensitizing or desensitizing is timing. It is when you stop the stimulus that is important. Again it is back to the simple learning theory. The horse will learn to repeat a strategy that seems to carry some benefit. For example, if you try to touch him with clippers and he breaks loose or kicks you and the stimulus stops (you take the clippers away), he will learn that it's a reasonable strategy for coping with an undesirable situation and will probably repeat the same action next time. If this is repeated several times, you will have created a new learned pattern. Equally, if you don't stop with the clippers until the horse is quiet and accepting, you will have taught him that standing still is a good strategy and he will adopt that next time.

Fortunately, if you make a mistake and unwittingly condition an undesired reaction, you will usually be able to change it and replace it with a new pattern because horses learn extremely fast. This is what helps them adapt to new situations in the wild; however, they also have long memories. Old patterns are not forgotten, they are just replaced with something more current. Rather like painting a new picture over something on a canvas, you can't erase what was there before, and

occasionally, especially in times of stress, these old behaviours are triggered, taking everyone by surprise.

Sensitizing

Once we have desensitized the horse to the things he finds scary and helped him become less reactive, we need him to become sensitive and responsive to our commands and requests.

There are numerous methods available – some use voice commands as stimuli, some involve food treats as rewards and so on. Each can be used to good effect but they can also be ineffective if not backed up by a more motivating factor such as pressure. Horses don't use voice commands or food and as such these methods are not specific to the species. If we are interested in being on their wavelength, it's a good idea to learn more about how horses communicate with each other and to incorporate some elements of this into our training.

Fundamentally, horses use intention and feel as stimuli, and support these with the application of pressure and its release when the desired behaviour is achieved.

Applying pressure

We have talked about why and when pressure is applied, but not about what type or how.

We may need to control our horses up close, or from a safe distance and this involves different techniques. We can cause our horses to yield from the physical pressure of touch (which we call direct feel) or from psychological pressure without touching (which we call indirect feel or suggestion). In both cases, initial stimulus (sometimes called a cue) should be the subtlest signal possible and be supported by just enough pressure (and no more) to cause the horse to respond (rewarded by its instant release). However, it can be difficult to know how much will be just enough, so to be fair to the horse the most cautious approach is to apply it in stages, gradually increasing the pressure by degrees to the point where he responds.

If you don't start with the subtleness of a cue, your horse will never be given the opportunity to respond to it. If you want lightness in your training, you have to offer it. This may sound obvious but, unless it's pointed out, many people omit this stage from their instructions. This is probably because they don't think the horse will respond, and it is true that he possibly won't do to start with. Equally, if you don't increase the pressure until you get a response, you won't achieve your aim.

These degrees of pressure can be applied in different ways, with either a steady or a rhythmic quality. A simplification of this would be that direct feel is usually steady, and indirect feel is usually rhythmic, but there are exceptions. A good rule of thumb is that lightness is steady, but if you need to get firmer, you may find rhythm helps create yielding.

So, what is light and what is firm?

Think of the range of pressure that horses use on each other. The lightest pressure would be a thought or a look, and at the other end of the spectrum the firmest might be a kick or a bite. When asserting dominance over each other (or us), horses will use as much of that range as necessary to get the response they desire, and we need to be prepared to do the same. Their strongest assertions rarely come out of the blue, and there are almost always preceding signals

that increase in intensity as if to say: I suggest you ... I am asking you ... I am telling you ... I insist you ...! In times of threat, these stages may come so close together that they seem to merge into one dramatic action, but horses generally give warnings before they act violently as it is not in their interests to injure each other, and they generally avoid conflict if possible.

If your horse doesn't respond to a request with a low degree of pressure, you need to increase it in stages. Each stage should last about two seconds to give him the opportunity to respond before going up to the next stage if needed – that is, do as little as possible but as much as necessary to get the response you are looking for. When you do achieve it, even for a moment, you must release the pressure instantly because that is the part that will teach the horse which response you want. (If the time frame is longer than two seconds per stage, the horse may not relate it to the preceding stage.)

Remember that he probably has no idea what you are looking for from him. He will simply repeat an action that offers him release from pressure and will learn to respond to the cue or lighter stages and not wait for it to become firm.

Note that unless you are defending your personal space from hostile invasion, I am not suggesting that your highest degree of pressure would ever need to be as hard as one horse kicking another as this would only cause him to become defensive, even though he may perform the task you have asked for. However, you do need to be effective and this can be a challenge for some people, especially nice ladies! If you ask softly, then a bit firmer, then a bit firmer again, then quit before you get a response, you will teach the horse that if he ignores your signals long enough, you will give up, and that comfort can be had by simply 'out waiting' you!

There is never any place for violence or anger. These are signs of a lack of knowledge and self-control – they result in fear and confusion and are damaging and counterproductive to training.

How emotion influences feet

Confusion is the biggest cause of the stress behaviours or 'problems' we encounter in training. It leads to a sense of threat to which the horse is hard-wired to react with his feet one way or another. It is wise to always bear in mind that however well trained he may be, a horse's survival instinct is only ever just under the surface.

A sense of threat always makes a horse tense. Stress will make him need to stay straighter and want to move his feet more, thus relaxation, softness and suppleness cannot exist.

If you try to *make* a horse become soft, the result will be the opposite. This is sometimes called opposition reflex. His instinct tells him to brace and to stay straight for a possible speedy exit (the straightness allows the hindquarters to be engaged as this is needed for propulsion).

When a horse's body does not follow its nose through a bend, it is because of some holding in his body, but the stiffness may originate in the mind. If he is open to the idea and not holding a defensive posture, the bend will be smooth and correct.

If you can reduce the amount confusion by making your communication clearer, ask for less and reward more, you will gradually find your horse becomes more confident and the resistance disappears.

Therefore having a clear intention of what you want and a clear strategy of how to achieve it is the key to success, and the exercises in this book will help you develop both.

How your position influences movement

If you apply pressure in a certain direction, you will get a predictable result. The way you are facing will have a huge influence on this. It can be very effective to think of the energy that is transmitted through your intention as a laser beam or water jet coming out of your *belly button* – belly button power! Where you point that power is the part of the horse that will yield.

Understanding this directional power is very important. A fractional change in your position can have a huge impact. Whether you are controlling by touch (direct feel) or suggestion (indirect feel), the direction of your energy in relation to the driveline is critical.

Driveline

Put simply, the driveline is a conceptual division between the front and back of the horse. If you are in front of the horse and point your energy towards his tail, you will cause him to move backwards. If you stand beside his neck and direct your energy through his neck, he will move his front end over. In both cases, you are in front of the driveline creating different effects. It is the same with the hindquarters.

When riding, its presence is usually described as being 'in front of' or 'behind' the horse's movement. And on Figure 1, which demonstrates pressure applied and the resulting direction of movement, it is shown in its central position, where the rider sits, as the rider's balance and leg position impacts alot on the horse's movement.

However, what is difficult to master about the driveline is that it is not always in the same place, especially when you are on the ground. It depends on the circumstances. It may move up the neck, or even be in the eye. As you will discover in the exercises that follow, anything that affects the horse's emotions, and therefore his need to move his feet, will affect the driveline. If you are not achieving the desired direction when asking your horse to move, check your position in relation to the driveline. Sometimes you may just be standing in the wrong place, or directing your belly button the wrong way. Since it is moveable, the trick is to learn to feel for it and that takes a lot of practise. One of the many benefits of working with horses loose or at liberty is that you don't have the rope to help you if you get out of place and so learning to position yourself correctly becomes vital for success in controlling their feet (the same is true when herding other animals such as geese, sheep or cattle).

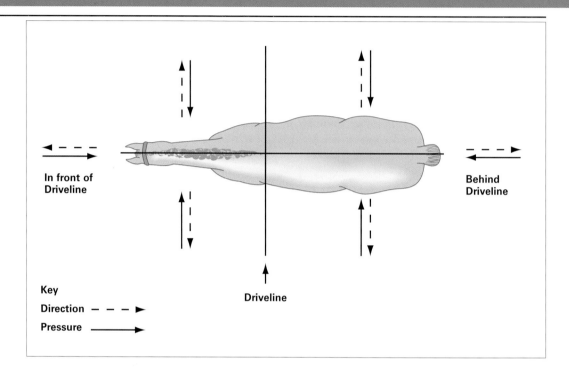

Key

Direction – – – ►
Pressure ————►

To control our horse, we need to be able to move him in all the directions he can go and be able to do it by touching or not touching. *Simple!*

Well, it is simple, but that doesn't mean easy, since the horse is programmed to do the opposite of what man 'the predator' wants and has many ways to evade our requests.

The fundamentals of movement

Since controlling the horse's movement is key, and he can only move in a certain number of directions, the basis of our training is to sensitize him to pressure applied directly (touch) and indirectly (suggestion), and to teach him to yield in fundamental directions. These fundamental directions are:

❑ Forwards
❑ Backwards
❑ Hindquarters
❑ Forequarters
❑ (Lateral flexion) (in brackets because it is not really a direction and doesn't involve moving the feet – but is essential nevertheless).

Up and down are also directions the horse can move and are included in exercises later in the book; however, for simplicity, they are not part of the fundamental list.

How can we simplify the cause and effect of specific movements and how do we obtain directional control with predicable results?

Think of a sheepdog driving a flock of sheep. The dog instinctively knows where to be to move the flock in any direction. He knows how much pressure to apply, when and where to apply it, and when to stop (or he is told by his master). The flock moves as a fluid but cohesive group to which the dog constantly adjusts his direction, feel and timing.

It's the same with a handler and a horse and the results of pressure applied are just as predictable, or can be made so.

Like the dog, if we want to turn the front end of the horse (our flock), we need to put pressure near the front. This may seem obvious, but many people try to send their horse out on the lunge by waving a stick at his hindquarters and wonder why he turns to face them!

Fundamentals: forwards

A horse that truly leads will lead anywhere.

Teaching your horse to yield to a feel from a halter is one of the most basic and essential requirements, and yet there are many situations where we find the horse has other ideas about the direction he wants to go and suddenly we have problems. Coming forwards from a feel on the halter is actually yielding away from something – that is, pressure on the back or the head and under the jaw. When a foal first wears a halter, he will often resist this feel (opposition reflex) and fight the applied pressure by going backwards and, in all too many cases, rear up and fall over. It's a similar pattern when horses pull back when tied up. We often take for granted the horse's ability to lead until we try to lead him somewhere he doesn't want to go, or tie him somewhere he doesn't want to stay, and then we find out, sometimes with dramatic consequences, that the horse only yields forwards off pressure behind his ears when it suits him or he is confident.

Yielding to a feel means softly following the halter in whichever direction the handler indicates. This means not leaning on it, not barging through it and not planting the feet and refusing to move. It also means going at the pace and distance requested without resistance.

Teaching your horse to lead (from both the nearside and the offside) is one of the most basic skills, and is largely taken for granted until we are in a difficult situation where suddenly the horse is not so easy to control. When this happens, many people resort to equipment that enforces their request. While this may relieve the symptoms, it doesn't really solve the problem, which is that the horse doesn't share your idea, or would rather not be with you. Think of it as a communication breakdown. If we could cause the horse to be happy to walk or jog with us wherever we were heading, we wouldn't need strong equipment, or perhaps he would even follow without any equipment (to an indirect feel) – just like horses do with each other!

If we have a horse that pulls on the halter, we often hang onto it harder and this can create a vicious circle as the horse becomes more determined to get away the more we try and hold him back. Learning to apply pressure only when needed and not hanging on in case something happens is quite alien to many of us, so work on leading is a prerequisite that we should not take for granted.

Fundamentals: backwards

Being able to back your horse out of your space is a basic requirement. Horses are usually too close and spend far too much time in a person's space and this can be dangerous. Many people almost seem to 'wear' their horses and do not know how to back them away effectively, or see any reason to.

Again, understanding why this happens is the key. Controlling footfall is how horses assert themselves over each other and if your horse causes you to move out of his way by coming into your space, this may well be what he is doing to you. The more you back down and step aside, the more you prove to your horse that he can control you and the more you will encourage him to push you around.

Fundamentals: hindquarters yield

Yielding the hindquarters is a fundamental move that can make profound changes in the relationship between you and your horse. It is one of the most important and useful exercises you can do to encourage your horse to be with you mentally, emotionally and physically.

Sounds good! Can one exercise really do all those things?

Mental, emotional and physical states are closely intertwined since what we think and do are usually based on what we feel and it is the same for a horse, though we often forget it. When a horse (our prey animal) becomes scared, his first instinct is to run. In very simplistic terms, instinct is located in the right side of the brain. A horse uses this side when he reacts automatically – without thinking. It is the right side of the brain that is usually responsible for accidents around horses! Not all instinct is bad: eating, suckling, social behaviour, drinking and so on are examples of right-brain behaviour; and from a horse's point of view it's good to run first and ask questions later – it has served the species well for millions of years.

But for humans it is usually preferable to have a horse that thinks – that uses the left side of his brain and that responds rather than reacts.

There are 'left-brained' behaviours that are undesirable to us also – some horses will kick in left brain, bolt, squash you against a wall, refuse to load in a trailer, undo the stable door, or simply turn away, pull the rope out of your hand and calmly jog off. These are learned behaviours, usually prompted by some previously distressing occasion but now embedded as a habit or deliberate strategy and executed with precision!

So what has yielding the hindquarters got to do with all this? One way to think of it is to go back to the image of the 'right-brained' reactive horse running from something scary. He runs a certain distance until he crosses what is often referred to as the flight line (a comfort threshold) and then what? He *thinks* – he wonders if whatever it was is still a threat. So he stops and turns to check if he has run far enough. At this point he has disengaged his hindquarters and could be said to be in left brain. Now he may decide that it is safe to stay where he is, or that he needs to run some more.

The left- and right- brain concept is metaphorical and often used to describe how humans differ too. Of course, neurologically it is far more complex than this but it serves as a useful model for our purposes.

As unlikely as it may seem, you can help a horse to change from 'right-brain' type behaviour to 'left-brain' type behaviour. This can be achieved by practising disengaging the hindquarters, and giving him the opportunity to turn and face his fears when he has had a fright, which is an enormous help in encouraging him to become a more thinking horse as he learns that he can survive frightening situations.

Yielding the hindquarters is a submissive move. A horse will not turn his rump on a more dominant horse, and asking your horse to yield his rump away from you can replicate this sort of response. With some horses this is all you need to do to persuade them to literally follow you around, even without a rope.

On a physical level, when you disengage the hindquarters, you take the horse's power away. The power comes from the engagement of the hindquarters and is very desirable in some situations and not in others. You are well advised to make sure your horse is with you mentally and emotionally before engaging his physical power or events can go wrong very quickly. Knowing how to disengage and take a horse's power away on the ground or in the saddle can help you get a dangerous situation quickly back under control.

Fundamentals: forequarters yield

The aim of this fundamental pre-requisite is to move the horse's forequarters around in isolation from the hind end in order to perform a turn on the haunches.

Yielding the forequarters is extremely important both for steering when you are riding and for safety on the ground, as many horses use their shoulders to push into your personal space and cause you to move out of their way – or tread on you if you don't!

Therefore we learn to do this by touching, using the steady contact of direct feel, and also from a distance using indirect feel to drive the horse's front end away.

In both forms, the exercises teach your horse to elevate his forehand by shifting his weight to the hindquarters. When he does, this he will make the turn without falling forwards on the forehand (remember all this is building towards what we want when riding).

Fundamentals: lateral flexion

Lateral flexion is a barometer of acceptance.

If a horse is resistant to an idea or an action, it will be in his mind and show in his body. If a horse cannot give physically, more often than not this is because he is resistant in his mind. For example, a horse may seem stiff laterally if you ask him to bring his head round and yet when he has a tickle on his hip he can scratch it with his teeth! The resistance is gone when the idea is his.

Lateral flexion, as its name suggests, is essentially bend to the side, starting at the poll and going through to the tail. The horse's ribcage cannot actually bend much compared with that of a human, cat or dog, because his vertebral column is less flexible, but he can slide the barrel of his body to the outside, allowing the inside hip and inside shoulder to come closer together and so giving the illusion of bend.

This flexion starts at the atlas/axis joint where the skull connects to the vertebral column – it is not just a bend through the neck, though some horses have more movement in the poll than others, depending on their conformation. A large wing of atlas and large jaw can limit the amount of flexion that is possible. (Check the distance between your horse's jaw and atlas bones to get a realistic idea of how much he can flex here – two fingers is ideal.) The extension of lateral flexion is bend through the body.

Protecting your personal space

The first objective you need to establish when working with a horse is your own personal safety zone. This is of paramount importance when you are around horses. I often see horses pushing, barging, or biting their owners or causing them to move their feet (see 'The feet are connected to the mind, page 28). Therefore the first fundamental pre-requisite is to know how to protect your space from invasion.

How do I do this?

Imagine you have a bubble all the way around you at about arm's length from your body. Learn to think of this space as off limits to your horse unless he is invited in by you. Once you start taking notice of this bubble, you will be surprised how much your horse comes into in your space uninvited.

Stand with your arms outstretched and move them all the way around you to get the feel of the extent of your bubble (Figure 1). If your horse is already standing in your bubble, cause him to move backwards until he is not standing in your space anymore rather than moving your feet. Exercises 5 and 6 contain information on how to do this.

Block his entry by defending the wall of your bubble. You may do this with your hand, arm, rope or stick on the edge of your bubble (Figure

2). If you move your arm like a windscreen wiper at the edge of your bubble and the horse walks into it, he will receive a bump on his nose and think twice about doing it another time. To the horse this is very different from you stepping out of your bubble and hitting him on the nose. The consequences of his actions will be very clear to him and because he understands it, this process does not result in him becoming fearful around his head.

Double check

❑ Do not perform this action with anger, be firm but fair. Keep it unemotional and the horse will see you in a positive light rather than a negative one.
❑ Make sure your horse stays outside your bubble once you've moved him. You need to set clear boundaries and be consistent.

1

Reminders

❑ If you move your feet, your horse may think you are showing submission; if you cause your horse to move his feet, you are showing that you are in charge.

❑ Match the horse's velocity – in other words, if he comes into your space gently, you don't need to respond violently, just firmly enough to keep him out. However, if he is going to trample on you, you should defend your space as strongly as you can as your life may depend on it!

❑ The more threatening you find your horse's behaviour, the bigger your bubble should become. He is only allowed in when you feel you can trust him to be respectful. Understanding this principle alone could save you from injury around horses every day.

Problem solving

❑ He still comes into your space – you were not effective enough, and may need to repeat this exercise several times until he understands where your boundaries are and that he must respect your space.

❑ He becomes defensive and looks worried – you probably did too much. Just smile and rub him with the stick to reassure him at arm's length (see Exercise 2).

Special information

Be aware that the horse doesn't always come forwards into your space. He can push on you with ribs, shoulders or hindquarters and cause you to move out of his way, sometimes it can be very subtle, but every time you fail to notice or do something about it puts him another notch above you in his mind so make sure you are fair by being consistent.

Note

I am not suggesting that you should never have your horse near you, or that you should not be able to stroke or scratch him or even smother him in kisses if you want to, but do make sure it happens when it is your idea rather than his, especially in the early stages of establishing respect and communication between you.

HORSEMAN'S TIPS
Do as little as possible, but as much as necessary.

2

Desensitizing

Helping your horse become more confident in his environment is an important process and a vast subject that could fill a whole book in itself.

How do I do this?

A good place to start is to check that your horse is not scared of you or your equipment, so you will learn to use progressive desensitization to make sure you can touch him all over his body with your hand first, then your rope and then building up to your stick (see 'Desensitizing', page 20). Once he is confident in these, you can move on to other things you might encounter in the big wide world that might cause your horse to 'spook'. These could be anything but are likely to include saddle, ropes round legs and body, plastic bags, tarpaulin, people jumping around,

paste wormers, footballs, umbrellas, fly sprays, clippers, farrier work, bicycles and traffic.

For the purpose of this exercise I will refer to 'the object', as the process is much the same for them all.

Make sure your body language is neutral. You want your horse to sense that you don't require anything from him. Keep your energy low. If you are nervous, he will pick up on it, so remember to breathe, keep calm and make your movements slow but not stealthy – you don't want to look like a predator!

Show him the object and let him sniff it or nibble it if he chooses to. You want to encourage his curiosity. Gradually see if you can get closer, perhaps touching him on his shoulder or neck (Figure 1). The further back towards his tail you go, the more likely he will be to go forward; the further towards his nose, the more likely he will go backwards. Each horse is individual, so it is a matter of trial and error. Some horses will actually come closer to you and try to barge you and the object out of their way, so be alert and know how to protect your space (see Exercise 1; also see 'Driveline', page 23).

1

See if there's a place where your horse can tolerate the object enough to stand still while you rub him with it. Rest here awhile, to reward the behaviour that you want, then start to rub again rhythmically, moving on round his body using this method of approach a little at a time. If he is accepting, retreat again and gradually build up to doing this all around the horse. He may move, and at this point don't approach any further but don't stop either or, as said earlier, that will only teach him to move. Just let him walk around you and not away from you (Figure 2). Breathe and smile, showing him that you don't want to harm him. Eventually he will stop, as walking is not having the desired effect and is not serving any purpose. Keep rubbing until he looks more relaxed and is able to keep his feet still. This is the time to stop.

2

Your horse may lick his lips and chew, as if he is chewing over the idea. He is learning at this point, so keep the pressure off him and allow him some time to think.

Repeat the process, progressively building up to the point where the horse can tolerate the object anywhere around his body, including under his belly, up and down and between his legs, and does not need to be held with the rope and can stand still with his head lowered so his poll is below his wither (see Exercise 52) or with lateral flexion (see Exercise 11).

Problem solving

❑ He becomes scared – if you hold him back, he will just want to move even more, so allow him to move around you not away from you and keep him facing his fear.

❑ If he is really troubled, keep the object further away (have an assistant) or walk away from him with the object so it does not threaten him (Figure 3). As you walk away, he may become curious and start to want to sniff the object. This is great, just take your time and go through the process above, starting from a greater distance if necessary.

❑ If the object is static, lead him past or around it at a distance and gradually become closer by degrees, stopping to reward when he tries to be brave, rather than trying to walk him straight up to it.

Remember

❑ *Take time* – patience is everything here. If you become cross or frustrated, you will undo all the good you've achieved and your horse will reconfirm that you are not trustworthy.

❑ Whether you think it's justified or not, if horses are scared, they are truly scared – they don't make it up. If you get annoyed, you will only deepen the negative association your horse has with the situation or object.

❑ Desensitizing is an ongoing process. Every new thing that comes along that might scare your horses should be treated in this way.

Benefits

When your horse stops reacting like a prey animal and gains the confidence to think his way through problems, you will have more fun and stay safer. (For more information on desensitizing to specific issues, see Chapter 5.)

Moving on

Sometimes, horses look as if they are accepting when they are standing still but then explode when you perform the same desensitizing in movement. This is because they are in 'freeze' mode or have become introvert (see 'Reading horses', page 14). Once your horse can tolerate objects when standing still, always double check they are still acceptable to him when he is moving his feet.

3

Yield forwards – direct feel

In this exercise, you will teach the horse how to follow feel on the halter and come towards you.

How do I do this?

- ❑ Stand in front of your horse with a space of at least 1.8 metres (6 feet) between you and have your rope laid over your open hand.
- ❑ Make sure your horse is looking at you with both eyes and both ears.
- ❑ Smile and look inviting.
- ❑ Think of your belly button power in reverse – 'drawing' rather than 'driving'.
- ❑ Draw your open hand towards your body so that it just lifts the clip on the rope and contact is made. Your horse should ideally yield to this little amount of pressure and come towards you (Figure 1).

- ❑ If he doesn't move forwards, start to comb the rope with both hands open back towards your body – this will put a little more feel on the halter.
- ❑ If he still doesn't come, close your hands on the rope and continue to comb it while slipping the rope but exerting a steady feel on the halter.
- ❑ If he still doesn't come towards you, keep your hands still and exert a firm hold on the halter until your horse steps forwards into release (Figure 2).

Remember

- ❑ You are not trying to drag your horse towards you. Offer him a light feel and increase this by degrees until it is firm enough for him to want to do something about it. The instant he steps, open your hands as if the rope is hot (Figure 3) – comfort is his reward.
- ❑ If you try to pull your horse forwards, towards you, he will be more inclined to dig his toes in and go backwards.
- ❑ Imagine you are like a fence post that your horse is attached to. It doesn't pull when he doesn't yield, it is just there and he finds instant release when he steps towards it.
- ❑ Reward the slightest try from the horse and gradually build up.

1

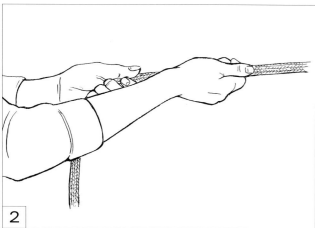

2

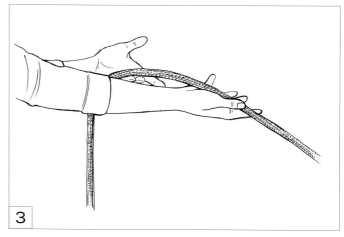

3

Problem solving

- ❏ He leans on you with his toes dug in – rather than pull harder, move from one side to the other in order to change his balance over his front legs and cause him to step. Release and repeat until he is no longer resisting and will come straight forwards.

- ❏ He is very reluctant to move – use your stick behind his driveline as you feel on the line to encourage him to put more effort into following your feel. Flick the string of the stick so that it lands on his hindquarters (Figure 4). He may move sideways to start with, so be ready to change your stick into the other hand (passed under the rope) to counterbalance this while keeping the feel on the halter. Only release when he steps towards you.

Hints

- ❏ Remember to do as little as possible. If you become energetic with your stick, your horse will be more likely to go away from you. Keep your body language soft and inviting.

- ❏ Some horses find it intimidating to step towards their handler. It often helps if you step backwards to increase the space between you both and give him somewhere to go.

Benefits

Teaching your horse to yield to a feel from something in front of him can help him learn not to pull back.

Moving on

- ❏ Teach your horse to become so responsive that he will trot towards you from just a light application of pressure.

- ❏ Try this using indirect feel by giving the horse a cue to follow, such as beckoning with your finger before you use the halter.

- ❏ Will he follow your finger wherever you go?

4

Yield forwards – indirect feel

As we have discussed, getting your horse to go forwards is fundamental and there are lots of different ways to achieve this.

The previous exercise asked the horse to move forwards towards you, Exercise 13 tests your control using a more familiar technique but this exercise is excellent for retraining a horse who plants his feet and won't move forwards. You will learn to drive him forwards from stimulus behind the driveline, just as you do when you are riding.

How do I do this?

❏ Start by standing facing forwards at your horse's shoulder, say, on his near side.

❏ Place your rope in your left hand with your arm across your body. Your stick should be in your right hand, resting on your horse's back where the saddle sits (Figure 1).

❏ Lift your energy and focus your belly button forwards to where you want to go.

❏ Extend your left arm in front of you and point your finger forwards so your horse can see it but the rope is not exerting feel on the halter. This is the cue you want him to follow (Figure 2).

❏ If he doesn't move, extend your lead rope forwards so he feels the halter on the back of his head and under the jaw.

❏ If he doesn't follow the feel of the halter to go forwards, slide the stick backwards so it's over his rump and lightly tap on top of his rump to ask him to follow your suggestion to move forwards.

❏ Only when he steps should you start to walk with him and rest your stick back in the neutral position where the saddle goes.

1

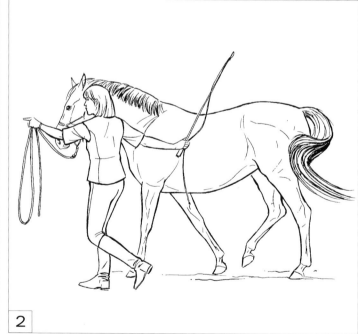

2

Problem solving

❏ He doesn't move – continue the rhythmic tapping on his rump while giving him the cue to step forwards. You don't need to tap hard, just be consistent till he moves and reward his effort.

❏ He walks a bit then stops – go through the process again.

❏ He walks forwards but cuts across your path – bring the stick forward to block or turn him (see Exercise 10).

Remember

❏ You want him to learn to follow the cue, so make sure you always offer it before tapping on his rump.

❏ Keep your energy projecting forwards and try not to look back at him constantly. Learn to feel for him.

❏ Practise this exercise from both sides.

Benefits

Many horses plant their feet and refuse to move, especially when asked to take the front of a ride. Being able to drive forwards ahead of you like this is excellent for helping your horse to become braver about taking the lead and for letting him know you have the ability to control his footfall.

This is one of the building blocks for teaching your horse to load himself in a trailer.

Moving on

❏ Do this at trot.

❏ Aim to reach the stage where he trots when you trot. And to be able to do this without using your rope or stick.

HORSEMAN'S TIPS

When a foal is born, his mother encourages him to stand up and moves him in front of her by nipping him on the rump or root of his tail, rather like you are doing in this exercise.

Yield backwards – direct feel

In this exercise, you are going to ask your horse to yield softly back from a direct feel on his nose.

How do I do this?

❏ Stand beside your horse's head facing him and place your hand on his nose with your fingers touching each side of the bridge of his nose about where the noseband sits (not obstructing his airway).

❏ He may fight you off, or try to walk through you, but aim to keep your hand in place until he is settled and he accepts you touching him there.

❏ Once he is still and not resisting or pushing on you, lift your energy, focus it behind him with clear intention and squeeze gently on the bridge of his nose (Figure 1).

❏ When he has given one step back, reward him immediately by releasing the pressure, but try to keep your hand on his nose. You can rub him to say thank you if your horse likes that, but watch that he doesn't take the step forward again! You will gradually build up to more steps back using gentle feel.

Remember

❏ Squeeze on the bridge of the nose – don't push him backwards as you will be using force and this will change your balance. You are just exerting pressure either side of his nose.

❏ Keep your focus and encourage him to go back straight.

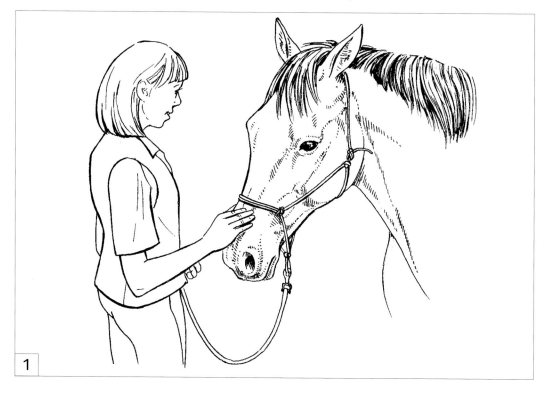

1

Problem solving

❑ He fights your hand on his nose – some horses find this difficult to tolerate, especially if they have had restrictive tack on their noses, such as a tight noseband. It can bring out the claustrophobic in him, so just try to keep your hand there, or stroke him gently until he can accept it before asking for movement.

❑ He won't move – use the halter to gently rock his head over the front foot that needs to move and ask him to take a lateral step first. This usually frees up the feet after a few attempts.
❑ Make your pressure firmer if necessary and if he still doesn't move, rhythmically flick the end of your rope (or stick) towards the foot that needs to move, making contact if needed until he moves it back (Figure 2).

2

❑ He tries to evade by dropping his head down – stamp your foot on the ground to discourage this and if necessary let his nose run into your knee coming up the other way.
❑ He throws his head up – try to keep your hand there (sometimes difficult with a large horse, but persevere) and spend time encouraging him to accept your hand on his nose using the process described in Exercise 2.

Benefits

❑ You will be able to keep your horse at arm's length outside your bubble.
❑ Yielding backwards from the nose sets you up for backup when riding.
❑ You will be able to develop your communication to get in time with his footfall and be able to specify which of his feet move.

Moving on

Once your horse is reliably following your feel backwards, you can start to specify which foot to move. Ask whichever forefoot looks ready to move first to take a step back by using your thumb or forefinger on the side of his nose, whichever is on the same side as the chosen foot (Figure 3), in a backwards direction.

This is to enable you to communicate with individual feet and release the pressure in between. As your horse goes back, move your footfall in time with his, so your body does what his body does and you learn to be in rhythm with his stride.

If he is truly soft, yielding and balanced, backwards will be a two-time gait as he will move his feet in diagonal pairs, like trot.

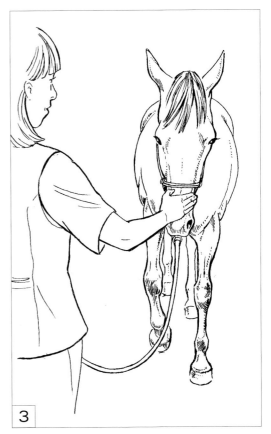

3

Yield backwards – indirect feel

Very often a horse is outside your personal space but not far enough for safety, so it's important to develop the ability to control his direction without waiting until he's close enough to touch.

In this exercise, you will practise backing up your horse from a distance.

How do I do this?

❑ Position your horse outside your bubble to (at least 1.8 metres/6 feet away) and make sure he is facing you with both eyes and both ears.

❑ Focus on a point in the distance behind him, stand tall and lift your energy to let him know that you want something.

❑ Straighten your arm that is holding the rope and rhythmically pulse your finger towards his chest. The rope should be loose enough not to move the halter at this stage (Figure 1).

❑ If he doesn't move back, send a pulse down the rope so that it moves the clip where it joins the halter and he feels a vibration from the noseband.

❑ If that doesn't work, flick the end of the rope or your stick towards his legs and walk forwards towards him (Figure 2). If he is still standing when you get to him, touch him firmly and rhythmically with your rope or stick on the chest between his legs until he moves backwards.

1

2

Remember

❏ It is important for your safety that he understands your instructions. If he doesn't respond to the subtle degrees of pressure, you will need to be more effective.

❏ As soon as he steps back, reward him with release. Soon it will take very little pressure.

❏ Start with one step and build up as your horse understands what you want.

Problem solving

❏ Your horse becomes defensive and goes backwards too much – you may have used more pressure than necessary, or you need to spend more time desensitizing him.

❏ He comes forwards through your pressure – he may be defensive or challenging your authority (all the more reason why you need to practise this exercise). Do whatever it takes to stop him and back him up – do your best not to step backwards as you will show him that he is in charge.

❏ He goes off to one side rather than back up – yield the hindquarters to straighten him up and try again (see Exercise 8).

Very often, a horse will go back and then persistently step forwards again – be more persistent than he is!

Moving on

Once your horse understands this basic form, you can increase the distance between you both, driving him backwards without moving your feet.

HORSEMAN'S TIPS

Keeping your stimulus aimed low (chest or below) will help prevent your horse going back with his head up and back hollow, which is undesirable.

A true back-up is a two-time gait.

Yield hindquarters – direct feel

As you have read, this is one of the most useful ways you can move your horse around, so work on it until you really understand it as you will find many examples of it in different forms in this book.

You will need to ask your horse to step his hindquarters away from you while keeping his body softly flexed around you and his front feet quite still (you may know this as turn on the forehand).

How do I do this?

❑ Stand at your horse's rib cage with low energy and ask for lateral flexion without movement (see Exercise 11).

❑ Adjust your position so that you are standing by his hindquarters facing through his body. Imagine he is a gate and you are going to open it and walk through as it pivots on its hinge (the forequarters).

❑ Keeping the feel on the line to maintain the flexion but not to pull him round, lift your energy up, focus on a point in the distance and ask him to take a step over by touching the middle of his hindquarters with the back of your hand (because it is light but does not tickle like fingertips can) (Figure 1).

up to a full turn. The inside foreleg should stay fairly still, picking up and putting down in roughly the same place as the horse walks himself around this leg.

❑ Once he understands to yield to this feel repeat the exercise, this time touching him just behind the girth, where your leg will be when riding. This will build the link between the commands on the ground and in the saddle (Figure 2).

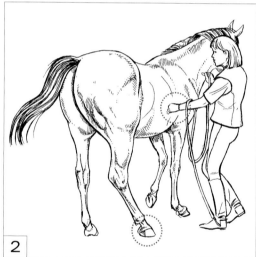

2

❑ Practise from both sides and aim to reach the stage where he can walk around his inside foreleg as he lifts and replaces it in more or less the same spot (preferably not pivoting on it as this is not good for his joints and encourages him to load the inside shoulder).

1

❑ When he moves away, you should be still in the same place but with more space between you. The idea is that he works out how to find release. This will motivate him better than if you push him round, which will encourage him to become heavier.

❑ Once he understands the idea and moves from a light feel, you can move your feet, walking in an arc so that he softly yields a quarter turn on the forehand. Gradually build

Remember

❑ As soon as he moves, he should find release. Don't ask for many steps to start with.

❑ Don't lean or shove, as you will not be in balance when he moves and the release will not be instant. You will just encourage him to shove back.

❑ The further that he steps under with his inside hind leg, the more elastic and supple he will become.

Problem solving

- ❏ He goes forward around you – lift your rein hand and this should lift his shoulder and change his weight. Put some rhythm pulses in the rein if necessary.
- ❏ He drops in on his shoulder – make sure you are not pulling him in on the rope.
- ❏ He doesn't want you to touch him and threatens to kick – use your stick to apply the pressure by degrees to the hindquarters, which keeps you out of his range (Figure 3). Once he understands and doesn't feel defensive, the kicking will stop and you will be able to touch him with your hand. Give it time.

Benefits

Apart from all the benefits listed opposite, this is an essential ingredient for all your lateral work as it teaches your horse to yield his hindquarters from your leg.

Moving on

Start to refine your signals so that one cue means one step. Ask with your hand on his flank when you want the inside hind foot to move across underneath him, then turn your rein hand over and give an indirect rein to ask the outside hind to move over (Figure 4) (see 'Rein positions', page 17).

3

4

- ❏ He moves away from you too much – he is feeling defensive and so is reacting instead of responding. Spend some time rubbing him with low energy and lateral flexion (Exercise 11). When he relaxes, he will not move so much.
- ❏ He won't move – gradually increase the rhythm pressure tapping on his hindquarters until it is uncomfortable (but not painful) enough that he can't ignore it – wait for him to find out how to release himself from discomfort and reward him. Repeat this until he doesn't wait for the pressure to increase.

TIPS

If he pivots around the outside foreleg, he is travelling backwards. This could mean that he is defensive or that or your position is not ideal (see 'Driveline', page 23).

HORSEMAN'S TIPS

If you have clear intention, you won't need to use force. Force is unbalancing.

This is the key to having an independent seat and applies on the ground just as much as in the saddle.

Yield hindquarters – indirect feel

This exercise shows you how to control your horse's hindquarters from a distance. If you can control the hindquarters, you can control the whole horse. Without touching, you will ask your horse to step his hindquarters away from you and turn to face you (you may know this as turn on the forehand).

How do I do this?

❑ Stand about 1.8 metres (6 feet) from your horse's shoulders, facing him and run your hand down the line to ask for lateral flexion (see Exercise 11). Turn to look intently at his hindquarters.

❑ Walk in a 'C' shape towards his hindquarters and turn your wrist to give an indirect rein signal on the lead rope, making sure you don't pull his front end towards you.

❑ Keep focusing your energy and belly button power towards the horse's hindquarters (not towards his front end) and if your energy is not enough to cause him to yield,

start rhythmically moving the stick (or end of your rope) towards that area of his body (Figure 1).

Hints

As in Exercise 7, the idea is that your horse walks around his inside foreleg, which lifts and replaces in the same spot. It may help to imagine that he is a gate and you are going to open it and walk through as it pivots on its hinge (the forequarters).

Start with a step or two and gradually build up to a full turn, driving his hindquarters away from you as you walk towards him.

1

Remember

❑ As soon as he moves, he should find release. Don't ask for many steps to start with.

❑ Don't chase him round, or you will cause him to feel defensive, but be effective and walk towards him with purpose as a more dominant horse would.

❑ Practise from both sides.

❑ The more the horse steps under with his inside hind leg, the more elastic and supple he will become.

Problem solving

❑ He goes forward around you – lift your rein hand and this should lift his shoulder and change his weight. Put some rhythm pulses in the rein and if necessary pulses to bump the halter on his nose and discourage him from moving forwards. Make sure you are directing your energy through his hindquarters, not behind them (Figure 2).

❑ He drops in on his shoulder – make sure you are not pulling him in on the rope. Flick the tail end of the rope at his shoulder if necessary.

❑ He moves away from you too much – he is feeling defensive and so is reacting instead of responding. Check you are not using more pressure than necessary. See how little it takes.

❑ He doesn't yield as you approach – increase the pressure and, if needed, tap him firmly on the hindquarters with your stick or the end of your rope and reward when he moves. Repeat this until he doesn't wait for the pressure to increase.

❑ He braces his body and turns his forequarters away or his hindquarters towards you instead – you don't have enough lateral flexion.

Benefits

Disengaging the hindquarters takes the horse's power away. You can use it to stop him, make transitions, cause him see you differently and help him learn to control his emotions.

Moving on

Once your horse understands the idea, you can try this starting from a metre or two in front of him and causing him to yield his quarters just by looking at them without you moving your feet – this is very useful for straightening a crooked back-up!

2

Yield the forequarters – direct feel

The aim is to build up to where the horse, bending in the direction of the turn, walks forwards around the inside hind foot (on the opposite side to you) – picking it up and putting it down in virtually the same spot (you may know this as turn on the haunches). This manoeuvre is practised on the ground, simulating the action of the rider's aids, so that the horse becomes familiar with the movement, learns to rebalance and will perform it with understanding and acceptance when ridden.

How do I do this?

❏ Stand beside your horse's neck facing him.
❏ Place one hand on his lower jaw under the noseband of the halter, and the other hand on his shoulder muscle near his elbow (Figure 1).

❏ Without asking him to move, ask him to turn his nose away from you a little so he is looking in the direction you want his forehand to go (see Exercise 11).
❏ Focus through is neck and project your energy where you want him to go. Keeping his neck bent in the direction of the turn, ask him to step over by applying pressure by degrees on his shoulder. When he moves aside release the pressure immediately. Start with one step and gradually build up to a full turn (Figure 2).

Double check

❏ Check that your horse moves over, not forwards or backwards.
❏ Make sure that you don't lose the bend when the shoulders step across – you will need to step with him to keep his nose facing into the turn.
❏ Be sure to practise this from both sides.

Benefits

Your horse will become lighter and therefore more manoeuvrable through using his hindquarters better and counteracting his natural inclination to push out or forwards through the shoulder.

Hints

Begin with one step at a time, releasing when your horse tries. Remember, he doesn't know what you want, but will learn very quickly what response gets him a release and next time he will put more effort into a strategy that works for him.

It may help to think of your horse as a gate, with his hindquarters being the hinge end and the forequarters being the latch end that opens before you as you walk through. This often clarifies where you should be focusing and directing your energy (Figure 3).

Problem solving

❏ He moves too much – stop, make sure you are clear about what you are going to ask for and break it down into its individual components, one step at a time. If he still moves his feet too much, you may need to keep turning him for a few revolutions until he doesn't want to turn any more and starts

1

2

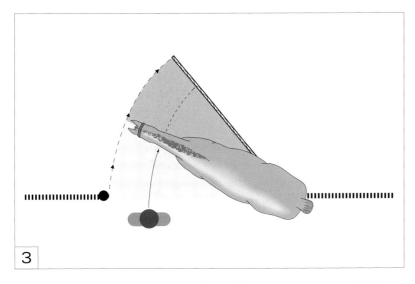

3

When he accepts the idea, his body will relax and you will be able to specify which feet move and which stay still.

❏ The shoulders stay still and the hindquarters moves around – you have probably bent his head round too far.

Reminders

❏ Where you direct your energy and focus will have a strong effect on the direction your horse moves in. Check your position in relation to the driveline.

❏ Make sure you practise this from both sides.

Moving on

Once your horse has the basic concept of this and is successfully making a turn on the haunches with lightness, you can refine your commands so that you communicate with individual feet, as you want them to move. This is where you will simulate the rider's aids to be in rhythm with the horse's footfall.

The pressure on the jaw simulates the direct or open rein and controls the inside (right in Figure 4) foreleg, and the pressure on the shoulder simulates the supporting rein and controls the outside (left) foreleg (Figure 5).

Thus, when you want the inside leg to lift, ask with the hand on the jaw, and when it is the turn of the outside foreleg to come across use the hand on the shoulder. Only ask when the relevant leg is on the ground, or you will lose the benefit of this refinement. Release when the chosen leg is lifted – in this way you will learn to tune into your horse's rhythm and to control one step at a time. (For more information, see 'Rein positions and responsibilities', page 17.)

to work out what you want so you will give him release.

❏ He does not move at all – increase the pressure by degrees (see 'Applying pressure', page 21) until it is quite firm and he cannot ignore your command. Hold it and wait until he makes a try, then release and start again.

❏ He goes backwards – he may be feeling a little defensive. Use the halter to reposition him at the starting place rather than allowing him to move your feet and ask him to flex again. Wait till he is soft through is body and then ask him to move the shoulder one step.

❏ He goes forwards, leaning on the halter – discourage this by rattling it to prevent him pushing through it. Again, try not to let him pull you off your feet.

❏ He moves around but the hindquarters will not stay still – you probably don't have true lateral flexion (see 'Lateral flexion', page 27) and he is holding through his outside ribs.

4

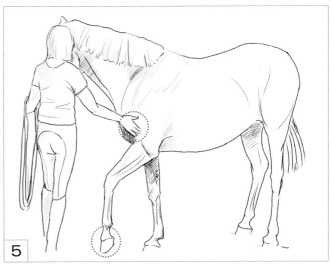

5

Yield the forequarters – indirect feel

If you are going to be run over by a horse entering your space, you will want to be able to deflect him before it's too late! In such a situation, having the ability to turn his front end away from you at a distance would be very useful (you may know this as turn on the haunches).

As in Exercise 9, here you will learn how to yield his front end over, only this time without touching him. You can gradually build this up to greater and greater distances.

How do I do this?

❑ Stand facing through your horse's neck as in Exercise 9 with your stick held horizontally in both hands parallel to his neck. Whichever side you do this, you will need your rope held only in the hand nearest your horse's shoulder, not slack or tight but just short enough to make contact on the halter if he walks forward.

❑ Lift your energy and focus through his neck and tap the air with the stick about 45cm (18 inches) from him to ask him to yield his forequarters away (Figure 1). Angle the stick so that his nose turns first, followed by his neck and shoulders (Figure 2).

❑ When he stops, release the pressure by pointing the stick to the floor, pivoting it in the hand nearest his shoulder.

❑ Start with one step and build up till you can do a complete turn on the haunches.

HORSEMAN'S TIPS

The stick is used to begin with because it is not unlike the way horses steer others with their necks.

Problem solving

❑ Horse goes forward – he should walk into the feel of the halter within a stride. Send a pulse down the rein to discourage him from going in that direction. You may need to adjust your position in relation to the driveline by coming further forwards if the problem persists.

❑ He goes backwards – again check your position – is your belly button pointing where you want him to go? Reposition him using your line, rather than moving your feet and try once more. He may still go backwards, but if you are confident you are in the right position, keep your focus strong and keep trying to send him where you want him to go. Eventually he will work out that backwards does not achieve release. As soon as he steps across, release and reward him.

❑ He doesn't move when you tap the air around him – make contact by rhythmically tapping on his neck (don't be tempted to shove him, just keep tapping gently). If that doesn't work, increase the pressure so it is a firm tap and then just keep it consistent until he tries.

❑ He moves his hindquarters instead of his forequarters – you have probably bent his head around too far.

1

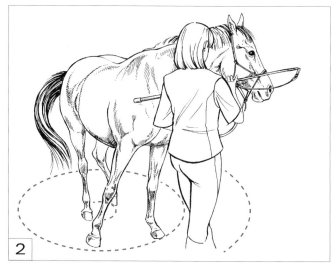

2

Double check

❑ Ensure your horse is not defensive about the stick. Check that you can rub all over his head with the stick before you begin.

❑ Make sure you don't have the rein in the hand nearest his nose as this will pull him back on to you and cause confusion.

❑ Make sure the rein is not too long or you will end up behind his shoulder.

Remember

Try to keep his nose facing in the direction of the turn – if he is looking back at you, he will reverse the bend. It is preferable that he is bent in the direction of the turn and walks around the inside hind (furthest from you) as this means he is thinking forwards rather than backwards.

This can be difficult to get right as there are many ways the horse can out manoeuvre you when you are not touching. Don't worry – take it slowly and break it down for you and your horse to understand. It takes patience and practice.

Benefits

❑ It enables you to control his forequarters from a distance – keeping you safer.

❑ It is great for stopping horses that barge you with their shoulders.

❑ It is essential preparation for sending your horse around you on a circle.

Moving on

❑ Test your accuracy – see if you can cause your horse to turn around the hind foot furthest from you (marking time). You will need to feel for the driveline and be neither in front or behind it.

❑ Try to do this using the rope horizontally instead of the stick, or just by projecting your energy and have your horse yield as you walk through his space.

❑ Aim to do it from further away.

Lateral flexion

The importance of lateral flexion in training is very often underestimated. It can tell you a great deal about your horse's state of mind as well as his body, as it is the opposite of tension and brace. If you have soft flexion through the poll and the body, it shows that you have relaxation in the horse and that his mind and therefore his body are open to your suggestions. If you don't have soft flexion, it indicates that you may well run into resistance.

How do I do this?

❑ Stand at the shoulder with your rope in your outside hand facing forwards.

❑ Place the back of your hand nearest your horse's flank on the girth area to ask him to move his ribs away but keep his feet still (Figure 1).

❑ You may find that he looks around at you automatically, which is what you want. If he doesn't, lift the rope gently until he starts to yield his head round while still keeping your hand on his ribs (Figure 2).

❑ Release and repeat until your horse looks round at you when you touch his ribs – one day this will be your inside leg softly asking for bend.

Benefits

Lateral flexion tells you a great deal about your horse's acceptance and confidence in you and your training. It indicates relaxation. He will not be able to keep his feet still if he is tense as the outside of his body will be tight and not allow the ribs to move to the outside; consequently, when he brings his head round, his feet will move.

Remember, lateral flexion in the presence of a predator is a vulnerable position for a horse, and in the wild it would only happen as that predator tried to suffocate him. Bear in mind that opposition to this is natural, and help him overcome his fears and gain trust.

Teaching your horse not to brace against your rein is fundamental.

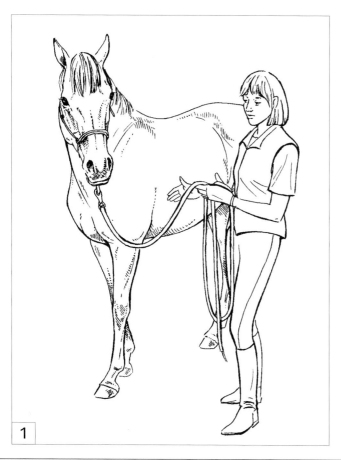

1

2

Problem solving

❏ Your horse doesn't willingly bring his head around when you ask – keep your hand softly on his ribs and put a little more tension on the rope. Be sure not to pull him round, just give him a clear feel to encourage him to find release. Set it up and wait – it might take some time! Don't be tempted to make him. As soon as he softens, even a little, release and then try again.

❏ Your horse appears to have tuned you out and gone to sleep – this can be a typical reaction by those horses who have learned to lean on pressure. If this happens, put a bit of vibration down the line so he just can't ignore it – he will soon start looking for a way to obtain comfort.

❏ Your horse will not keep his feet still – he is probably too tense and wants to keep his body straight. You can easily check if the resistance arises from some physical incapacity by offering a carrot near to his flank – most horses can reach when its their idea! (If he cannot, you should seek the advice of your vet or other suitably qualified professional.)

❏ Your horse won't stand still – make sure your body language is neutral (try yawning – it releases tension in both of you) and your belly button is facing forward. Sometimes it helps him understand if you ask by putting your hand on his nose first and showing him the flex you want. Once he grasps the idea and can do it without moving his feet, go back to doing it with the halter.

Remember

❏ Don't try to make him do this, set it up so that he finds the release himself.

❏ You will probably need to repeat this many times until he understands the idea.

❏ If your horse can reach round to his flank for a carrot but won't flex to your feel, the resistance is in his mind.

❏ If he is full of energy or not relaxed at the start, you are going to find this exercise difficult – pick a time when he is quiet to begin teaching this.

HORSEMAN'S TIPS
You can't get true softness through force.

GROUND WORK

THE EXERCISES

In Chapter 2, you learned the basic alphabet of the language of the horse – now you will learn how to put those elements together words and sentences. You are ready for the exercises that follow if you:

❑ understand position, driveline and how to influence direction of specific areas of the horse.

❑ can isolate the front end, back end, go forwards and backwards.

❑ know the difference between direct and indirect feel, how to apply pressure in stages and when to release.

❑ know what an indirect, direct and supporting rein/ stick are and what they do.

❑ understand disengaging the hindquarters.

❑ understand flexion and how tension affects it.

If you are not sure about any of these points, go back over the fundamentals in chapter two again since they are the essential building blocks of your horse's foundation.

Everything that you are going to learn in this section of the book should be done with respect to the horse, with feel and with finesse. You will learn how to balance pressure and release and about causing things to happen rather than making them happen. You will also come to understand how to do as little as possible and as much as necessary to be effective.

To get the most from this book, try to be open to the honest feedback you will be given by the best teacher you could ever have – your horse!

Halter on and off safely

In this exercise, you will learn how to teach your horse to allow you to put on and take off any kind halter smoothly and safely.

How do I do this?

It's a good idea to be organized before you start. If you tie the halter with a quick release knot (Figure 1), double over the rope and hang it through the throatlatch whenever it is not in use, this will prevent it from getting in a tangle and it can be hung on a hook ready for use (Figure 2).

❏ When you approach your horse, take the rope and place it around his neck.
❏ Stand beside your horse's shoulder facing forwards and put your right arm over the top of his neck.
❏ Hold the halter in your left hand just underneath the knot and pass it under his neck so you can undo the quick release knot with your right hand (Figure 3). Now you have the headpiece around his neck.
❏ Don't let go of the halter, just ask him to bring his head around towards you (see Exercise 11) and place his nose in the halter

(Figure 4). Your hands are now perfectly positioned to do up the knot and secure the halter and at no time have you had to let go of it or your horse (Figure 5).
❏ To take the halter off, do the same procedure in reverse, making sure his head is softly flexed towards you before slipping the halter off his nose.

Benefits

❏ Being particular about this will help your horse learn to have good manners when being caught and set free.
❏ The flexion means his hindquarters are more likely to go away from you than towards you, which keeps you safer.
❏ You can do the whole process without letting go of him or the halter, so you always have some control and a way of asking for flexion.
❏ You don't throw the headpiece over and risk hitting yourself or your horse in the eye.

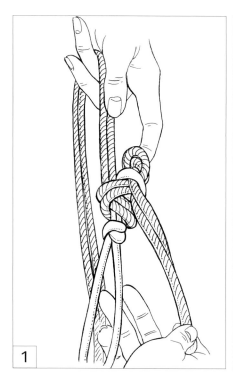

1

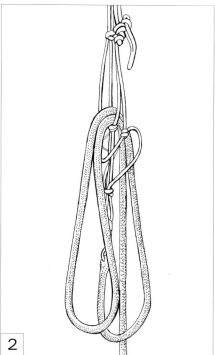

2

3

4

To tie the knot – follow Figure 6 and practise until you are sure it's right. This knot is called a 'sheet bend' and will neither slip nor become over tight. Tuck any excess away so that it can't flap in your horse's eye.

5

Remember
❑ Keep your feet still and wait until your horse's feet are still too.
❑ You can do this from both sides. If you turn the halter inside out, the knot will do up on the off side.

Problem solving
❑ Your horse will not bend and tries to avoid the halter – put another halter on as best you can and leave it on while you practise putting a second one on and off using this technique. It will give you more ability to control the situation while you retrain him.
❑ He turns away from you as you take the halter off – disengage the hindquarters to take his power away and bring his head towards you. Practise your flexion until it is really good and use a second halter so when you slip one off, he finds that you still have control. Practise until he is soft and patiently waits until you are ready before attempting this with just one halter.

HORSEMAN'S TIPS

Practise this at a quiet time in a safe place to start with. Work on it until it becomes second nature and it will stand you in good stead should a challenging situation arise.

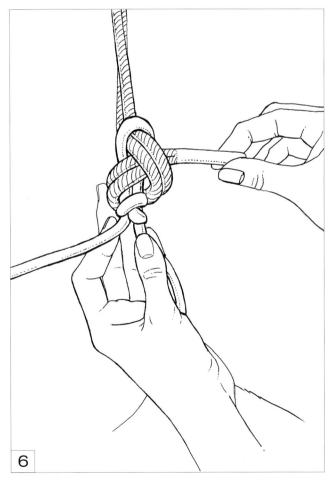

6

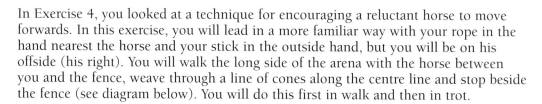

EXERCISE

13

Lead in serpetine from the offside

In Exercise 4, you looked at a technique for encouraging a reluctant horse to move forwards. In this exercise, you will lead in a more familiar way with your rope in the hand nearest the horse and your stick in the outside hand, but you will be on his offside (his right). You will walk the long side of the arena with the horse between you and the fence, weave through a line of cones along the centre line and stop beside the fence (see diagram below). You will do this first in walk and then in trot.

How do I do this?

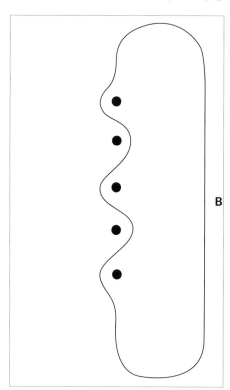

This is a simple exercise but it shows whether your horse is with you or not, and doing it from the offside shows up whether you or your horse are one sided. Some horses won't lead from the offside at all as they are so used to seeing us out of their left eye.

The aim is to have your horse yield to the slightest feel on the line, maintain distance on a soft contact and not hold back, run past you or switch sides on you.

- ❏ Stand beside your horse's right side facing forwards.
- ❏ Hold the rope in your left hand 30–45 cms (12–18 inches) below the clip.
- ❏ Hold your stick in your right hand with it pointed down to the floor and out behind you.
- ❏ To move forwards, extend your hand forwards and ask him to step (Figure 1).
- ❏ Starting at B, lead him on the right rein along the long side of the arena.
- ❏ Turn up the centre line and weave between the markers in a serpentine.
- ❏ Turn right at C and halt at B.
- ❏ Now repeat in trot.
- ❏ Change the rein and repeat, still staying on the offside.

Double check

Face forwards and focus where you want to go. Think about your energy level and have the energy you want your horse to have.

The halter should be exerting a light but consistent forwards feel on the line. Open your hand and try leading with the rope lying across it – that's how little pressure you should have. If

your horse doesn't step forwards (and the rope slips across your hand), point the stick behind you towards his hindquarters to encourage him to follow up, but don't turn around, just keep facing forwards and cause him to catch up.

Hints

- ❏ Position yourself just behind his jaw so that when you extend your arm forwards to lead him he can feel it on the halter.
- ❏ Don't hang on to the line, even the weight of your arm is heavy and will cause him to deaden to your feel or to fight for release.
- ❏ If he lags behind, use the end of the line or a stick behind his midline to ask him to put more effort in. Keep facing forwards – if you look back, your belly button power will tend to stop him.
- ❏ Many of you will be able to do this exercise at home, but not necessarily in new surroundings. Suddenly your horse either moves too much or won't move at all! This tells you about his confidence level. The more you work through these exercises, the more confidence you will both have.

1

B

Benefits

❑ Your horse will learn to follow the feel in the halter and stay with you in different directions.
❑ You will learn how to offer him feel and focus and how your energy affects his.
❑ You will both become more even sided.

Problem solving

❑ He doesn't step forward – use your stick (or the end of the rope if you don't have a stick) behind his driveline. Create some energy back there by moving the stick up and down and touching his hindquarters if necessary (Figure 2).

2

❑ He rushes past you – turn and walk the other way so he is behind you again, repeat till he learns not to rush past.
❑ He consistently pulls forward and leans on the halter – put some firm rhythm down the line or put the stick in front to block him (see Exercise 14).
❑ He barges you out of the way – see the basic information on blocking his entry into your personal space (Exercise 1).

If you can't do it, start on the nearside and then progress to the offside.

Moving on

❑ Check you can control his position and pace to maintain a set distance between you by repeating the exercise with his head alongside your shoulder, then behind you, then his shoulder alongside yours. First at walk, then at trot.
❑ Do it with indirect feel, following a cue from your finger as shown in Exercise .
❑ Aim to be in step with his footfall and alter your energy to adjust his speed.

Stop and back up straight while leading

This is an essential skill in leading, just as important as going forwards.

If you want to stop, slow down or back up, your horse should listen to you and follow your commands.

1

2

How do I do this?

It helps to begin this exercise with a fence on the other side of your horse from you (bear in mind you could and should practise leading him from both sides).

❑ Continuing from Exercise 13, lead your horse from the offside with him between you and the fence. Your rope should be in your left hand and your stick in the right. You should be facing forwards with your shoulder about level with his jaw, that is, in front of the driveline but not in front of his eye.

❑ Keep focusing forwards and when you want to stop, breathe out, tuck your pelvis under and rock your shoulders back a little as you stop your body quite sharply. This gives him a clear visual cue (Figure 1).

❑ If he doesn't stop, lift your hand that is holding the rein so that it lifts the knot on the halter to let him feel that you want him to stop. Repeat this several times until he stops on your body cue.

❑ Once he has learned the stop, you can begin on the backup. Lean your body back a little and keep your feet moving as if you are walking backwards on the spot (this will become a cue for him to back up). Lift the rein in rhythm with your footfall so the movement is felt on his nose to ask him to back up (Figure 2). You can increase this pressure to a firm bump if necessary, but keep it rhythmic – don't pull. As he steps, you step with him.

❑ Soon you will only have to stop your own body and back up and he will follow your cue.

3

Problem solving

❏ He doesn't stop when you ask with low pressure – increase the pressure in the rhythm and bring the stick in front of his nose. If he walks into it, so be it. He will learn the consequences of his actions and begin to pay more attention to your earlier signals. It is important that he stops, so be effective and fair – for example, unfair would be to let him walk into the stick without the preceding cue.

❏ Make sure you are not too close to the fence as it may make him feel claustrophobic and more likely to need to keep his feet moving – and therefore more difficult to stop.

❏ He turns across you – bring your stick forwards so it is parallel with his neck to keep his head straight (Figure 3).

❏ He stops but doesn't back up – again, increase the rhythmic pressure and use the stick to support your request if necessary. Reward the slightest try, and repeat till he understands and follows with lightness.

Remember

❏ The fence is there to keep his hindquarters from swinging away from you. Practise this until you can do it without the fence and stay straight.

❏ Practise from both sides.

❏ Keep your stick low so he doesn't back up with a high head and hollow back.

❏ Be in rhythm with your horse's footfall, forwards and backwards.

Moving on

Once your horse starts to read your body language, you will find that he will walk, slow down and stop in step with you – to the point where you will scarcely need the rope, or stick.

HORSEMAN'S TIPS
Your body should do what you want your horse's body to do. Stop with your hindquarters underneath and shoulders lifted!

Preparation for a circle

There are many exercises on a circle that will benefit your horse's training. But first you have to cause him to go around you – which some people struggle with. The problem is often that they can't send the front end around them because the horse keeps turning to face them. This is usually because they put their pressure towards the hindquarters instead of the forequarters, or the horse doesn't understand what is needed. This exercise prepares for the first part of the circle, also called the 'send'.

How do I do this?

❏ Start with your horse facing you about 1.2 metres (4 feet) away. In this instance, we are going to send him to your right as if he were about to go on a right rein, but for now we only want his front end to go across and the hind end to stay still, so he will be making about a quarter turn on the haunches away from you.

❏ Imagine a circle with your horse's hindquarters at the centre. You will stay on the track and he will step his front end across 90 degrees.

❏ With your horse standing still, take a couple of steps to your right along the track so that you are now on your horse's left side looking at him.

❏ With your rope in your right hand, extend your arm out and give a direct rein so that your horse feels the halter asking him to bring his front end across so that he puts you on his right side (Figure 1).

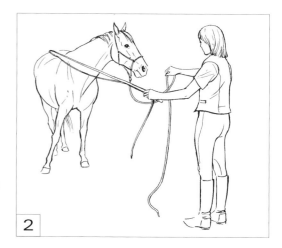

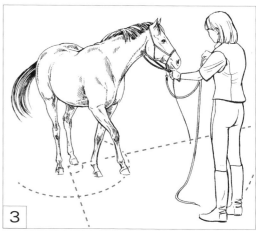

❏ If he doesn't follow the feel on the line, support the turn by lifting your stick in your left hand and giving some indirect pressure towards his neck (just behind his ears) to help drive him towards the feel on the line (Figures 2 and 3).

❏ When he moves his forehand across release, give him comfort for a few moments and then step to his left side again and repeat. This way you could gradually build up to a turn on the haunches with you walking a circle in front of him, but as preparation for sending your horse out on a circle you only need a quarter turn.

Double check

- ❏ Make sure he moves his front end across and keeps the hind end still.
- ❏ Keep to your track – don't let him change your focus or direction.

Problem solving

- ❏ He walks forward – put some rhythm pulses down the line so the halter bumps on his nose to discourage the forward drift. If he still comes forward, use your stick in front of his nose to block him.
- ❏ He won't move over because his feet are stuck – use the stick to tap him with rhythm on his shoulder with more and more purpose until he moves.
- ❏ He moves over but then moves his hindquarters away too so he's facing you again – make sure you gave him enough line and didn't accidentally pull his head back towards you.

If you just can't get it, repeat the work in Exercise 10, which is the same exercise but from a different position.

Remember

- ❏ Reward the try with comfort so he knows he is doing what you want.
- ❏ Make sure you can do this from both sides to send him on both reins.

Moving on

When asking your horse to step to the left, encourage him to move his left foot first in response to your direct rein. The supporting (stick) should then ask the right foot to come across. This helps him begin a turn with an elevated inside shoulder and refines your communication so one cue equals one step.

HORSEMAN'S TIPS

Horses usually favour one rein, which is often the left rein, and is thought to possibly be because of how they lie in their mother's womb.

If you find one side easier than another, help your horse learn the exercise on his easy side but then make sure you spend more time working on the other side to make them even.

Simple circle

The idea of this exercise is to help you understand the basic concept of sending your horse around you on a circle from a distance while you stay relatively still and practise all the skills of directional control you learned in Chapter 2.

You are going to back your horse away from you, ask him to circle around you maintaining gait for three circuits and then turn to face you.

How do I do this?

❑ Pick a spot that will be the centre of your circle and put a marker on it – for example, a small bag with sand in it or a handful of wood shavings (not big enough to trip over!). With your horse facing you, ask him to go backwards using indirect feel until he is at least 2.5 metres (8 feet) away from

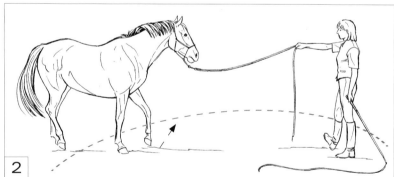

you. Backing up puts his weight on his hindquarters, lightens his front end and clears your personal space (Figure 1).

❑ *Without you stepping backwards*, send his forequarters away using a direct rein and support from the stick if necessary as covered in Exercise 15. As he goes, allow the rein to slip through your hand to 3 or 3.5 metres (10 or 12 feet) (Figure 2). Ideally you want your horse to walk calmly around you to start with. Transitions between the gaits is handled in Exercise 17.

❑ Once he walks on, relax your body posture and hold your rein in neutral position with feel in the line (that is, not tight or dragging on the floor) (Figure 3). Keep turning with him as he walks – only use the stick if he changes gait or the pace within the gait. Otherwise trust him to do what you have asked.

❑ When he has walked three circuits, run your hand down the rein to feel for the connection with the horse and ask him to disengage his hindquarters by yielding them away from your indirect pressure (as in Exercise 8) (Figures 4 and 5). Encourage him to stay out on the circle when he disengages and not rush in on top of you. When he has paused there for a moment, ask him to come and stand with you for a rest. This helps him start to associate you with comfort but keeps the discipline of respecting your space (Figure 6).

❑ Once you can do this successfully on both reins, try it in trot and then in canter and alter the number of circuits, sometimes more and sometimes less – keep him guessing. (Choosing a number simply helps you make a plan and your intention helps you carry it out.)

Problem solving

❑ You can't send him around you – practise Exercise 15.

❑ He goes off like a rocket – be more subtle with your pressure. You may only need a hand signal – remember to do as little as possible.

❑ He won't disengage – shorten the rope, but

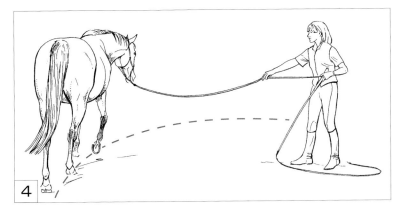

4

5

6

hindquarters, whichever is pushing on your space, until he moves out again.

❑ He falls in towards you when you ask him to stop – lifting your rope hand will sometimes be enough to stop him as it will lift his head which alters his balance, helping him not fall forwards.

Sometimes horses just need to move their feet, so if he is going faster than you intended, or bucking and plunging, it's acceptable to let off that steam as long as he is not too close to you. So remember to adjust the size of your personal bubble according to your horse's mood – if he is calm and soft, your bubble can be smaller than if he is exuberant or threatening. Once he has used up some energy, he may be in a better frame of mind to pay attention to you – just like young children at school, you need to find the balance between work and play.

See how subtle you can make your commands – horsemanship is about feel and timing.

Reminder

❑ You won't control your horse's footfall if you are not aware of your own. Keep them as still as possible, and don't step backwards as you will encourage your horse into your space.

❑ Keep your horse out on the circle and do not allow him to cut in.

Note

❑ Smaller circles are harder work for your horse but you may have more influence. A bigger circle requires better communication to keep the situation under control.

❑ With a green horse, start slow and small and build up to higher paces on bigger circles (you can walk with him to make the circle bigger on the same length of line – it's acceptable to move your feet if it's your conscious decision). As your horse develops balance and posture, the circle can become smaller again at higher paces.

Benefits

❑ Your horse learns to move around you and that you control his footfall.

❑ He will learn to listen to your commands from a greater distance.

❑ It opens the door to many other exercises.

HORSEMAN'S TIPS

Try not to use the stick while he is doing what you want, because the horse soon learns to tune it out if it has no meaning, or learns to lean on the constant command and not think for himself. Either way, you are wearing out the effectiveness of your subtle request, meaning you will have to do more in future to get the same result.

---

no less than 1.8 metres (6 feet), and keep your energy focused on his hindquarters until he stops. Then practise Exercise 8 until it is really good.

❑ He disengages but comes in towards you too much – make sure you have not pulled him in on the rope. Send a pulse down the rope if necessary to discourage forwards and keep him out of your space.

❑ He cuts in on you, dropping the feel on the line and pushing his ribs or hindquarters towards you – gently flick the string on your stick towards the underside of his ribs, or towards his

Transitions on a circle

Once your horse understands the basic circle, you need to be able to adjust his gait.
This exercise is about learning signals for upward and downward transitions. The beauty of these signals is that they can be applied to any gait, which means you and the horse have fewer commands to learn.
In this example, you will be moving from walk to trot and back to walk.

How do I do this?

It's all about your energy and teaching your horse to read and respond to it.

❑ Ask your horse to go around you in walk on a right rein, as per Exercise 16. As he is walking, your energy should be quite low and your body relaxed since he is doing what you've asked. Now take a deep breath, sand still and lift your energy so your horse can tell you want something.

❑ Make sure you have connection down the line, which is in your right hand, lift your right shoulder, straighten your arm and give him a clear direct rein with your right hand to ask for trot. You should see that this puts some feel on the halter – if it doesn't, your rein is too long (or horse too close). He must be able to feel the halter has gone forward, and his job is to hurry up to stay within it. Keep your belly button pointing behind the driveline (Figure 1).

❑ If he doesn't trot, keep the direction on the line and lift your stick in your left hand 180 degrees away from your right hand. If he still doesn't trot, swing the stick out behind his tail, and if this doesn't have the desired effect, swing the stick so the string touches the root of his tail.

❑ As soon as he trots, stop the pressure and go to a neutral stance. This will quickly teach him what he needs to do to find release from the pressure, and you will soon discover that he will respond to the lift in your energy and a slight feel on the rein.

❑ Trot a couple of circuits and then, pointing your belly button in front of the driveline, breathe out, drop your energy and send a gentle pulse down the line so the halter just bounces on his nose. If he doesn't walk, send stronger rhythmic pulses down the line, and if he still doesn't respond as you want, point your stick under the rope and in front of his nose (Figure 2) – you can move it up and down if necessary, gradually increasing the energy in front of him until he comes back to walk, though it doesn't matter if it takes a whole circuit. If you hassle him too much, he may become defensive and want to rush. Don't *make* him slow down, *help* him slow down. He will soon understand your meaning and respond to your energy, and if you don't make him feel wrong, he will be more willing to try.

❑ Play with the transitions (on both reins) going from walk to trot to walk, and then add canter.

Benefits

Making transitions between the gaits is one of the key ways to improve your horse's balance and way of going as they encourage him to use his hindquarters better and lift his forehand. They also encourage him to listen, think and respond to your signals.

Hints

❑ Be clear about your body language. Energy up for upward transition, and down for downward – ensure your body is doing what you want your horse's body to do.
❑ Always give clear direction down the line before lifting the stick. Otherwise, it's as if you are shouting at him before you've even asked him.

Problem solving

❑ Upward transitions – if your horse doesn't have enough 'go' and won't make the transition, you may have to touch him firmly on the rump with the string on the stick. Even if he doesn't make the transition but speeds up a bit, reward this attempt by taking the pressure off and then go through the process again repeatedly until he realizes that discomfort will follow if he doesn't make an effort. It is very tempting to just use the higher pressure if you don't think he will respond to lightness but this is a mistake. Always offer lightness and back up your request with progressive pressure until you get a try. This is the key to lightness in the horse. If you don't offer him lightness, he will never respond to it!

❑ Downward transitions – if he rushes or won't slow down, allow him to travel a bit longer until he has moved his feet enough to become less emotional. Use the degrees of pressure described opposite to let him know what you want and wait until he responds. You can slow him down or stop him by partially or fully disengaging the hindquarters as in Exercise 16, and start afresh if necessary.

Remember

❑ Stay unemotional. Don't chase him to go or make him slow. Be cool and collected and that will help you be clear for your horse.
❑ See how refined your signals can become once your horse understands.
❑ Many people like to use voice commands, especially for transitions because the tone used can be helpful. If you use voice commands to support your requests, make sure you still use your body language and are ready to reinforce if necessary.
❑ Don't make it the horse's job to learn our language.

Moving on

❑ When your horse really understands and is responding well, you can try more difficult transitions – for example, walk to canter to walk and also start to include halt and back up (see Exercise 25).
❑ Ask for transitions using your breath as a cue. Breathe in for upward and out for downward transitions – you might be surprised how perceptive your horse is!

Experiencing the horse's posture

As in shown in Chapter 1 (see 'Balance and biomechanics', page 14), you need to be aware of your horse's posture because he was built to run, not to carry weight. To carry weight without damaging himself, his posture has to change. Before considering how to influence your horse's physical way of going, you need to understand basic biomechanics and what a balanced posture is. This is best achieved by simulation, helping you obtain a clear feeling of this before working on it with your horse.

How do I do this?

Apologies for this but this is an experiential guide and you need to get on your *hands* and *knees* with this page of the book open on the floor between your hands where you can read it.

So, are you ready? Then we'll begin! Follow the steps below and take time over each one to really feel it. It might seem a bit eccentric but the insights it will give you are well worth it.

❑ **Step 1** 'Stand' on all fours in a neutral position, that is, four square with your weight evenly distributed over your hands and knees and with your back and neck straight. Notice that nothing is particularly in tension – it's an easy posture if you're not moving.

❑ **Step 2** Slowly, keeping your shoulders level and without shifting your weight back, lift your right fore (hand). Notice the muscles you need to use in your stomach and the tension it creates over your loin area. Now stand square again.

❑ **Step 3** Repeat step 2, but this time start with a hollow back and notice what happens to your head and neck and how the strain over your loins increases (Figure 1).

❑ **Step 4** From neutral again, move your weight forwards and see how it feels in your arms, shoulders, neck and back. Now try lifting your right fore! Notice that if you can do this at all, it is by putting your ribs to the right and your head to the left as a counter balance. Your withers and right shoulder have dropped and the strain on the left foreleg is enormous. (This is a posture that I commonly see when horses are circling – sometimes because they are defensive and thinking about leaving, and sometimes because they are on the forehand and down in the wither – either way, we need to address it to prepare them for riding.)

❑ **Step 5** Return to neutral. Now lift your right hind leg up and under your belly button. Notice how this changes the flexion through your ribs and your neck, right down to your nose, which now feels like it wants to go to the right. If you were circling to the right, this would be the correct bend and you would be said to be straight on the circle.

1

- **Step 6** This time from neutral, move your weight back over your hindquarters and try to lift your forelegs, one at a time and then both together – easier isn't it!
- **Step 7** From the neutral position, use your stomach muscles to tuck your 'tail' under. Don't shift your weight back for a moment, just notice that your back has risen and your head and neck feel more comfortable dropping down a bit. Again it's not that easy to lift a foreleg and the strain is taken on the opposite foreleg and shoulder.
- **Step 8** Now move your weight back over your hind legs and see how much more your back arches up and your withers are lifted, yet your head and neck want to stretch down (Figure 2). Your whole top line feels longer and now it's easy to lift your front legs and there is no strain in your back.

That's it for now, you can get up again!

Remember

Engagement gives the horse power, which you want when his heart and mind are tuned to positive reflexes. If he has opposition reflexes to your ideas, disengagement is vital for safety because it takes his power away.

Benefits

This exercise will help you understand that by asking your horse to flex on the circle, moving his ribs to the outside and his inside hind underneath him more, his back will lift and so lighten the front end. His nose will start to follow the direction of travel and the rest of his body will follow his nose. The more he works from behind, the more his withers will lift and his nose will come to the vertical, just as you experienced on the floor. Your horse will soon learn and develop muscles to hold this new frame even on straight lines and with light contact – this is self-carriage.

2

EXERCISE 19

Improve posture on a circle

One of the best uses of a circle is to work on your horse's posture and balance to prepare him for riding. Left to his own devices, he is likely to fall on his forehand, look to the outside and not use his hindquarters for propulsion as much as he could. In this exercise, you will learn how to create bend, improve his posture and encourage him to work better from behind without the use of additional equipment, first in walk and then in trot and canter.

How do I do this?

Carry out Exercise 18 first so you have a clear idea of what you are aiming for.

- ❏ Ask your horse to go around you in a circle at walk.
- ❏ Keep a feel on the line as you turn with him.
- ❏ Think about your horse's spine – if you had a bird's eye view, would his spine follow the same arc as the circle?
- ❏ Try to feel if any part of his body is pushing on your space – for example, if he is looking to the outside of the circle his ribs will probably be pushed in a little towards you, so he will not have the correct bend through his body.
- ❏ Point your stick at whichever part of his body needs to yield to the shape of the circle (Figure 1).
- ❏ If he is not using his hindquarters actively, generate activity with the inside hind leg by aiming your pressure at his hindquarters so that he steps underneath himself more (Figure 2).

- ❏ You may need to use the stick with rhythm, and even flick the string and make contact to get him to yield. As he does so, take the pressure off him again.

This will take many repetitions, but you will start to notice that as the hindquarters works underneath better, his ribs go to the outside, his back rounds and his head drops.

Problem solving

- ❏ Your horse just goes faster when you direct your stick at him – he will probably do this when you put one leg on when you are riding too. He has not learned that pressure here doesn't mean go faster, it means yield. Make sure your energy is low and you are not doing more than necessary. If he keeps getting faster, push his hindquarters further out as a partial disengagement to take his power away and start again, or send pulses down the rein to slow him as in Exercise 17.
- ❏ He keeps disengaging and turning to face you when you want him to keep going – don't make him feel wrong for doing this. If you

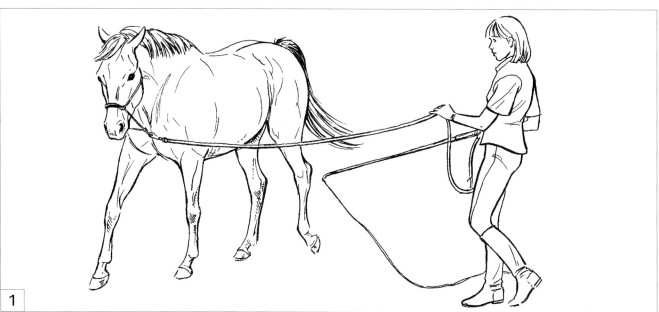

1

have been practising your hindquarters yield, he will think this is what you want and be trying to do what you've asked for – just help him understand this is different by giving him direction on the rein while you shape his body with the stick.

❑ He falls in on the shoulder – point your stick to that area.

If he is stepping under his own belly button and using his back properly, he should automatically stop looking to the outside and be following his nose better around the circle, giving a lighter feel on the line. Some horses still manage to work well from behind yet flex to the outside at the poll and lean on the halter. In this case, you can put some vibration down the line to the halter to remind him to lead with his nose, releasing as soon as he softens. In doing this, be careful you don't pull him in – point the stick at his shoulder if necessary to keep him out.

Remember
❑ This is not a quick fix. You are asking your horse to change his posture, which takes time and

effort. Don't ask for too long at a time – he needs to build strength to hold this frame.

❑ Your horse pushing on you can be very subtle and hard to notice until you get tuned to it – try to feel his bubble pushing on yours.

❑ This may take a few sessions to achieve, you must be patient.

❑ Practise on both reins.

❑ Build up to trot and canter.

Hints
❑ Ask the inside hind to step into the track of the outside fore for a few steps at a time. You may find it difficult to see a change in his body but it will be more obvious in his head carriage. Note, however, that the change in head carriage is effected by working on the hind end!

❑ When you use the stick towards his body make it an upward motion to cause him to lift his belly or inside leg.

Benefits
Your horse will be able to find true self-carriage rather than being held in place by equipment. This will help when you are riding too.

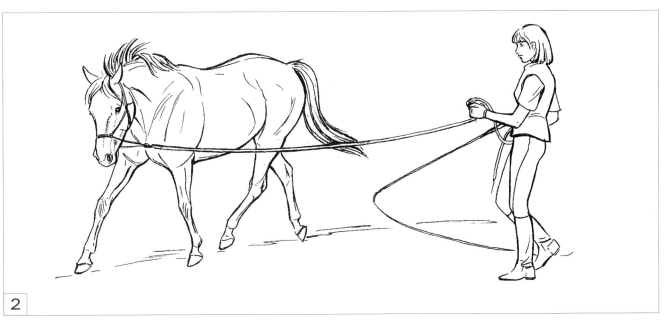

2

Circle at short range

In this version of circling, you will stay close to the horse in order to work on his posture more effectively at different gaits, to teach him to follow your body language and to work in the same gait as you.

How do I do this?

Make sure you can do the fundamental Exercise 10, only this time you will have a light contact on the rope, which will be shorter than your stick.

- ❏ Stand at your horse's shoulder, focus forward and bring your energy up.
- ❏ Ask him to step forwards to follow a feel on the halter, followed by a light tap on his hindquarters if necessary to encourage him to step.
- ❏ Walk forwards with him, staying at his shoulder and keeping enough feel on the line to keep a little lateral flexion towards you as you walk in a circle of about 10 metres. Your stick (in the hand nearest him) should rest in the middle of his back when he is doing as you have asked (Figure 1).
- ❏ If you sense him pushing or leaning in with his ribs or shoulders, use your stick rhythmically on that part of his body to ask him to yield away again, while keeping his nose flexed towards you. His body should be soft and moving in an arc around you.

- ❏ Lift your energy again and ask for trot by trotting yourself (tap him on the rump if necessary) (Figure 2).

Hints

Think of using your stick like the bow of a violin when you ask his body to yield. It has a circular motion, making an upward sweep on contact with the horse which has a lifting effect.

Reminders

- ❏ You are looking for flexion throughout the body and soft contact in the line.
- ❏ Your horse should hold himself upright, not down in the shoulder or leaning in.
- ❏ Practise this from both sides.

Benefits

- ❏ This exercise is good for teaching your horse to move on the circle in the correct bend.
- ❏ It tunes you into thinking about whether your horse is leaning in or pushing on you and how he is carrying himself on the circle.
- ❏ Working close up enables you to work in a concentrated way.

1

2

- You can use this exercise for doing upward and downward transitions to improve the horse's balance.
- Shows you if your horse gets worried by movement close up at higher gaits
- Keeps you fit!

Problem solving
- He bends around you too much – pivot your stick forwards so it is parallel with his neck to straighten him. Make sure you are not holding back with your rein. You should be keeping a feel but it must travel with him.
- He gets excited or agitated when you move into higher gaits – he may find your movement disconcerting so close up. Do some work on desensitizing him to you jumping up and down and being really active around him – don't let him train you to be stiller and stiller as it will work against you both in the long run.
- He doesn't make the downward transition when you do – remember to breathe out, lift your line and pivot the stick so it lies parallel to his neck (same technique as used in Exercise 14).

Moving on
- Ask your horse to canter alongside you as you canter (you will need to make the circle bigger) (Figure 3).

- Play around with transitions and reach a level where your horse will simply follow whichever gait you move in, using just your energy or breathing for the transition.

3

Using markers on a circle

In this exercise, you are going to put some of your skills together and test your accuracy and timing by having your horse circling and using the markers to make accurate transitions from a distance.

Set up
Place two markers near X in the centre of the arena either side of the centre line about 1.8 metres (6 feet) apart. These will be on the edge of your circle.

How do I do this?
❑ Stand in the centre of the circle with your horse standing between the two markers facing you (see diagram below).

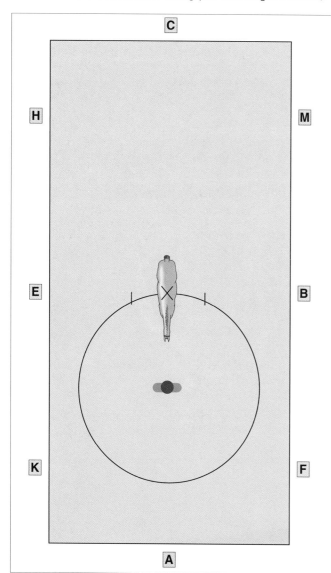

❑ Send him out around the marker on the right rein in walk (Figure 1). Walk one circuit.
❑ Make an upward transition to trot when he crosses the centre line between the markers.
❑ Trot two circuits, and canter next time he reaches the markers. Canter three circuits.
❑ Make downward transitions in the same place, trot for two circuits and walk for one, then ask him to come back to you by disengaging his hindquarters and walking between the markers and down the centre line (Figure 2).
❑ Reward.

Remember
❑ Don't move your feet away from the centre of the circle, just turn on the spot as your horse goes around you.
❑ Being able to control your horse's gait and his direction is a challenge that increases with distance.
❑ Practise on both reins.
❑ Do as little as possible but as much as necessary to make yourself understood.
❑ Only support with your stick if your horse has not responded to clear direction on your rein first.

Benefits
❑ This exercise tests your accuracy.
❑ Having a clear plan will help you transmit your intention to your horse.

Problem solving
All the elements needed for success in this exercise have been covered in Exercises 16, 17 and 27. Don't worry if something is not working, just break it down into smaller pieces and then recombine it when all the elements are achievable.

Moving on
Reach a level to where you can begin the exercise by backing your horse from the centre of the circle to go between the markers (see Exercise 27).

HORSEMAN'S TIPS
Remember, the lead horse in a group can and will control the gait and direction of the others.

1

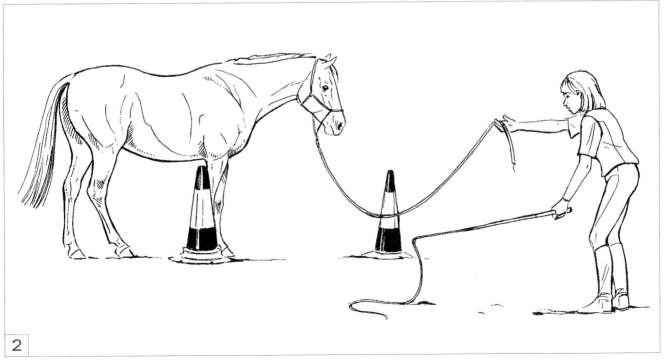

2

EXERCISE
22

Change direction through a circle

This is one way to change direction on a circle, keeping the forwards rhythm and momentum and asking your horse to follow his nose through the centre of the circle in a graceful 'S' shape to change the rein (see diagram below).

How do I do this?

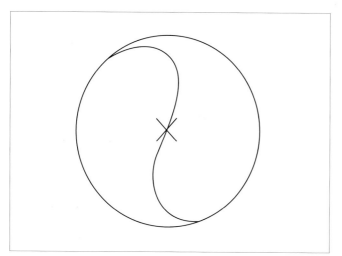

❑ Ask your horse to walk around you on a circle.
❑ Feel for a connection down the line and start to walk backwards in a gentle spiral, drawing him towards you but maintaining the distance between you as you both keep walking (Figure 1).
❑ As he starts to face you, keep going backwards and swap hands by passing your stick under the rope (Figure 2).
❑ Give a direct rein to indicate the new direction you want him to go, supporting with the stick to send his neck or shoulder (Figures 3 and 4).
❑ Go back and stand in the centre of your circle.
❑ Once you can do this well in walk, build up to trot.

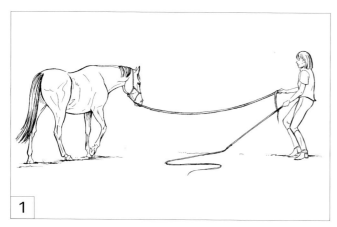

1

2

3

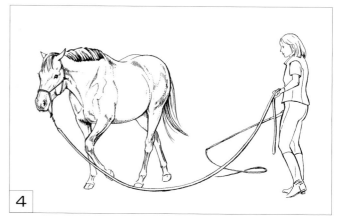

4

Double check

Your horse should not be looking to the outside of the circle before you begin. Make sure he has the correct bend to start with.

Reminders

❏ The idea is that he doesn't fall in through the shoulder, so make the curve gradual to start with until he gets the idea and be sure not to pull him in.

❏ Keep the momentum.

Problem solving

❏ He doesn't face you when you spiral – use partial hindquarters disengagement to cause him to face you and try to keep him flowing forward.

❏ He won't come towards you – practice Exercise 3.

You can't keep the momentum – think of a driveline in your horse's eye that divides the eye in half. Make sure you are in the front half of his eye when you start to draw him in (see diagram below).

Benefits

❏ This exercise shows that your horse is following feel.

❏ It is useful to be able to change direction without having to reel him in and start again.

❏ This exercise is a pre-requisite for canter lead changes on line.

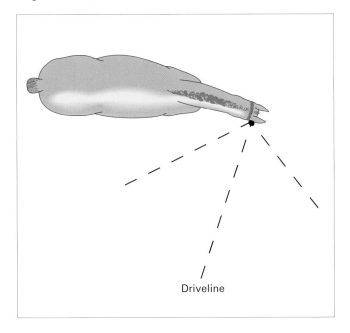
Driveline

Change direction over hindquarters

Instead of coming through the centre of a circle to change direction, you can also ask your horse to turn over his hindquarters while remaining out on the circle.

1

3

2

How do I do this?

❑ Start with your horse walking around you in a circle on the right rein, preferably on the end of a 3.5 metre (12 foot) line.

❑ Swap your rope into your left hand and your stick into your right, but keep your arms crossed so the stick is still on your left side, pointing behind your horse, and is underneath your rope.

❑ Put some energy towards his hindquarters (Figure 1) so that it moves slightly to the outside as he steps well under himself (he should keep his front legs on the track and not come closer).

❑ Now your rope is in the correct hand to lead his front end with a direct rein and ask him to change direction and go off on the left rein (Figure 2). Bring your stick to your right side and support the neck and shoulders for the turn (Figure 3).

Hints

Start slowly and try to keep your feet still. The idea is that your horse brings his hindquarters well underneath him so he can make the change of direction with a light forehand.

Reminders

Feel for your horse – don't pull his head in, instead, drive his quarters away.

Benefits

❑ This exercise builds agility and power because it really gets the hindquarters working underneath the horse.

❑ It tests your ability to influence his direction over a greater distance.

❑ It is a great exercise for developing your dexterity and rope handling skills.

❑ It is good for energizing a lazy horse.

Problem solving

❑ He becomes flustered and goes backwards instead of crossing his forequarters into the other direction – you have probably done this too fast. Slow it all down and make sure you both understand the elements before putting them together.

❑ He just gets faster and continues on the same rein – until he learns the new pattern slow everything down and put the hindquarters further out so you have two eyes facing you and his body is straight before asking for the new direction. If he is still looking to the right, that is the way he will go.

❑ He comes in too close – be quicker to give the new direction and send his front end more convincingly.

Moving on

When you and your horse understand the feel and timing try this in trot, and even canter.

HORSEMAN'S TIPS

Find the balance between this and getting your horse to come to you for comfort, otherwise you may lose your draw.

Changes of direction while travelling along a line

Building on Exercise 23, see if you can cause your horse to make a change of direction every half circle as you travel forwards in a straight line down the arena (see diagram below).

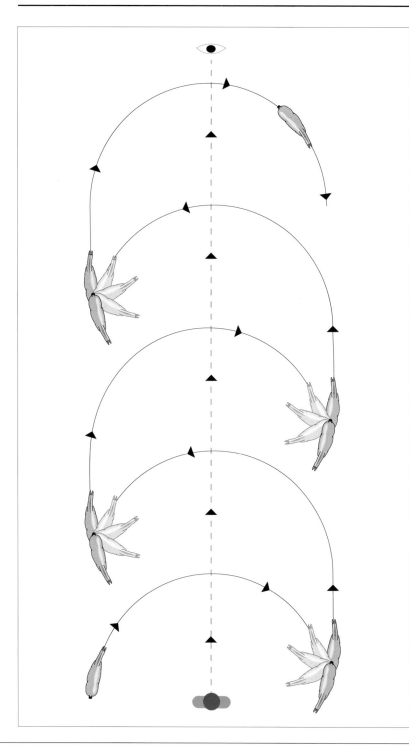

How do I do this?

Exactly as in the last exercise but this time walk forwards and ask your horse to change direction every time he comes parallel with your shoulder. You will need to change hands to the crossed position whenever the horse crosses the line you are walking. Then you will be ready to make a change of direction over the hindquarters and send him the other way. Repeat several times so you travel at least 30 metres.

Hint

❑ So that you don't get too tied up with your rope and stick, do this at walk first – even if you can do the previous exercise at trot or canter, because events will happen very fast and you need to be organized!

❑ Drag one of your feet in the sand as you travel – you can then look back and see how straight you were.

❑ Try to be graceful and allow the exercise to flow. It should look like you and your horse are dancing.

Benefits

❏ An excellent exercise for improving your rope-handling skills.
❏ Helps a horse get to where he can handle your requests coming one after another and still keep his emotions under control.

Remember

❏ Focus on a point in the distance and walk straight towards it.
❏ Keep your horse out on the end of the line, don't let him drop the feel and get too close to you.
❏ Using the full length of the rope will give you more time between turns and provide space if your horse becomes excited.
❏ When you get to the end, give him a break as a reward.
❏ Keep your communication as subtle as possible and as clear as necessary.

Problem solving

❏ You can't do it – there is just a hole in your preparation. Go back and improve it so you set up yourself and your horse for success.
❏ You miss the moment when your horse is level with your shoulder – don't worry, just let him travel a full circuit before trying again.

Moving on

Yes, you guessed it – try at trot and then canter! You will find your horse makes flying lead changes at every turn.

HORSEMAN'S TIPS

When you learn a language, you have to learn the individual words first before you can make your first clumsy sentences. One day, eventually, if you are passionate enough to practise, you will become fluent and it all becomes effortless.

Backwards from a fence

This exercise tests whether you can control your horse's footfall while controlling your own, so you are going to sit on a fence and ask him to back up straight for 3.5 metres (see diagram below).

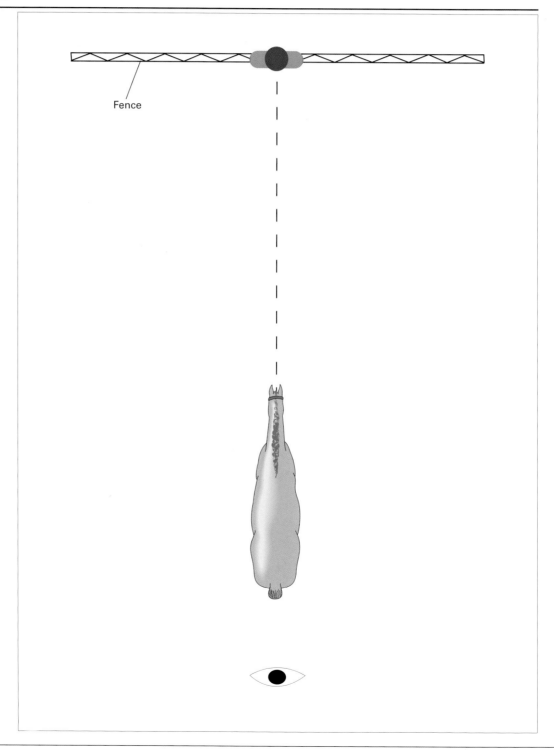

Fence

How do I do this?

❏ Pick a good strong fence or gate to sit on.
❏ Have your horse facing you and close enough that you can rub him on his head.
❏ Ask him to back away from direct feel on his nose until he reaches arm's length.
❏ Then go to indirect feel and aim to drive him backwards to the end of the line.
❏ Give him comfort at the end of the line as a reward.

Reminders

❏ If you rush, your horse is more likely to go crooked.
❏ Try to point your energy low, at his chest or below – by being a bit taller you may make him go back with his head up if you are not careful.
❏ Reward with comfort, for longer than you think. This will motivate him to put more effort into it the next time.

Benefits

Sitting on the fence can really highlight if your horse usually gets you to move your feet when doing these kinds of exercises.

Problem solving

❏ Hindquarters are crooked – straighten them up using indirect pressure to that area (see Exercise 8).
❏ Your horse tries to push you off the fence – defend your bubble! (See Exercise 1.)
❏ Your horse doesn't feel confident with you higher up – spend some time getting his confidence with this, after all, this is more like the height you will be when riding him.

Moving on

Try putting a couple of markers about 3.5 metres from the fence and back him between them while sitting on the fence.

Back and over

Here you will combine backwards and yielding the forequarters to achieve a backup around a corner or on a circle (see diagram below).

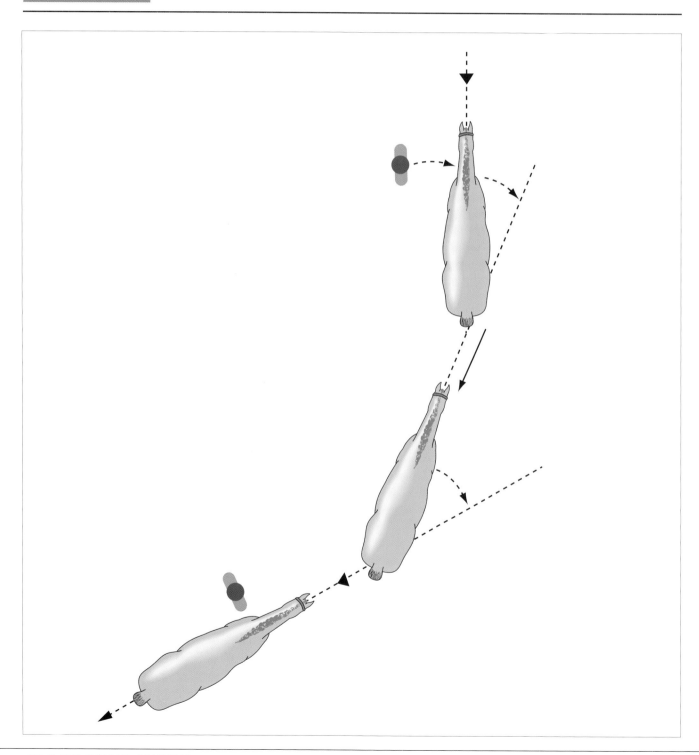

How do I do this?

- ❑ Stand along side your horse and face forwards with your rope in the hand furthest from him and stick in the one nearest him.
- ❑ Ask him to back up a few steps (Figure 1).
- ❑ Turn and face through him and ask him to yield his forequarters away from you a step, keeping his hindquarters still (Figure 2).
- ❑ Reward him and then repeat – back up and step over, back up and step over.

You will find your horse is walking around a bend backwards.

Remember

- ❑ Build this up a few steps at a time.
- ❑ Give comfort when he's followed your instructions correctly – it will motivate him to do the same next time.

Problem solving

Since you have hopefully practised the elements of this manoeuvre many times by now, the most likely problem you will encounter is that you try to put these together too quickly and confuse your horse.

Benefits

- ❑ It gives you the ability to back you horse around a corner.
- ❑ It can be used to straighten your horse if he crosses in front of you while trying to back in a straight line (such as Exercise 14 but with the rope in the other hand).

Moving on

Increase the distance between you. Build it up to where you can ask him to back around you in a circle while you stand in the middle. Then try adding this to your transitions from walk!

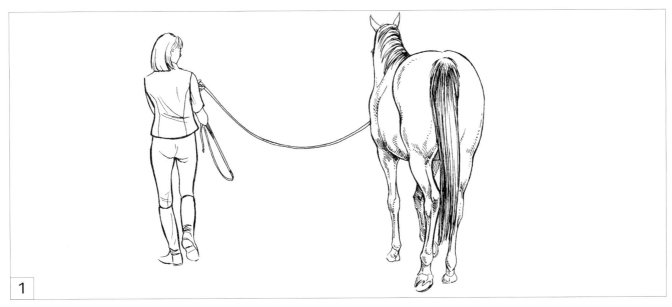

1

2

Back between two markers

The aim of this exercise is to be able to ask your horse to go backwards between two markers while you stand still (see diagram below).

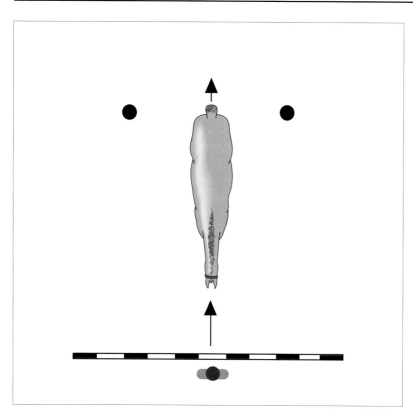

Set up
Put two cones or buckets on the ground about 1.8 metres apart and lay a pole alongside them about 2.5 metres away

How do I do this?
Back your horse through the markers while you stay the other side of the pole.

Problem solving
❏ Your horse will go backwards until he gets near the markers then swings his hindquarters to avoid the challenge – lead him through forwards first, stop between the markers and make it a place of comfort. Bring him forward one step, and back him up to rest between the markers. Build it up from there one step at a time.

❏ All goes well while he is between the markers but doesn't like them behind him – you have not created enough comfort there. Try moving them wider apart until he is confident, then close them together again. Exercises 6 and 41 will help you with this.

Remember
❏ Your horse doesn't know what you want. Work on the elements separately before you put them together.
❏ Anything behind the driveline will tend to make him go forwards.
❏ Use the fundamental groundskills you learned in Chapter 2 to reposition him without moving your feet!
❏ The narrower or taller the markers, the more claustrophobic he will feel and the harder it will be.

Benefits
❏ It makes you think!
❏ Your horse has a blind spot directly behind him (and right in front of his eyes), so it's a big test of trust and communication for him to follow your directions to go somewhere he can't see.
❏ Your horse will gain more trust in you as he learns that you never ask anything that has undesirable consequences.
❏ It's good for practising your directional control, using indirect feel.

Moving on
Move the cones further from the pole.

HORSEMAN'S TIPS
Set it up for success – think laterally!

EXERCISE 28

Steer backwards around a figure of eight – direct feel

A figure of eight is such a useful shape as it works the horse on both reins. This time you are going to back around it, which will help you with steering backwards – if you can steer, you can also stay straight (see diagram below).

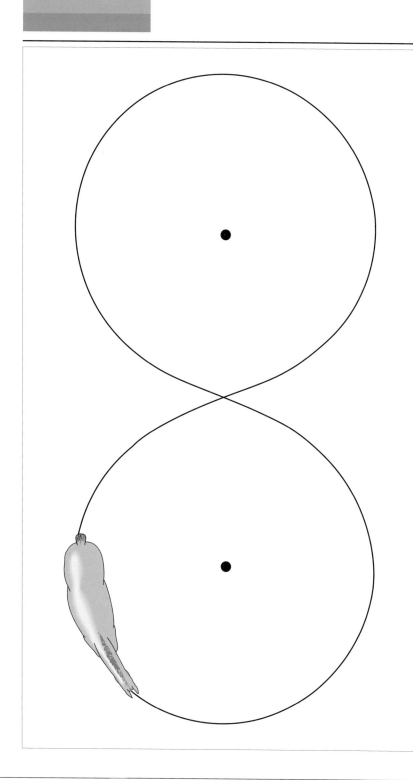

Set up
Place two markers 3.5 metres apart.

How do I do this?
❑ Stand to the side of your horse's nose, facing backwards.
❑ Using direct feel off his nose, ask your horse to softly yield backwards around and between the markers.

Reminders
❑ Make sure your horse is not braced against you. Encourage him to be soft in your hand before asking him to move his feet.
❑ Make sure you are not pushing with your hand. If his feet do not move freely, use your stick or the end of your rope to put some rhythm towards his feet.
❑ Try to stay on your chosen track – don't let your horse deflect your focus or shut you down.

Problem solving
❑ Your horse's feet are stuck – make sure he can back up straight. If he can and is just confused, move his nose from side to side and rock him over his front feet until they move, then continue backwards making the loops bigger if necessary.
❑ You can't steer – tip his nose the opposite way to where you want his hindquarters to go.
❑ You horse throws his head about to shake you off – go back to fundamentals and practise backwards off the nose.

Benefits
It checks your steering, focus and positioning.

Moving on
Try doing this using indirect feel from a greater distance.

Manouevre around a figure of eight – indirect feel

This is a combination of Exercises 27 and 28, only this time you are going to ask your horse to make a figure of eight around the markers while you keep your feet still (see diagram below)!

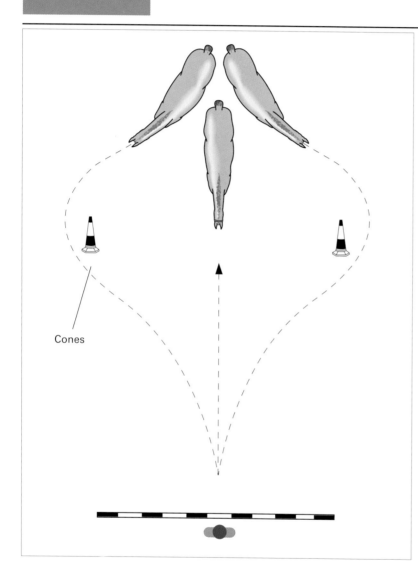

Cones

Set up
As for Exercise 27.

How do I do this?
❑ Stand behind the pole and ask your horse to back between the markers, then step around one of them (still facing you) and come forward towards you.
❑ Send him back through the markers again and around the other side and back to you.
❑ Send him back between the markers again and stop.

Remember
❑ Do not move from behind your pole.
❑ At all times the horse should be facing you.
❑ Slow and right has much more value than fast and wrong.

Problem solving
The most likely problems have already been dealt with in the earlier exercises. Try to separate out the elements that are not working and spend some time dealing with them, then put them all together and try again.
   Be creative and find ways to help your horse help you.

Moving on
❑ Increase the distance from the markers to the pole.
❑ Put the markers closer together.
❑ Use taller markers – for example, barrels, which are more claustrophobic.
❑ Try making the figure of eight by sending your horse forwards away from you between the markers.
❑ Once you have mastered sideways in exercises 33 to 38, come back to this exercise and send your horse around the figure of eight by including sideways to manoeuvre around the markers – while keeping your feet still.

HORSEMAN'S TIPS

Strive to make your training a win–win situation for you and your horse.

Back up to touch a fence

Horses are very sensitive to objects behind them – especially when they can't see them. So this exercise works on building trust and confidence to back up until your horse can rest his tail on a fence at a specific point (see diagram below).

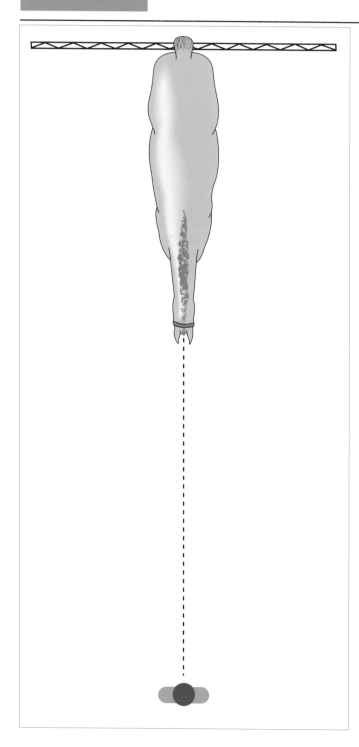

How do I do this?

❑ Pick an arena marker point, say C, and stand on the centre line about 4.5 metres away.
❑ Face C with your horse also positioned on the centre line facing you.
❑ Using indirect feel and keeping your feet still, ask him to back straight to C and rest his tail on the marker.

Benefits

❑ He will learn to trust that objects behind him need not be cause for concern. This can help with breeching bars, vet stocks, trailer ramps and so on.
❑ It challenges your ability to keep the backup straight.

Problem solving

❑ He gets close but then swings his hindquarters to the side – this is normal, you need to stop just before he swings. Give comfort and ask for only one step at a time. By now you should be able to yield his hindquarters without moving your feet – straighten him up and start again.
❑ He really can't tolerate it – do more desensitizing around his hindquarters with ropes, sticks and other objects. Also practise backing between markers and developing confidence in small spaces (see Exercise 41), then come back to this exercise.

Remember

❑ If this is difficult, it tells you that he still lacks confidence with objects behind him.
❑ There is no time limit!

Back over a pole

This exercise will tell you a lot about your horse's understanding and acceptance if he can negotiate tasks and challenges while going backwards without becoming flustered. It also helps him improve his awareness of where his feet are. In this example, you are going to ask your horse to walk back over a pole from direct feel on his nose.

How do I do this?

This is similar to fundamental Exercise 5, backing the horse from his nose, but with added challenge.

Make sure your horse is confident to walk over the pole forwards first, and that he can stop with the pole underneath him.

Focusing on a point behind him, ask him to back up, lifting his feet over the pole (Figure 1).

Remember

❑ This is a big challenge for some horses. Don't be too straight line in your thinking.
❑ Horses hate the feeling of having their feet caught up as it prevents them running away. Use a heavy pole so it doesn't move if he catches it.
❑ This is a claustrophobic experience for the horse as his space is constricted.

❑ If you push him, he will push you – use rhythmic pressure if he is not yielding, but reward one step at a time.

Problem solving

❑ He will back up without the pole but not with it there – start with the pole underneath him, by coming forwards over it, and just ask the front feet to step back over it. Use your stick or rope end to support your request if he doesn't yield to the feel on his nose. Give him comfort when he tries and build up as his confidence grows.
❑ He pushes past you when you ask – horses push through pressure when emotional, and are sensitive to objects behind them. Be firm about defending your bubble and think how you can break the exercise down so he can gain confidence and succeed.

1

- ❏ He won't even go over the pole forwards
  – he's not ready for backwards! Work on
  going over forwards.

Moving on

- ❏ Do it from a distance using indirect feel.
- ❏ Make the pole bigger, such as a telegraph
  pole or try backing him up a step (avoid a
  concrete step) or onto a box, such as in
  exercise 48.

HORSEMAN'S TIPS

*Horses are extremely sensitive to objects
behind them. This exercise helps counteract
the instinct to push forwards, and helps him
deal with the claustrophobic feeling that the
pole can create.*

Back along a pole

This exercise is much the same as the last one, only this time you will ask your horse to back up the length of the pole with it lying between his legs.

How do I do this?

Make sure you can do Exercise 31 and that your horse is not concerned about having the pole underneath him.

- ❏ Stand at one end of the pole and without moving your feet, send your horse around to the far end of the pole and ask him to turn and face you.
- ❏ Ask him to walk towards you with the pole between his front and hind legs.
- ❏ When he gets to you stop and give comfort.
- ❏ Ask him to back along the pole to the far end using direct feel (Figure 1).

Benefit

This exercise is a test of trust, communication and straightness.

Reminder

- ❏ He doesn't have any idea what you want, so it's up to you to make it clear.
- ❏ Keep your focus and try hard not to move your feet.
- ❏ Do one step at a time. Help him understand or you will cause anxiety.

Problem solving

- ❏ He keeps stepping sideways over the pole – slow it all down. It will give you time to make a subtle correction.

Hint

Horses quickly lose confidence if over faced by something they don't understand. Get your preparation really good and you will set your horse up with the right mindset for succeeding at working out this puzzle.

1

Preparation for sideways

This exercise puts together your ability to move the hindquarters and the forequarters independently and shows you how to cause the horse to move sideways around you (see diagram below).

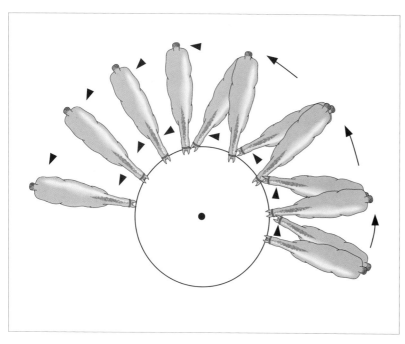

How do I do it?

- ❏ Start with your horse facing you at arm's length. In this example, you will ask your horse to go around you to his right (but obviously practise it both ways).
- ❏ Hold the knot on the halter under his chin in your left hand with your arm straight. Using a direct rein, ask him to step his front end across to his right, so he is at an angle to you (Figure 1).
- ❏ Use an indirect rein to ask his hindquarters to step to the right to catch up with the front, so he faces you again (Figure 2). Your stick will be in your right hand, and is there to guide and support your requests if necessary by making a circular motion, sweeping upwards towards him in a lifting action.
- ❏ Try to keep your feet still – you are just going to turn on the spot as he moves around you.
- ❏ Once he has the idea of moving his front end and then back end in a kind of zig-zag, you can start to use your stick parallel to his body to encourage him to step his whole body sideways around you in an arc while you face each other. You will need to use your rein much less (Figure 3).

Remember

- ❏ Keep your arm straight, holding the halter so that he doesn't push forwards on you.
- ❏ Try to stay light with the halter, don't hang on to his head.
- ❏ Direct rein controls the front, indirect controls the back. Once he is moving fully sideways your rein can be neutral.

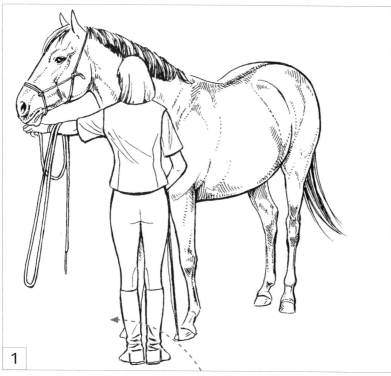

1

Problem solving

❏ He tries to walk through you – put some rhythm in the halter and rattle it quite firmly if necessary, he must stay out of your bubble.

❏ He fights for his head – you are probably hanging on too much.

❏ He will step his forequarters or hindquarters but not both together – this may be the first time he has moved fully laterally. Practise the isolations until they are easy and they will more or less flow into moving together. If you need to use more rhythmic pressure, touch his flank with your stick to simulate your leg.

❏ He becomes defensive – break it down and use less pressure.

❏ He plants his feet – shift his balance to get his feet moving and try again.

Benefits

❏ This is an effective way to introduce the concept of sideways, and most horses pick it up quickly when they have already learned the elements.

❏ He has to balance to move sideways without falling forwards.

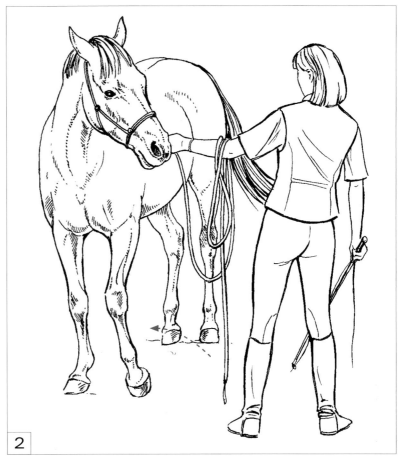

2

3

Sideways from in front

Following on from Exercise 33, instead of turning on the spot you will now step sideways with your horse, keeping him at arm's length (see diagram below).

How do I do this?

Start with your horse in front of you, and encourage him to move his feet sideways around you. When he is doing this without resistance, step sideways yourself, travelling at the same rate as your horse in a straight line (Figure 1).

Remember

❏ At all times you should be facing him, stepping sideways.
❏ Keep your arm outstretched – your horse should be staying within the halter and yielding away from your stick, which is parallel to his body.
❏ Don't ask for many steps to start with and reward the try.

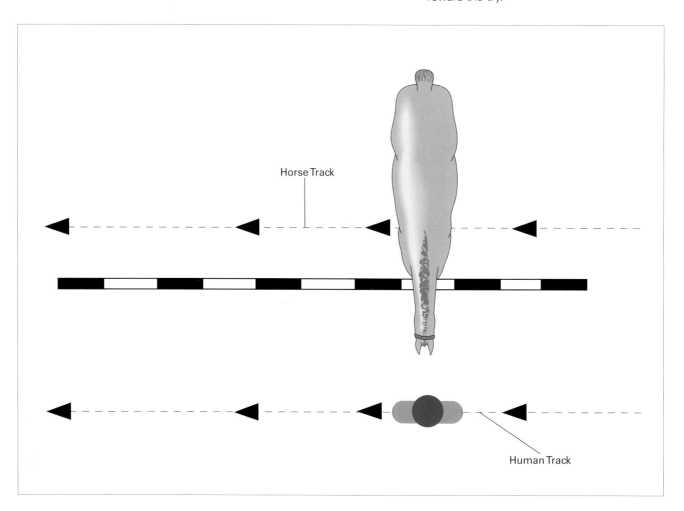

Horse Track

Human Track

Problem solving

❏ He stalls once you start walking sideways
– go back to the zig-zag as in the Exercise
33 to get his feet moving and try again. It's
acceptable if he is at a slight angle to start
with if this helps.

❏ You and he are not travelling in a straight line
– lay a line of poles on the floor as a guide
(Figure 2)

Benefits

❏ This exercise tests your preparation.

❏ It teaches your horse to lift his belly, which
will help the movement become two beat
instead of four.

Moving on

❏ To begin with it is acceptable if your horse's
body is straight, but aim to encourage him
to turn his nose towards the direction of
travel. He will need to be yielding to feel on
the halter and from your stick creating the
movement for this to be successful.

❏ Up to now you have been holding the knot
under his jaw and doing the exercise from
close range. Once you have mastered that
try to do the same exercise with distance
between you – 1 metre, 2 metres, 4 metres.

1

35

Sideways from the flank – direct feel

Having taught your horse to go sideways without touching, you are now going to ask him to yield sideways to your direct feel to simulate what you will do when riding.

How do I do this?

❏ Stand just in front of your horse's shoulder facing through him and have one hand on the halter below his jaw and the other on his flank where your leg will be when riding.
❏ Focus on a point in the direction you want to go and lift your energy. Ask his nose to point slightly in the direction of travel (away from you) and use light pressure on his flank to ask him to step sideways (Figure 1).

Benefits

❏ This exercise teaches your horse to be light to your leg for riding.
❏ It helps you develop a feel for how your leg position adjusts to control the hindquarters.

Problem solving

❏ Your horse doesn't understand and doesn't move off the flank – this is quite common. Break it down by asking the front end to go first then the back end (use your hand further back) and build up as a zig-zag to begin with (see Exercise 33). Gradually bring your hand back to your leg position around the girth so he can travel sideways from there.
❏ Your horse goes forward – bump the noseband to deter this and make sure you are not behind the driveline.

Remember

❏ He should travel sideways along the line of your focus.
❏ Encourage him to lead with his nose.
❏ Use a fence or pole to help you if necessary to start with.

Moving on

Aim to be in rhythm with your horse's foot fall. Your hand on his flank stimulates the hind leg on the same side. Reach a level where you only use it when the hind leg is on the floor, and release as he picks it up and moves it over. This will enable you to keep the lightness in your legs (if you keep the pressure on all the time he can learn to tune it out and you will have to use more leg to get a result).

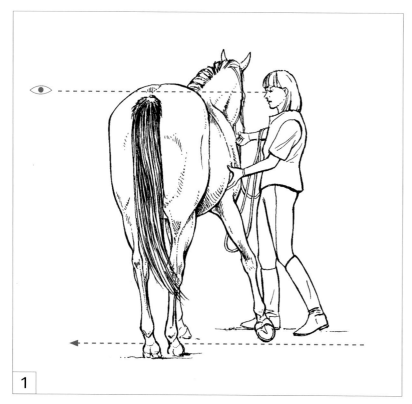

1

HORSEMAN'S TIPS

❏ *When you are up to travelling a few metres, drag your toe in the sand as you go and look back afterwards to see how straight you were.*
❏ *The reason for going fully sideways is to teach the horse not to fall on the forehand.*
❏ *When he is truly flowing and balanced, his feet will move in diagonal pairs.*

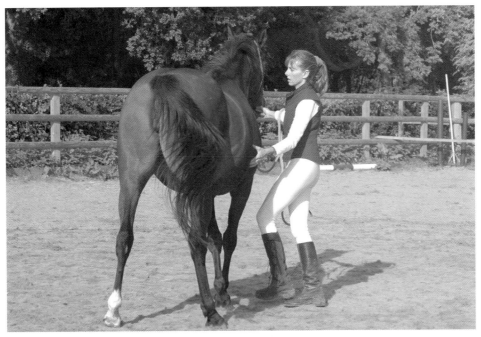

Sideways from the flank – indirect feel

Now you have given the horse the idea about going sideways from the flank and he has learned what he needs to do with his balance to achieve it, you can do it from a distance using indirect feel. The best way to start this is to send him sideways along a fence line for a short distance, remaining calm in walk and rewarding with comfort while facing the fence.

How do I do this?

Stand with your back to the fence, facing your horse and back him away from you at least 3 metres. Send him in an arc around you and towards the fence, just like the beginning of a circle (Exercise 16). As he approaches the fence, turn and walk towards him, sending him sideways away from you along the rail for a short distance (Figure 1).

Hints

❏ Make sure you keep a strong focus ahead of you down the fence.
❏ Don't travel faster than your horse, you are meant to be driving him in front of you.
❏ Keeping a good distance away – 2.5 to 3 metres – makes this exercise work better.
❏ Beginning the sideways out of forward momentum will help him keep going laterally.
❏ Drive whichever part of his body needs to go.
❏ Make sure you are not pulling him back with your rein, extend your arm parallel to the fence.

Problem solving

❏ He stalls and you end up too close to him – start again and put more energy into sending him ahead of you.
❏ He goes straight and forwards down the fence instead of sideways – slow down and put more energy towards yielding his hindquarters until he faces the fence.

❏ He turns to face you – send the front end. You may have a zig-zag for a bit, this is fine, and will iron out when he gets the idea.
❏ He goes backwards away from the fence or changes direction and runs the other way – lots of horses get emotional about this, the fence makes them feel claustrophobic and they can get quite animated in their opposition! Keep cool, keep your energy low and make sure you are not trying to chase him down the fence. Just continue to give him clear direction with your rein and support with your stick and let him find the way to solve the puzzle. Reward him immediately he takes a step sideways.

Remember

❏ The two preceding exercises are preparation for this.
❏ He doesn't have to go far down the fence – reward him when he travels sideways.
❏ Offer your rein so he can travel, and put energy to is hindquarters to keep up with his nose.
❏ Once he is travelling, try to keep your pressure very low. Once he has the idea, it should only need your focus and stick held parallel to his body to keep him going.
❏ Use a substantial and safe fence, and stay on the fence line.
❏ If you have done your preparation, you should be able to do this just by applying your pressure to his bubble, not his body.

Moving on

All the sideways exercises so far have used something in front of the horse to stop him going forwards. Once he knows the movement and is balanced, check if you can do it without the fence, and just use a pulse down the rein if he goes forwards.

As with everything here, the idea is to set yourself and the horse up for success, so you could use a pole on the ground first, and then perhaps a rope, before trying to go sideways without any guide.

1

Sideways straddling a pole

Another variation on the many things you can do with a simple pole.
   If you can back your horse over a pole (Exercise 31) and go sideways (Exercises 34, 35 and 36), you can try combining your skills to ask your horse to go sideways with the pole underneath him.

How do I do this?

❑ Position your horse with the pole underneath him, and make sure he is confident with it and happy to stand there.
❑ Ask him to yield his forequarters over a step or two, and then yield the hindquarters to catch up.
❑ Reward him with comfort.
❑ Repeat this zig-zag motion until he is confident and knows what you want, then ask him to move front and hind end together so that he travels laterally along the pole (Figure 1).

Remember

❑ Focus your belly button power on the part of his body that needs to move.
❑ Do it slowly and build up to more steps

Problem solving

❑ He tries to go forwards or backwards over the pole –have your hand on the halter so you can communicate with him.
❑ He cannot keep the pole underneath – spend more time leading forwards, backing and resting over the pole to help him become more confident.

Moving on

❑ Once this exercise is working well, try to do it from a greater distance of, say, 2 metres, both from the side and from in front.
❑ Try raising the pole off the ground on blocks or going over something more bulky such as a barrel on its side.

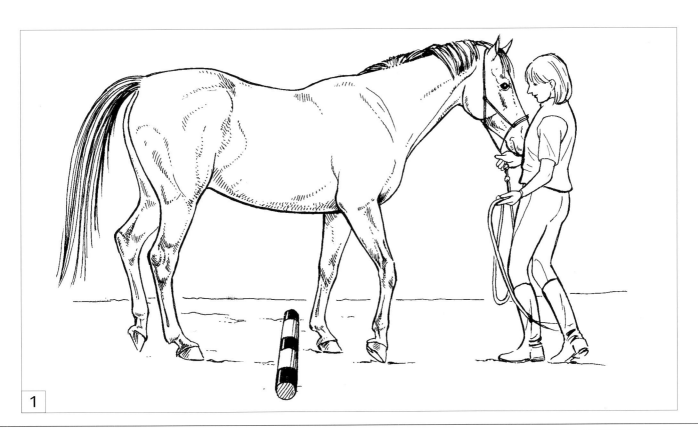

1

Sideways on a circle

This one is a combination of Exercises 21 and 34. To help you succeed, make sure you have developed your skills so that you can cause your horse to go sideways from a greater distance, at least 3 metres, without him drifting forwards.

In this exercise, you will have him walking around you in a circle, and at the first marker, travelling sideways for a short distance before stopping at the second marker (see diagram below).

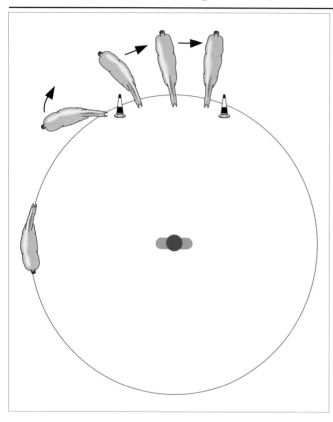

Set up

As for Exercise 21 – using markers on the circle, but this time put them 3 metres apart.

How do I do this?

❏ Have your horse walking around you in a circle and feel for a connection down the line.
❏ As he reaches the first marker, focus on his hindquarters so that they move out until he is facing you (Figure 1), keeping the momentum and travelling sideways to the second marker (Figure 2).
❏ Stop and reward.

Benefits

❏ The markers give you a clear goal, which will help develop accuracy and purpose.
❏ This exercise teaches your horse to adjust from forward to lateral movements.
❏ It builds towards one of the ridden exercises.

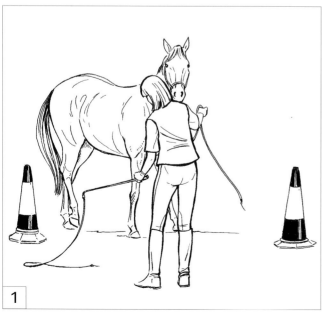

1

2

Remember

❏ Set yourself and the horse up for success – make sure you can do it at closer range before attempting it from greater distances (Exercise 34).
❏ Be aware of your horse's posture on the circle. The better balanced he is, the less he will drift forwards when you ask for sideways.
❏ Balance quantity with quality.
❏ Keep your feet still.
❏ Keep his front feet on the track of the circle.
❏ Do the exercise on both reins.

HORSEMAN'S TIPS

If you can learn to think laterally about how to approach suggested exercises like this, you will be well on your way to thinking like a horseman.

Problem solving

❏ Your horse falls in towards the centre of the circle when you ask for sideways – put rhythm pulses down your rope to prevent this (see Exercise 6).

This is quite a challenging exercise, but all the ingredients for success have been covered in the preceding pages. Look for ways to make it more understandable to your horse – have your rope shorter, or make the markers closer together and so on.

Don't be too straight line in your thinking.

Moving on

Try it in trot.

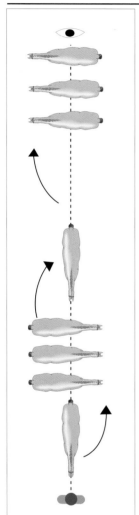

Sideslip down centre line

This exercise will test your accuracy as you alternately ask your horse to yield backwards and sideways down the centre line of the arena, without going off course (see diagram below).

How do I do this?
❑ Back your horse away from you so there is at least 3 metres between you and he is looking at you with both eyes (Figure 1).

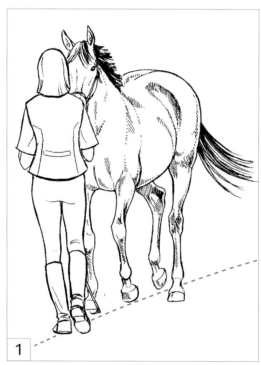

1

2

❑ Without moving your feet off the centre line, ask him to yield his forequarters over to one side so that he is across your path and you are looking at his flank (Figure 2).
❑ Ask him to go sideways for a few steps, and travel with him, maintaining the same distance between you (Figure 3).
❑ Drop your energy so he stops.
❑ Swap hands on your rope and stick so your arms are crossed (Figure 4) and ask him to yield his hindquarters and turn to face you again (Figure 5).
❑ Back him up, and ask him to yield the forequarters the other way this time.
❑ At all times, keep your eyes on a focus point in the distance.
The idea is that you walk in a straight line and the horse travels along the line also, sometimes backwards and sometimes sideways.

Reminders
❑ You don't have to do this in a hurry. If you go too fast, your horse will become confused and lose confidence.
❑ This is just a combination of previously practised elements.
❑ Try to keep the distance the same between you – don't catch your horse up, drive him ahead of you.
❑ Keep your phases as low as possible.
❑ You don't have to use an arena – you could use any marker to go towards.

Benefits
This exercise shows how much control you have over a distance.

Problem solving
The line he travels is wonky! – you are probably going too fast or need to practise the elements in isolation.
   You could mark the centre line in the sand with wood shavings or coloured chalk before you start as a guide to help you.

3

Moving on
❑ Try doing this without the stick.
❑ Do it from the end of the 3.5 metre line.

HORSEMAN'S TIPS

Try dragging your foot behind you to make a mark in the sand as you walk – you will be able to look back and see how straight you actually were!

4

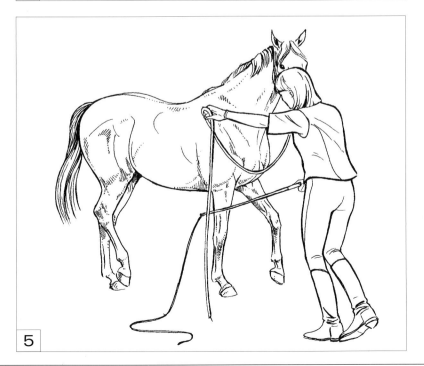

5

Place the foot
from Ken Faulkner

This exercise will help you become really accurate in controlling your horse's footfall as you isolate and control the placement of each foot in turn onto a marker.

It teaches you how to influence his body in subtle ways and helps him to tune in and listen to your commands.

How do I do this?

With your horse facing you, throw a marker (such as a small sand bag or the string from your stick 3.5 metres behind him and cause him to go to it and place his left fore on it (Figure 1) – without moving your feet! Do this with each foot in turn.

Remember

❏ Your horse has no idea what you want, so be very clear, but keep your signals subtle or you will cause too much movement and overshoot the marker.
❏ Think of the quality of the feel you are offering your horse – the idea is to create understanding, not force an issue.
❏ Do it slowly, positioning and manoeuvring the horse one step at a time, rewarding the try.
❏ Remember to focus on the area of his body you want to move.

Double check

❏ Check that you understand how each rein position controls the movement of each individual foot (see 'Rein positions and responsibilities, page 17).
❏ Don't move your feet.
❏ Do as little as possible but as much as is necessary.

Problem solving

❏ Not sure how to approach it – make sure you and he can do the fundamentals exercises in Chapter 2. This is just a combination of all those directions.
❏ Don't have enough control over that distance – that's fine to begin with. You can put the marker a bit closer (but no closer than 2.5 metres – this is supposed to be challenging!) and work up to the full distance.
❏ Your horse is spooky about the marker – desensitize him to it around his legs and feet first (Exercise 2).

Benefits

❏ This exercise will help you refine your communication skills for directional control.
❏ It will help you become really accurate and teach your horse to wait for your signals one step at a time.

Note

This exercise is quite a challenge and shows you that horses know very well where their feet are – think about that next time one treads on your toe!

HORSEMAN'S TIPS

Becoming subtle means doing less sooner so you don't have to do more later.

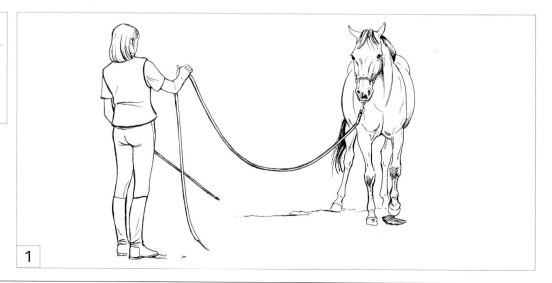

1

Confidence in small spaces

This exercise uses a simple arrangement of a pole and two barrels to create a narrow space along the side of a fence. The idea is to ask the horse to go through the space calmly when you ask him and turn to face you afterwards. Gradually, your horse will gain confidence to the point where he can stop in the narrowed space, or even go backwards through it. (See diagram below.)

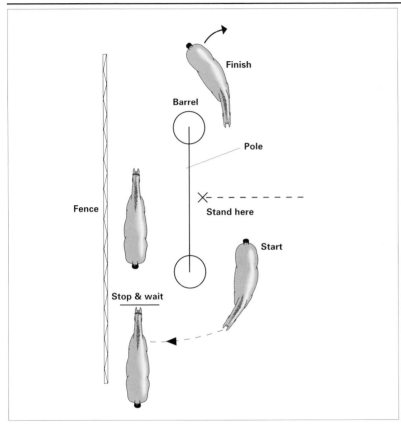

How do I do this?

❑ Place two barrels or blocks about 2 metres from the fence and place a pole on top so that it is parallel to the fence.

❑ Stand at the middle of the pole with it between you and the fence and try not to move your feet from there. The pole is there to protect you as the horse goes through the gap and to help you stop him from crowding you.

❑ Send your horse away from you to the first barrel at the entrance to the 'corridor' and ask him to stand there parallel to the fence, facing the narrowed gap (Figure 1).

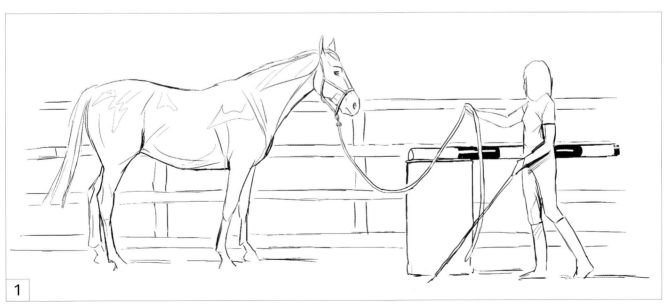

1

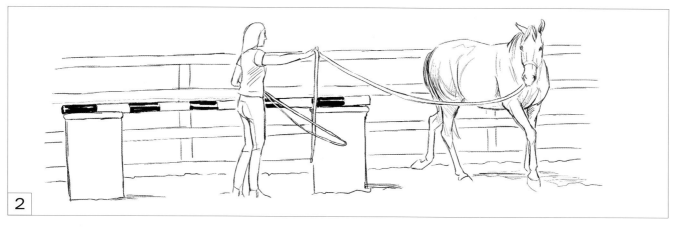

2

3

- *Don't* let him rush into the corridor – wait until he is settled and calmly standing facing the entrance. Then using feel on the halter and line, ask him to go through the narrow space and out the other side (Figure 2).
- Don't worry at this stage if he rushes once you have asked him to go through – you want him to feel he can get out of the 'trap'. But make sure he doesn't push on the pole you are standing by.
- When he has gone around the end of the pole, ask him to disengage his hindquarters and turn to face you. Give him comfort for

doing this by leaving him alone or rubbing him with the stick, but try to keep him at arm's length outside your personal space as this exercise can cause some horses to become quite agitated until they gain confidence and become less claustrophobic (Figure 3).
- Repeat the exercise several times on each rein until your horse is calm and no longer feels the need to rush through the space.
- Gradually build up to the point where he is happy to stop and get comfort in the small space (Figure 4).

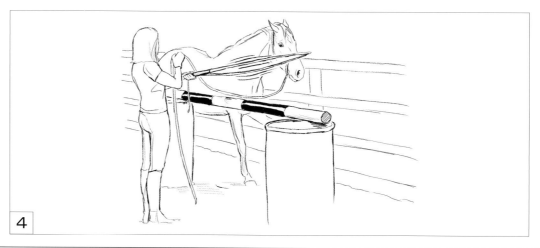

4

*Windy weather often
powerfully increases
your horse's degree
of claustrophobia
and sense of being
trapped. He may feel
the need to stay out in
the open because he
needs to be extra alert
to danger when he
can't hear if predators
are rustling in the
bushes. This explains
why many horses will
not use a field shelter
in bad weather.*

Double check

❑ Check that you keep your feet still and control your horse from a distance – you will need at least 2 metres of line between you and him.
❑ Ensure he doesn't rush through the gap before you are ready (imagine it is a doorway with a small child standing in it).
❑ Make sure that you don't chase him through with the stick – take the pressure off him when he is in the confined space or he will lose confidence.

Hints

❑ Give very clear direction on the line using a steady feel to bring him through or rhythm pulses on the line to stop him or back him up (see Exercise 14). Your stick is there to help you have influence over his footfall from a greater distance and to support your request for him to follow the feel on the line.
❑ The higher the pole, or the closer it is to the fence, the more claustrophobic the space will feel to the horse.

Benefits

❑ This is one of the most beneficial exercises you can do to help your horse control his natural fears. It is excellent for preparing your horse for a trailer, vet stocks, narrow gateways or anything else that might restrict his movement.
❑ It teaches him to learn to wait for you to give him instructions and to proceed calmly without rushing.

Reminders

❑ Be prepared to widen the gap to start with if your horse resists the idea of going through. The aim is to build confidence, so don't make it too challenging to begin with.
❑ Yield the hindquarters after he has gone through to help him think his way through the task (see Exercise 8).

Problem solving

❑ He won't go through – widen the gap, give clear direction on your rope line and support with the stick behind the driveline. Immediately stop asking when you see him try. Be patient and consistent and soon he will understand.
❑ He rushes through – allow this to start with as trying to slow him down will make him feel more trapped. Repeat until he feels more confident.
❑ He will walk through but not stop or back up – practise Exercises 8 and 27 first and then come back to this one and put them together.

Note

Being a prey animal, the horse is programmed by nature to be sceptical and suspicious of confined spaces or anything that restricts his ability to run for his life (including wearing tack and being ridden). While the modern horse lives a rather different life to his wild ancestors, we still see this instinctive behaviour demonstrated time and again in many different ways. Most common examples are: not loading in a trailer, pulling back, rushing through gateways or doorways, bucking when the saddle is girthed up and rushing off after a jump.

In order to reduce stress and danger to humans and horses, it is important to help horses overcome these issues and become more comfortable with the lifestyle we impose on them.

Moving on

Once he is relaxed with this, try hanging some flapping plastic over the pole, or have someone banging on the barrel like a drum while you do this exercise. Remember – repeat it until your horse becomes confident, don't stop while he is still worried. Reward him by taking the pressure off when you achieve the response you want.

Go under something

Horses often find it challenging to go underneath something low, so this exercise is designed to help him understand how to negotiate this problem.

1

2

3

Equipment
You will need two sturdy road cones or barrels and a length of stout water piping (about 6 metres long); or two tall jump wings with a light pole and deep cups.

How do I do this?
❑ Place the pipe in the top of the cones or barrels, and position them at a distance apart that gives plenty of headroom (or put the pole on the highest setting on the wings).
❑ Standing at the side of the obstacle and without moving your feet, give clear direction on the rein and ask your horse to walk underneath and disengage his hindquarters on the other side so he turns to face you (Figures 1, 2 and 3).

Benefits
❑ This exercise gives your horse more confidence when it comes to everyday situations such as low stable doors or trailers.
❑ It helps him gain greater awareness of his own height.
❑ It develops his courage to go into a tight spot on his own.
❑ It presents a different and interesting challenge for both of you.

Problem solving
❑ Your horse won't go anywhere near it – take time. Let him sniff it, give clear direction on your rope, support your request with the stick or the end of your rope but use very sparingly and give him plenty of comfort when he makes a try.
❑ Your horse rushes through – no problem, his emotions have run down to his feet. Just disengage afterwards, give him long comfort and repeat until he is less emotional.
❑ You horse goes tries to duck between you and the obstacle – if you allow this, you are telling him its acceptable to run you over. Be very firm about protecting your space. This is the only direction that is totally off limits.

❑ Your horse is terrified of the pipe – take it out and use Exercise 2 to reach a level where you can rub your horse all over with the pipe before putting it back and trying again.

Remember
❑ Make it as easy as possible to begin with.
❑ Break the idea down, and rebuild it. Lead him through it to start with if that helps.
❑ If it goes wrong, it's a great opportunity to practise again!
❑ Don't chase him through this. You will need to keep your pressure very low or you will create resistance – the more subtle you can become the better.
❑ Never push him when he's trying.

Moving on
❑ Drop the height so he has to duck his head under (no lower than 5 cm above his withers).
❑ Reach a level where you can stop underneath and go backwards through it when standing beside the barrel or in front of him (Figure 4).
❑ Hang string or plastic on it so he has to brush through something.

4

Negotiate a maze

This is a great exercise as the lay out of poles is so versatile (see diagram below) – you can approach it in lots of different ways.

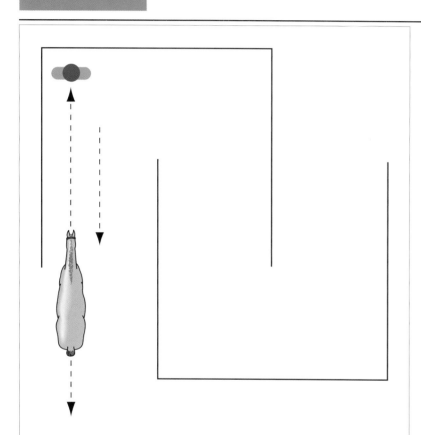

Remember

❏ The main consideration is to make a plan and stick to it, otherwise you will not have focus and your intention will not be clear to your horse.

❏ Challenges like this are designed to help you work out the holes in your preparation.

❏ Take it slowly, being careful to control your own feet as well as your horse's.

❏ Do it an easy way first before making it more difficult.

❏ Keep smiling – it's supposed to be fun!

Problem solving

The solutions to all the problems that can arise in this exercise are contained in Chapter 2.

HORSEMAN'S TIPS

Don't just do it the ways you find easy. All these exercises are to help you develop your skills, and to do that you have to stretch a bit – but not so much that you or your horse snap! The trick is to find the balance.

How do I do this?

Using direct or indirect feel from in front or alongside your horse, you could:

❏ Go forwards or backwards through it.
❏ Go forwards in, and back out.
❏ Go forwards out and back in.
❏ Back over the poles.
❏ Go sideways over the poles.
❏ Turn the corners by yielding the hindquarters or the forequarters.
❏ Or any combination thereof!

44

Confidence with water crossing

Many horses become concerned about water crossing, whether it is a river, a ditch or just a puddle.

This exercise shows you how to introduce water in a way that will build your horse's confidence in himself and in you.

HORSEMAN'S TIPS

Horses' eyes are different from human eyes. They do not have the same depth perception as we do because their eyes are not on the front of their head, so they cannot use binocular focus. Therefore, your horse cannot easily tell whether a puddle is 1 metre or 1 cm deep. He will need to drop and rotate his head in order to see the object better, and may paw at it to check the depth. If he is doing any of these, be happy – he is trying!

Set up

Assuming you don't have a river or large puddle in your arena, a good way to start this exercise is to use a strong water jump tray, or foot bath used for cattle, or even simulate water with a tarpaulin folded to about 2.5 metre by 1 metre and held down by two poles.

How do I do this?

The idea is much the same as for Exercise 41.
- ❑ Stand beside the obstacle and give clear direction on your lead rope to ask your horse to go closer to it (Figure 1).
- ❑ When he tries, reward him for a moment and then ask again. You can add some support

from your stick, but only to get him to try, not to make him cross. As he approaches, take the pressure off. He will soon start to associate the object with the comfort.
- ❑ Allow him to sniff, paw or chew the object if he wants to – he is learning what it's all about and you want to encourage his curiosity.
- ❑ If he jumps it, great – ask him to disengage afterwards and look at the object. Repeat until he is confident enough to tread on it, or even stand in the middle of it.

Reminder

If he learns that you never put him in danger and that you always show him how to solve a challenge, he will put his trust in you and follow your directions with confidence.

Hint

Try to keep your pressure very low – the more you get after him the worse he will feel about the whole thing.

Problem solving

- ❑ He won't go near it – use approach and retreat, find the threshold of his comfort zone and work around it. Don't be too straight line in your approach to this. Take it slowly, build trust and stretch his comfort zone gradually – it doesn't matter how long it takes. Sometimes doing it over several sessions is best – just make sure you end each session on a good note.
- ❑ He leaps over it but towards you – defend your bubble very firmly. Try not to step back as this will invite him to leap on top of you. Try to let him know your bubble is off limits, and make sure he is facing the object straight (if his shoulder or ribs are pointing towards you he will probably jump on you).

Moving on

Once he is happy with the simulation, try with the real thing, using the same technique until he has no fear.

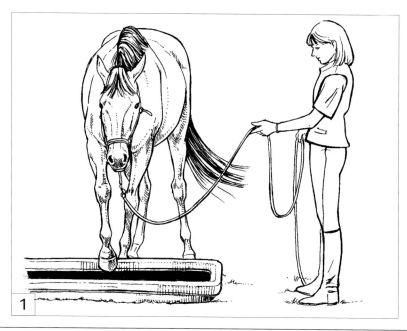

1

Jump over something

Whenever a horse's space is restricted, even from underneath, it can make him feel claustrophobic and anxious. In this exercise, you will work on control of footfall and build confidence to jump something while you are on the ground.

Equipment

You will need a jump without a high wing.

How do I do this?

First make sure you can do Exercises 16 (the simple circle) and 41 (confidence in small spaces).

❑ Start with a small jump, or even a pole on the ground if necessary. Just like the small spaces exercise, you stand still beside the obstacle and ask your horse to go around and over it, then turn to face you afterwards and rest.

❑ Repeat, gradually increasing the size of the jump as you go. You can do this out of a walk until the jump is the height of his knees, then he will need to put in more energy to get over it.

❑ If he clambers over it or knocks it down, stops and sniffs or chews it, don't worry. This is an alien idea to us but the horse needs time to understand the obstacle if he is to have confidence with it, so the above responses are preferable to him jumping too big and rushing off afterwards.

❑ Disengaging the hindquarters afterwards will help your horse to stay in left-brained 'thinking' mode.

❑ Once he is confident and knows that a jump is followed by comfort, you can make those comfort stops less frequent so that the jump can flow and become part of a circle or course (Figure 1).

Problem solving

❑ Your horse refuses the jump – don't chase him! The main consideration is to give clear direction and set it up so that he chooses to jump. Remember, horses are deeply sceptical and the more pressure you put on them to make something happen, the more likely you will be to cause opposition and he will form an unpleasant association with the jump. So give direction and support until he tries and then reward with comfort – even if he only sniffs the jump to start with. Repeat the procedure, give direction and reward the try until he jumps, then reward again.

❑ Your horse clambers through the jump – this is acceptable to start with, but once he is

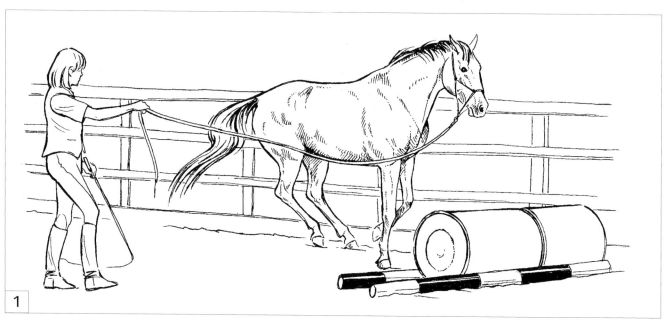

1

confident and as the jump becomes bigger, he needs to put more energy into it. Ask him to move in trot or canter, you can circle him away from the jump to get his stride flowing. Walk with him so the circle is not too small and then position yourself so his path will meet the centre of the jump.

❑ Your horse runs out between you and the jump – defend your bubble firmly. This is a 'no go' area.

❑ Your horse becomes agitated and runs around after the jump – remember his emotions run down to his feet. He is not confident and will jump with anxiety when you are riding. Disengage the hindquarters as best you can. Make the jump as unchallenging as possible and repeat until he is not so emotional.

Hint

If you are walking with your horse towards the jump, be aware of your position. If you get in front of the driveline on the approach, you may cause him to stop – be aware of where your belly button is pointing.

Remember

❑ Give the reward of comfort after the jump.
❑ Many horses will jump but this exercise helps them to jump with confidence – there's a difference.
❑ Don't make him jump, cause him to want to. If you can encourage him to see it as a puzzle he can solve, he is far more likely to enjoy his jumping and this will help when you are riding.
❑ Practise on both reins.

Benefits

❑ This exercise teaches your horse how to jump and adjust his balance without the added difficulty of carrying a rider.
❑ It encourage him to think and solve puzzles and makes challenges interesting.
❑ It helps him to overcome his feelings of claustrophobia.
❑ It will very often show if a horse is hiding a buck – a good point to know about before you get on!
❑ It improves your feel for positioning and timing.

Moving on

❑ Test your control by making the jump narrow (for example, a single barrel), or higher and wider, or drape items over or add other obstacles and make a course, maintaining gait in between and so on – use your imagination.
❑ Try asking him to jump towards you and stop in front of you. Try this over a narrow jump (Figure 2).
❑ Once things are working well you can take your horse out to jump logs, streams or go to a cross-country course and jump some fences on line.

2

Lead backwards from the tail

This exercise introduces an unusual way to lead your horse perhaps, but it takes the concept of following direct feel to a new level. If your horse truly understands how to yield, you will be able to lead him with lightness from any part of his body in any direction!

How do I do this?

Make sure that you can back your horse while standing at his shoulder facing forwards (see Exercise 14). And that he is not defensive when you are around his hindquarters with ropes and so on (see Exercises 2 and 49).

❏ In order to help keep him straight to start with, have him stand along the side of a fence with you at his flank, but not holding his tail yet. The rope should be in the hand nearest him and the stick in the other to help keep him straight.

❏ Using a rhythmic lifting motion with your rope ask him to back up while you stay by his side (you are just about on the driveline).

❏ When this works well, move further back behind the driveline and repeat.

❏ Then go to his hindquarters and lift his tail with the hand nearest him, put the rope and stick in the other hand.

❏ Put a steady, light feel on his tail to indicate that you would like him to yield to the feel (Figure 1). If he doesn't, put some rhythm pulses down the rope just as you did before.

❏ As soon as he moves backwards to find release, drop the tail and reward.

❏ Soon you will just ask from the tail and your horse will back up towards you.

Hints

❏ Don't start with the tail but start forward and work backwards, making it a gradual process that your horse understands.

❏ Stand slightly to the side of his hindquarters and use the end of his tail, so you are not in

1

kicking range (Figure 2) – but if your horse is trusting and confident and you have really worked on your preparation, this will not be an issue.

Reminders

Don't pull his tail! You are just applying a gentle feel. If you need to do more to get a response, use your rope.

Benefits

- ❏ This exercise is very useful for unloading backwards from a trailer.
- ❏ It helps your horse become more confident when you are behind him.
- ❏ It is a good test of trust and communication.
- ❏ It shows that your horse really understands how to yield.

Problem solving

- ❏ He turns towards the rope when it is lifted – improve your preparation (see Exercise 14). Put more rhythm pulses down the line. You can use your stick parallel to his neck to keep him straight if necessary.
- ❏ He looks worried – go back to what he can understand and make progress more slowly.

Moving on

- ❏ Ask him to yield his hindquarters towards you from his tail, or steer around a figure of eight.
- ❏ Try this exercise without touching. Stand behind and click your fingers to ask him to back up!

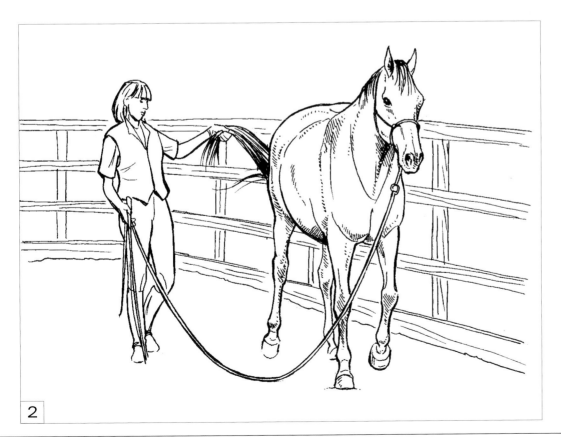

2

Lead from the foreleg

Horses need to move their feet for self-preservation. Getting their legs tangled up in things can cause a nasty accident if they panic to get free. Instead of avoiding the issue, it is safer for all concerned if you can progressively accustom your horse to be familiar and confident with this situation. In this exercise, you will teach your horse how to think his way through such an event, so that he learns to find release through yielding instead of fighting to be free.

How do I do it?

❏ Start by making sure your horse has no concerns about you touching all around his forelegs with your rope and stick (see Exercise 2), including when he is walking.

❏ Pass the rope around one foreleg and hold each end in your hands (can be the same 3.5 metre line that is attached to the halter or another one).

❏ Gently move it from side to side, up and down the leg and below the fetlock, again checking that he is not concerned. When this is working well, stand in front of him with the rope behind his pastern and exert a steady feel on the rope asking him to lift the foot forward (Figure 1).

❏ If he doesn't move it after a few seconds, increase the pressure to a firm resistance,

but don't try to pull him off his foot. The pressure should be just firm enough that it will cause him to look for release.

❏ As soon as he lifts the foot, release the pressure and rub with the rope (Figure 2). He doesn't need to go anywhere to start with, you are just teaching him to find the release.

❏ Once it is working well and he lifts his foot without much pressure, ask him to follow the feel on the rope forwards while the foot is in the air and place it down again. Encourage him to take a step forwards from the halter if necessary to rebalance himself. Reward him and repeat.

❏ Soon you will find that he will follow your feel and walk forwards freely from the rope around his leg, obtaining release at every he takes step.

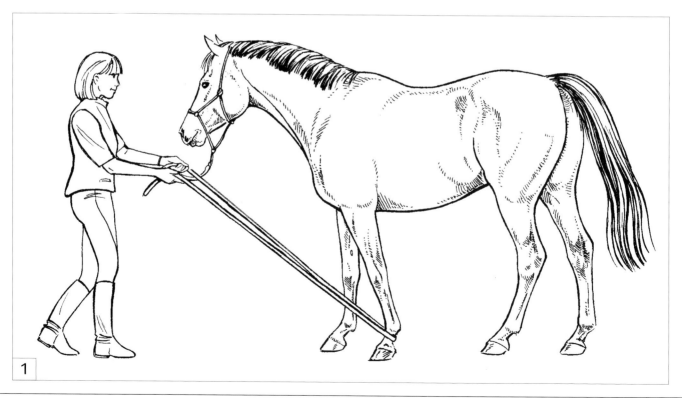

1

Benefits

- ❑ This exercise enables your horse to think his way through having his feet restricted, which might prevent an accident.
- ❑ It is a good test of trust and communication.
- ❑ It develops your feel and timing.
- ❑ It's a great preparation for the farrier.

Hints

It is sometimes easier to start with the rope at the back of the knee rather than the pastern.

Problem solving

- ❑ He panics and pulls back – drop one end of the rope. Your desensitizing was not thorough enough.
- ❑ He pulls the leg away – try to stay with him, keeping the feel the same and releasing when he stops bracing against you.
- ❑ He just doesn't move – tap the pastern rhythmically with your stick so he can't ignore you and makes a try.

Reminders

- ❑ You must release all pressure as soon as he yields or he will have no incentive to step and will not learn to look for release.
- ❑ Keep the pressure steady – no yanking.
- ❑ Stay in balance yourself – if you pull you will not release at the right time.
- ❑ Keep the rope in your hands so that you can drop it if necessary – never tie the rope around the leg.

Moving on

- ❑ Lead him in a circle, in either direction.
- ❑ Send him backwards by wiggling the rope with rhythm.

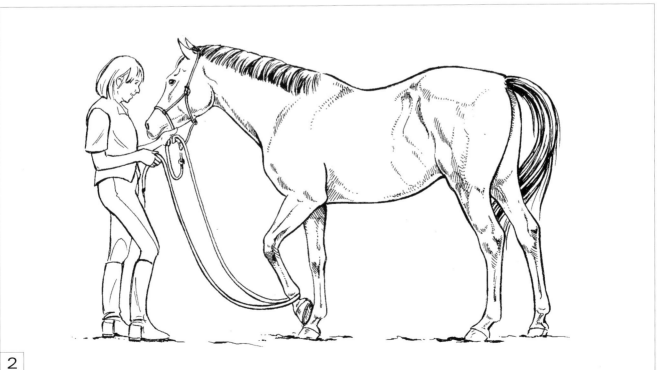

2

Stand on something

Horses are inherently sceptical and rightly suspicious of unusual, especially hollow-sounding, surfaces. However, sometimes we encounter these and may need our horses to stand on them – trailer ramps and floors, wooden bridges, weigh bridges and so on.

Apart from the fear of the footing not being secure, many horses seem to have balance problems on these surfaces and this exercise can help them to overcome these issues.

Equipment

You will need a box that is strong enough for your horse to stand on. A large sturdy pallet with a secured but detachable reinforced top made of 2cm (¾in) plywood is fine, inexpensive and easy to assemble (file or plane the corners and edges so they are rounded).

How do I do this?

❑ Lead your horse up to the box and encourage his curiosity by letting him sniff, chew or paw at it. The more noise he makes the better, he is desensitizing himself!

1

❑ Stand at the side and give direction on the rope that you would like him to step a foot on to it.

❑ Reward any try he makes by instantly taking the pressure off – even if he doesn't put his foot on it. Just a weight shift is enough of a try to begin with. Give him a moment and ask again.

❑ Reach a level where he can walk across the box, and build up to stopping on the box. Once you know he is not going to jump over it, you could try doing this from in front too (Figures 1 and 2).

Problem solving

❑ He won't go anywhere near it – give him time, walk around it, approach and retreat. Do some exercise somewhere else and bring him to the box to rest so he sees it as a place of comfort (see information on trailer loading – Exercise 100). Also, try taking the plywood top off and starting with just that on the ground. Try leading him across it first.

❑ He will go near it but not step on it – stand at the side giving clear direction on the rope and support with the stick used rhythmically behind the driveline. Reward the try and build one step at a time.

Remember

Use as little pressure as possible – increase by degrees if necessary, and instantly reward any try he makes.

HORSEMAN'S TIPS

Never ask while your horse is licking and chewing –give him a moment to consider what he just learned.

Be subtle – try just pointing at the foot you want to move, or tapping the air in front of it.

2

Moving on

❏ There are lots of things you can do with this.

❏ For horses who have balance problems (especially those that scramble or fall down in trailers, see Exercise 101), reach a level where he can move around on the box – for example, turn him with just his forehand on the box, or just his hind end.

❏ Stand him on it and turn around, one foot at a time, without scrambling.

❏ When it is really working well, see if you can back him onto it.

❏ Ask him to balance with three feet on and hang a chosen leg off the box (great stretching exercise for shoulders and hips).

❏ Ask him to stand on a see-saw (see Exercise 82 for more information on construction and how to approach this). Then see if you can cause your horse's posture to mirror yours and note how it changes his balance over the fulcrum (Figures 3 and 4).

Benefits

If you approach it carefully, calmly and consistently, the horse will be able to do all these and you will have helped him develop more confidence and more awareness of his feet and balance.

3

4

Unwind from a bind

A good test of whether your horse is trusting, yielding and thinking ('left brained') is to pass the rope from his halter, round behind him and ask him to wait with his head flexed away from you until you ask him to unwind himself from the rope.

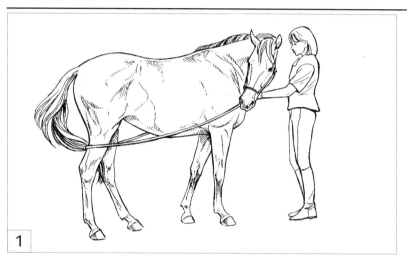

1

2

3

How do I do this?

Make sure all your fundamentals are working well – this will test them.

❑ Stand just to the left of his head with your left hand holding the halter and pass the rope over his head so it is on his right side and lying across his back.

❑ If he is confident with this, send pulses down the rope so it 'walks' along his back and drops down behind his tail but above his hocks. The rope should now surround him, going from the halter along the right side of his body, around his hindquarters and back to you at his head (tail end of the rope in your right hand).

❑ Ask his head to turn away from you, giving lateral flexion to the right – don't pull on the rope to achieve this but take up the resulting slack on the rope so it stays above his hocks (Figure 1).

❑ When he is softly flexed and standing still, let go of the halter, take a couple of steps backwards away from him and see if he can wait there for a few seconds.

❑ With your left hand, put some indirect pressure towards his eye (Figure 2) to ask him to yield to the weight of the lead rope and unwind by disengaging his hindquarters to turn and face you (you should be far enough away that his hindquarters can swing past you) (Figure 3).

Remember

❑ If your horse can't give lateral flexion without moving, or if he is not desensitized to your rope all around his body, you are not ready to do this exercise.

❑ If you use any force, your horse will not feel safe enough to keep his feet still.

❑ Take it slowly and give him confidence.

❑ Do it with him, not to him.

❑ Practise both sides.

Problem solving

❑ Your horse won't give the flexion away from you – work on this in isolation. When this works satisfactorily, pass the rope back to you over his withers and ask for flexion from there, but don't disengage from here as his hindquarters will swing into you.

❑ He gives flexion but moves his feet as soon as you let go of the halter – this is not uncommon, just repeat until he understands and feels comfortable with it.

❑ Your horse just stands there and won't move – drive his front end more and feel on the line around him exerting some pressure on the hindquarters. Don't pull him round though. If this is not working then he is not following feel well enough. Practise the fundamentals again.

Benefits

This exercise helps him learn not to panic when he is constricted, but to wait and follow instructions through the puzzle.

HORSEMAN'S TIPS

Lateral flexion towards you is a big challenge for many horses, but lateral flexion away from you and with a rope around the hindquarters requires a whole different level of trust and communication.

Change eyes through a turn

This is a clever way of changing sides without changing direction. It uses a combination of yielding the hindquarters and then the forequarters in a continuous flow with the effect that you start on one side of the horse and finish on the other side while you simply walk in a circle.

1

2

How do I do this?

❑ You can start this from either side of the horse, but let's imagine you are going to start on your horse's right, so he can see you out of his right eye.
❑ Face his hindquarter and use indirect pressure to ask him to yield away from you as you walk clockwise in an arc towards him.
❑ Focus your energy through his hip (Figure 1). If you have practiced this well from the fundamentals section, he will already know that you want him to step aside and turn to face you.
❑ As he starts to move, change the line into your left hand (Figure 2).
❑ As he yields and looks at you with two eyes, move slightly to your left to give him space as you continue walking and you will suddenly find you are now on his left side, yielding his forequarters, without having deviated from your circle (Figures 3 and 4).

Benefits

❑ This exercise is great for controlling footfall in a given area.
❑ It familiarizes your horse with transferring weight from forehand to haunches.
❑ It helps your horse become used to you appearing in one eye and then the next.
❑ It is good for keeping you focused on where you want to go.
❑ This is a pattern you can use in many situations. It is great for getting 'sticky' feet moving and for getting your horse to 'hook on' when you want to catch him or have him follow you at liberty.
❑ Shows if he favours one eye (normally the left).

Problem solving

❑ You don't understand the exercise – it sounds complicated but is actually extremely simple. Just practise yielding the hindquarters and forequarters using indirect feel as per the fundamentals section and then put them together in a flow while you walk in a circle.

- ❏ Your horse doesn't bring his head through to change sides – you don't have enough impulsion and energy in the disengagement, or you haven't stepped aside and given him room to bring his head through.
- ❏ Your horse gives you two eyes but then doesn't yield forequarters – focus your energy through his neck. Help him step across by supporting with the end of your rope or your stick if necessary, but by now you should be getting to where you can yield the horse in all directions with minimal support from the stick.
- ❏ Your horse barges forwards or goes backwards – you need to isolate the elements first so he understands what you want. Set him up for success!

Reminders

- ❏ Keep the bend in the direction of the turn at all times, but have softness in your rope.
- ❏ Try to do this without touching him.
- ❏ Practise from both sides.

HORSEMAN'S TIPS

If you over do this exercise, you may find your horse changes sides on you every time you yield his hindquarters and you will have lost control of his feet. Ring the changes and find the balance!

3

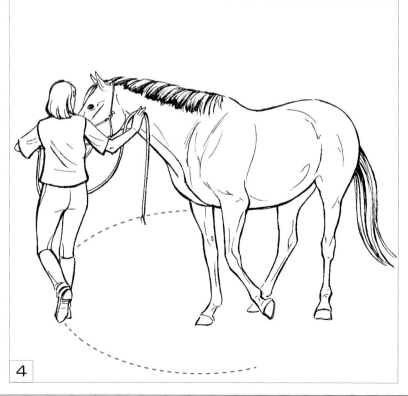

4

Drag something with confidence

One of the most horrible accidents you can have with a horse is to be dragged, and yet it is very useful to be able to ask your horse to pull something. This exercise helps your horse become familiar with the idea so it is not as alarming and may prevent an accident.

How do I do this?

Make sure that your horse leads well (Exercise 14), and that he is desensitized to ropes on the ground and around his legs and hindquarters (Exercises 47 and 49).

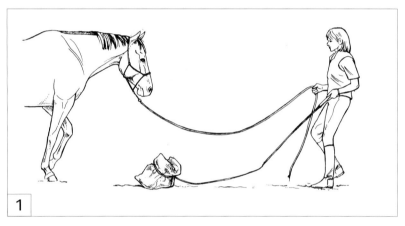

1

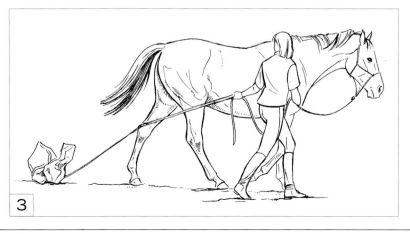

2

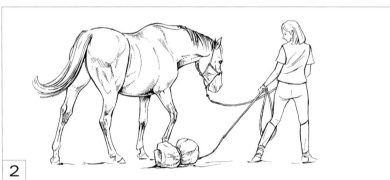

3

❏ Cut a thin but long, edible leafy branch from a tree and drag it in front of your horse as you walk backwards so he becomes interested in it and starts to follow it around. He will soon forget his anxiety as he starts snatching the leaves off it.

❏ As he becomes used to it, build up to where you can lead him in a circle around it. It might help to have an assistant drag the branch beside and behind him.

❏ Once he is settled with this, you are ready to introduce new objects, such as an old coat, or a plastic bag tied to a rope and you should not need the assistant.

❏ For each new object begin in the same way, dragging it away from him as he walks forwards (Figure 1).

❏ As he gains confidence, you can start to walk in a circle with the object along side him on the inside of the circle, keeping his head turned a little towards you (so he will move his hindquarters away from you and face the object if he becomes concerned) (Figure 2).

❏ Keep walking on the same rein, always with you on the inside. As he gains confidence, gradually feed the rope out so the object gets further behind his driveline (Figure 3).

❏ Build up to where he is happy to walk with it along side him before going straight.

Remember

You are dragging the object, not him. Do not attach it to him at any time.

Problem solving

❏ He freaks out when the object is on the floor – make sure he is happy with eating the leaves on the branch as you drag it forwards and add the other object so it drags along with the branch. If this still a problem, get a helper to drag it around in front of him at a safe distance while you just ask him to face it. If you take enough time and don't push for too much, you will find he eventually accepts it.

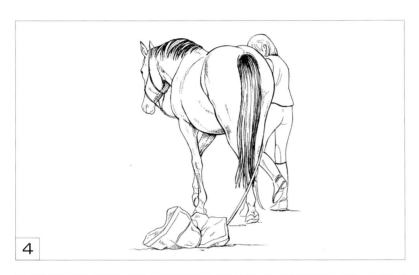

4

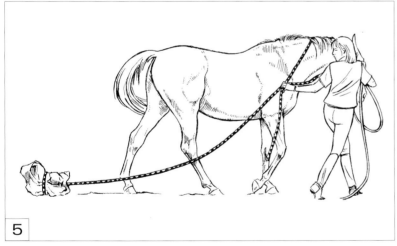

5

❏ He panics – disengage his hindquarters to face the object. You have more work to do on desensitizing. It tells you that your horse would not stop if you were dragged.

Benefits
❏ This is a good way to progressively encourage your horse to manage his concerns about objects dragging behind him, thus reducing the risk of an accident.
❏ This is a good beginning for carriage driving or for reaching the stage when he could help you pull something.

Moving on
Make sure you have desensitized him completely to ropes around his legs and hindquarters before trying to turn him away from you so he is on the inside, because the rope will go behind him and may spook him (Figure 4).
❏ You can reach the stage where you are able to hold the rope to the object in the hand nearest him, and eventually pass it round his neck like a collar so he feels the weight as he walks, but **never** tie it on (Figure 5).

HORSEMAN'S TIPS

Be aware that while some horses seem to accept objects in your hand, they may find them very spooky when they are on the ground, especially if they are moving. Using the branch works because it is a more natural way to introduce the concept.

Starting with it in front will engage his curiosity; starting with it behind may engage his flight instinct.

EXERCISE
52

Lower the head

It is useful to have a horse bring his head down for you for a number of reasons. It makes it easier to bridle him, or groom him, and it is a stance that can help him become both submissive and relaxed.

How do I do this?

Essentially he will learn to yield from a steady feel on the top of his head, either from your hand directly or the halter/bridle.

❏ Stand beside his jaw with one hand on the clasp of the lead rope and the other hand on his poll.
❏ Use your middle finger and thumb gently and steadily squeeze his poll as if testing a peach for ripeness (Figure 1).

❏ If he drops his head, even a millimetre, release all the pressure immediately. If he doesn't, squeeze a little more firmly, but no more than would be comfortable just above your own knee.
❏ If he still doesn't lower his head, use your other hand to put some downward pressure on the lead rope, just enough for him to want to find release. Hold until he tries and reward with comfort.
❏ Repeat until it is consistent.

Soon you will be able to lower his head with the slightest feel from your hand on his poll or from the halter.

Remember

❏ It's not about making it happen. Don't push or pull his head down, just be a passive resistance and let him look for the release.
❏ The pressure motivates, the release teaches.

Problem solving

❏ He can't tolerate you touching his poll – preparation by approach and retreat.
❏ He throws his head up when you apply pressure – try to stay with him if possible and keep your pressure the same so his strategy doesn't get him what he wants. Release when you feel the slightest yield downward (make sure you are standing to the side or you may get head butted!). If you rush it, you will get resistance – take it slowly
❏ Practise doing this from both sides.

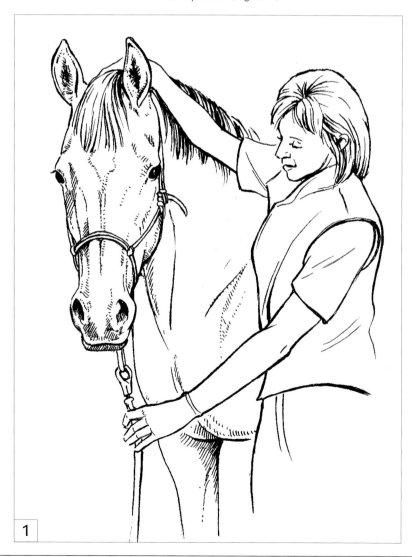

1

2

3

Benefits

❏ It teaches the horse to yield to a feel on the poll that can help him learn not to pull back while tied up, or not panic if he treads on his rope.

❏ It means you don't have to stretch when you want to bridle, groom or trim ears and so on.

Moving on

❏ Ask him to drop his head so his nose touches the floor .

❏ Encourage him to keep his head down while you put the halter or bridle on.

❏ Ask him to walk along with his head lower than his withers (Figure 3).

Throw the rope over the head

This is really a desensitizing exercise, getting your horse used to the rope being thrown over his head from one side to the other and working on any head shy issues he may have. But it also helps you develop feel, timing and coordination to improve your rope-handling skills.

How do I do it?

First make sure you can rub his head and neck all over with the rope in your hand and that you can pass the rope over his ears while he stands quietly and unconcerned. If he can't tolerate this, work on basic desensitizing of this area (Exercise 2) before going any further with this exercise.

❏ Stand with low energy at your horse's shoulder with the tail end of the rope in the hand nearest him and a big loop of the rope in the other hand. Swing the loop backwards and forwards so that you get a rhythm going.

❏ When it is swinging steadily, on a forward stroke open your hand and throw the rope over his head, still keeping hold of the end with the hand nearest his shoulder (Figure 1).

❏ Then throw it back again without moving your feet by reaching your arm over his withers and swinging the rope back over (Figure 2).

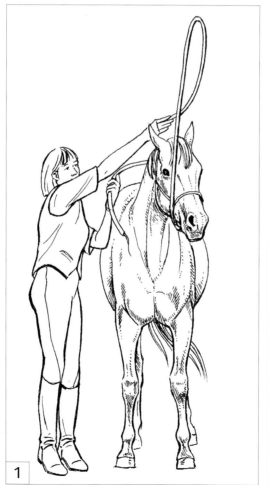

1

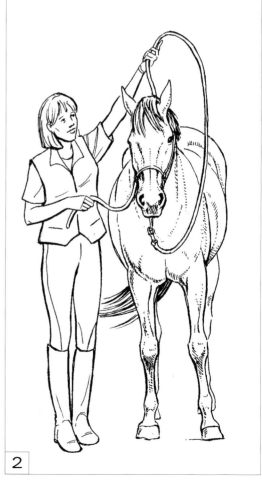

2

Remember

❑ You want your horse to read your body language. It should show him that you have no intention, and don't want him to do anything except relax.
❑ Practise from both sides.
❑ Working on your rope-handling skills away from the horse before trying this exercise is a good idea!

Benefits

❑ It teaches your horse to be less reactive and more tolerant.
❑ It is essential preparation if you are going to ride with one rein.

Problem solving

❑ Your horse is fine with the preparation but becomes jumpy when you throw the rope – work on your rhythm, make the throw really smooth and land it softly. Take time. Work on it till he can accept it – don't stop while he is still reactive.

❑ Your horse is very head shy – break it down into manageable pieces. Work on Exercise 2. Try standing on a box beside him and pass the rope over his head repeatedly until he accepts it before trying to throw it.

Note

Think laterally. There is no time limit on this – work on it over days or weeks if necessary and go at your horse's speed. You are doing this *for* him not *to* him!

Moving on

Once he has no opposition to this, you can try it from further back, so you are behind the driveline – for example, beside his flank, or even his hindquarters. Aim for him to accept it without needing to move his feet.

HORSEMAN'S TIPS

If you have been clear about your body language, your horse should by now be starting to tune into your intention and be able to tell the difference between rhythmic pressure that has intention behind it – requiring action – and rhythmic movement that doesn't have intention – requiring nothing but relaxation.

If an issue arises, it just means you and your horse have a difference of opinion and he is sceptical of what you are asking. Work out how to cause him to see matters your way.

Bridle with care

In this exercise, you will learn how to cause your horse to willingly help you put the bridle on by lowering his head and bringing it around for you.

How do I do this?
- Stand on your horse's left side, just in front of his shoulder.
- Have your bridle over your left arm, and pass the reins around the horse's neck.
- Ask him for lateral flexion (Exercise 11) while keeping his feet still.
- Then ask him to drop his head by touching his poll with your right hand (Exercise 52) so his head is around and down at a comfortable working height for you.
- Make sure you can rest your right forearm along the top of his neck with your hand between his ears (Figure 1).

1

- Pass the headpiece of the bridle to your right hand so it hangs down the front of his face with the bit just by his lips.
- With your left hand under his jaw, insert your finger into the side of his mouth where the

bit goes and tickle his tongue until he opens his mouth.
- The bit will be hanging in the right place for you to guide it into his mouth (Figure 2). Ease it up with your right hand and guide the headpiece over his right ear, then left – tips first (Figure 3). Then do up the throat lash etc.

- Taking the bridle off is a reversal of this process – ease the bit out slowly and make sure it doesn't catch his teeth. If you have the flexion, he will be less likely to throw his head up.

Remember
- Your horse should keep his head down and around for you throughout this exercise.
- Take time to relax the horse through this process. If he is tense, he will not be able to give you soft flexion.
- A negative association with the bridle will affect how he goes when you are riding.
- Just because the buckles are on the left doesn't mean you can't put the bridle on from the right. Improve your dexterity and practise bridling from both sides.

Benefits
- This exercise causes you to listen to the feedback your horse is giving you about the bridle.
- Once you master this, no horse will ever be too tall to bridle again.
- Make sure you are only bridling with your horse's permission.
- If he does move his feet, his hindquarters will be most likely to swing away from you if you have maintained flexion.

Problem solving
- Your horse won't stand still – ask yourself why he needs to move his feet. Is it anxiety or too much energy? Do you need to spend time desensitizing him or doing some ground exercises to get him more focused on you?

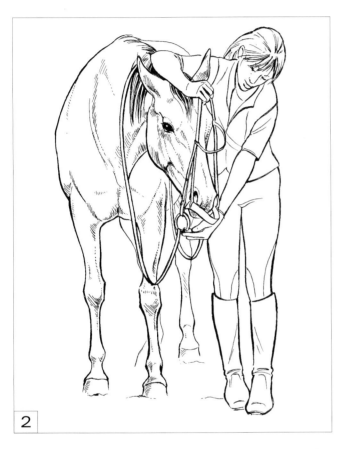

- ❏ Your horse walks all over you – go back to basics, teach him to respect your personal space and to yield from your pressure.
- ❏ He drops his head to the floor to hide from the bit – stamp the ground a couple of times and if necessary, let his nose bump into your knee coming up the other way.
- ❏ He drops his head fine until the bridle is there – he is clearly telling you something. Eliminate the cause of the problem and work on the symptoms.

HORSEMAN'S TIPS

Many horses object to being bridled and put their heads up out of reach or try to walk away – and many of them have good reason to. Ill-fitting or restrictive tack, sore ears, sharp teeth or a rider with bad hands can all make a horse want to avoid having a bridle on, so make sure your horse is not suffering because of any of these before expecting him to help you put the bridle on.

Seek something

You can change a horse's mind about something he has a negative association with if you can replace it with a positive association.

In this example, we will use a cone, but it could just as easily be an umbrella, a jump, a saddle, a trailer or anything your horse is not too keen on.

Unlike desensitizing, where you want the horse to become inactive or passive about something, now you will cause him to actively seek something that he previously avoided.

How do I do this?

❑ You will need to use the natural motivator of comfort to cause him to see matters in a different way.

❑ Place the object in the arena and ask your horse to circle past it in trot a number of times (as close as he feels he can).

❑ Wait until he is showing signs of slowing down and wanting to stop – these might include trotting with his head low, having his inside ear cocked towards you or looking at you with two eyes.

❑ As he approaches the object, give him the signal to disengage his hindquarters and stop by the object.

❑ Give him a long comfort spell, at least as long as he was trotting, plus a bit.

❑ Repeat this several times, until he is making a beeline for the object and would rather be close to it than having to work hard trotting around.

Remember

❑ Do this from both sides. Objects may look different to him out of different eyes.

❑ Be patient, your horse may need to move his feet quite a lot before wanting to stop by the object.

Benefits

❑ You can quickly cause your idea to become your horse's idea by making the right choice easy for him.

❑ It helps you to think and to watch his body language for his communication.

Problem solving

The object spooks him and he runs around moving his feet too much – do some basic desensitizing first (see Exercise 2).

Work away from the object and bring him closer to it just for the comfort stop. He will gradually change his mind about it, but it may take a few sessions.

HORSEMAN'S TIPS
You can make the experience even sweeter if he finds something he likes to eat at the object but don't use it every time or it will be the food he is seeking not the object.

Horse-friendly saddling

You will learn how approach the task in a horse-friendly way and to have your horse stand still and allow you to put the saddle on without the need for tying up.

1

2

Note

If only we listened more to the feedback our horses give us about saddles!

So many problems, in mind and body, are caused by ill-fitting saddles and so many incidents could be avoided if we took a little more time to gain our horse's acceptance of the saddle or looked for the reason if he can't accept it.

Note: if you suspect back pain and or a saddle that doesn't fit, seek the advice of a suitably qualified professional before proceeding with this exercise.

How do I do it?

First, let him sniff the numnah and saddle and have a good look at them. Ask for a little lateral flexion to the side you are standing on, rope in the hand nearest him and rub him all over first with the numnah and then the saddle as best you can, let him move his feet around you if he needs to. Keep rubbing until he stands still. Then stop for a moment. Repeat until he is no longer concerned about the saddle being moved about on his body. Do this from both sides.

Place the numnah on his back and stand beside his shoulder facing his tail with the rope in the hand nearest him, prop your saddle on your hip as shown in Figure 1. Pivoting on your foot, rhythmically swing the saddle in an arc two or three times from his nose to his withers (Figure 2). If he seems unconcerned, gently place the saddle on his back (Figure 3), watching his ears and head, which should still be flexed towards you (Figure 4). If he is still relaxed, ask him to step his front end across and change eyes on you so you can check the saddle and pad and let down the girth.

3

4

Move him back again to the original side (see if you can do this without moving your feet) and, facing his hindquarters, with the arm nearest him run the back of your hand and forearm down behind his elbow and under his belly to pick up the girth (Figure 5).

Do up the girth on a loose hole so it is secure but not tight. Ask him to move a few steps, yield the hindquarters, move backwards and so on so he becomes used to the feel of the saddle and girth, then tighten the girth a bit more but still not riding tight. Move him around a few more steps at close range

5

and then tighten again. Once the saddle is really secure, send him out on a circle in walk, trot and then canter. Show both reins and preferably pop over a small jump.

Hint

This saddling process should help your horse accept the saddle but it's good to check what happens when he starts moving at higher paces. Many horses will hide a buck at walk and trot but not so often in canter or after a jump. If there is one in him, it's best to know about it and let it out before you get on!

Benefits

❏ This exercise helps you to think about saddling in stages, making sure your horse accepts each stage before moving to the next one and helps prevent him getting resentful of the girth.
❏ This method is useful if your saddle is very heavy or you have a bad back. Launching it from your hip rather than trying to lift with your arms causes much less strain on your back than the usual method.

Problem solving

Your horse doesn't seem worried but walks around you in circles – if you have spent time desensitizing and you are convinced he doesn't have concerns about the saddle, you can teach him to stand by using reverse psychology.

Rather than trying to make him stand still, ask him to yield his hindquarters around repeatedly and then offer him the opportunity to stand still. Try the saddling again and repeat if necessary until he chooses to stand still while you put the saddle on.

Remember

❏ Give your horse the benefit of the doubt before using reverse psychology.
❏ The saddle causes constriction all around your horse's body and makes him feel claustrophobic, often causing him to feel the need to move his feet.
❏ Standing still does not mean he is relaxed. If he is tense, he will not give you flexion with still feet.
❏ Practise the whole process from both sides. Doing everything only from the near side goes back to military days and is not necessary today.

HORSEMAN'S TIPS

You should not have to tie your horse up to have him stand still to be saddled.

RIDDEN EXERCISES

THE EXERCISES

Leg and rein positions and responsibilities

In principle, it is widely accepted that the ability to manoeuvre, shape and control a horse should come mostly from the rider's intention, focus, balance, seat, legs (the 'natural' aids) and finally hands, but in practice if a rider drops the reins, there are few who can remain confident and balanced, let alone control a horse's speed and direction. This is because we humans are very reliant on our hands and if we are given reins, we are inclined to rely on them more than we should, which can dull the impact of the other aids and interfere with balance.

Hence the aim of the early exercises in this section is to suggest ways to help you control footfall with minimal use of the reins, so that sensitivity to the other aids is restored to the point that eventually your horse can understand commands to stop, go, turn, back up and go sideways with no reins at all. They will also help you develop an independent seat.

The goal is not that you should ride without reins! But simply that once your horse understands your other aids, the reins can be used with lightness for refining his posture and footfall. In this way, we are able to have horses that are softer in the mouth and more responsive to the hand.

By learning different leg and rein positions, it is possible to communicate with and place each one of your horse's legs in turn and to mould the shape of his body, therefore giving extreme precision to a movement while maintaining fluidity and lightness.

It is important to note that while these rein positions are learned in isolation to begin with, and sometimes exaggerated in order to help the horse and rider understand them, the aim is to recombine them and refine them to the point that the communication they convey is virtually imperceptible.

Something that often happens is that the exaggerated isolations are seen and thought to be the finished product. They are not the product; they are merely part of the process.

Rein/leg position	Controls
Neutral rein	Feels for connection and flexion, doesn't direct footfall
Indirect rein	Outside hind
Direct rein	Inside fore
Support rein	Outside fore
Inside leg	Inside hind
Outside leg	Supports outside hind or shoulder

Every aid here is directly related to what has been taught on the ground in preparation for riding. Don't forget that, just as on the ground, there are lots of different ways to achieve the same thing, and the suggestions presented here are just that. Since it is impossible to account for every scenario, just think of these skills as tools you can add to your tool kit, to be used as and when appropriate.

Some matters are universal and, without doubt, the clearer your intention, the stronger your focus, the better your balance, timing and feel, then the better your horse will understand your meaning.

Equipment

Whether you use a rope halter or a double bridle, it is how and why it is used that is the most important factor.

All equipment is designed for a purpose, and using it well for that purpose can bring great benefits to your riding. Problems occur when either the wrong equipment is used or the right equipment is used in the wrong way. If you use a severe bit because you can't stop your horse in anything less, or use spurs because your horse is dead to your leg, it suggests there is something wrong with the communication between you. The equipment you rely on may appear to help, but it's only masking the problem, which has a nasty habit of showing up in some other way!

I prefer to see people use a simple rope halter or hackamore for riding while they are going through the process of learning and developing a communication system between themselves and their horse. This is simply because it saves the horse's mouth until the situation is more refined, such as the rider developing an independent seat, balance and a better understanding with the horse. Therefore, in the ridden exercises we start with a halter using one rein at a time for learning the basics of control and you can build up to the use of the bridle as you go on. To tie up your 3.5 metre line to make two reins follow the diagrams below.

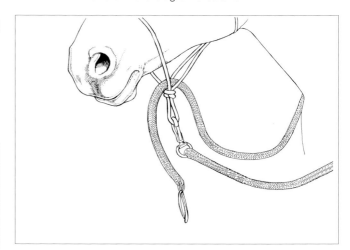

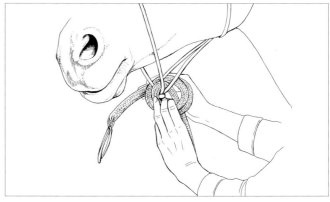

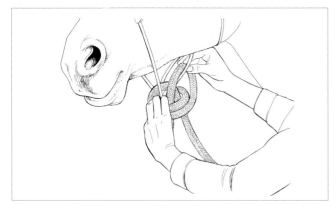

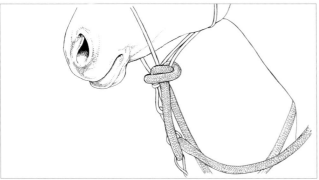

However, as pointed out earlier in this book, everything is offered as a suggestion and it is up to you to decide what equipment to use. Sometimes the thought of riding in a halter is too worrying for the rider who will in turn pass that down to the horse. So use whatever you feel confident with and as your skills develop, you may find that you can use simpler equipment.

Saddles too need to be thought about. An ill-fitting saddle can cause both behavioural and physical problems. You may want to train your horse to modify his behaviour but if he behaves a certain way because he is suffering discomfort from a saddle that doesn't fit, the training is both pointless and unfair. So always check with a suitably qualified professional that there are no obvious issues that need addressing with your equipment.

Riding bareback will improve your balance and help you get a close connection to your horse. Doing it for hours everyday might be uncomfortable for your horse as seatbones can be quite sharp, but it's a good to practise this from time to time and will do wonders for your riding. Start at slow gaits in an enclosed space with a soft surface, and gradually build up as your balance improves. A bareback pad is a good half-way house, giving some protection to the horse and some stability to you – don't use ones with stirrups as they are more likely to slide from side to side.

Just as on the ground, a stick can be a useful tool for guidance and support. For riding, you can use a long schooling whip type so you don't have to take your hand off the reins to touch the horse behind your leg, but they can sting even if used quite lightly, so I prefer to use a simple 1 metre bamboo garden cane, which is stiff but light and makes a noise even when used very lightly.

Prerequisites for riding

Before we ride, we should ensure that we can at least perform the fundamental ground exercises in this book (Chapter 3) and have a basic knowledge of how to assess if the horse is safe to mount or not (see 'Reading horses', page 14). As the horse has a mind of his own, we need to know what to do if things go wrong once we are up there.

The important point is not to 'steal' a ride on the horse. If he doesn't want to let you on, there may be a good chance he will let you off again before you are ready, or think of more and more ways to prevent you from getting on top next time! If your instinct tells you not to get on, I strongly advise you to listen to your own alarm bells. Don't give in to pressure to ride if you are fearful because – just as on the ground, your horse will be looking to you for guidance and assurance and if you can't give it, he too may become fearful, which is not a safe combination.

The horseman's approach is to work on the horse's mindset and help him become mentally, emotionally and physically prepared for being ridden. When this happens, the horse will willingly let you onto his back.

If your horse seems generally confident and calm, is prepared to let you move his feet around while wearing his saddle, is not braced through his body and is able to give you lateral flexion without moving his feet (in other words he is not displaying any opposition to your requests), he is probably ready to get on.

Even with all these 'pre-flight checks' in place, horses often have a habit of walking off as we try to mount, or stepping aside at the last minute from the mounting block. If you are satisfied that your horse is ready to ride, then Exercises 57 and 58 will teach him to help you get on.

Safety basics
❑ Always wear a helmet.
❑ Wear shoes with a heel.
❑ Never ride or jump alone.
❑ Check your tack and equipment regularly.

About the exercises

In choosing the following exercises, priority was given to those that would enhance understanding and acceptance and develop a broad range of skills for horse and rider. They are designed to improve communication for control and manoeuvrability, and work along side more traditional exercises to build a broad and solid foundation from which you can specialize in any discipline.

Mount from the ground

There is much discussion about the adverse effects mounting from the ground may have on your horse and your saddle. It is preferably not something you should do every day; however, being able to do it is important and it is a skill that should be practised from both sides of the horse.

In this exercise, you will learn how to teach your horse to stand still and to read his body language to know if he accepts you getting on.

Note

It's all very well writing a section on ridden exercises but we have to be able to get on first and sometimes that's easier said than done!

It is very common to see people lining their horse up by the mounting block and the horse stepping away just out of reach at the moment they go to get on. Some people get down, reposition the horse and try again – a process that often takes several attempts. Others move the mounting block to a new position along side the horse and, again, this process is often repeated a number of times as the horse tries to outmanoeuvre them. Finally, some either decide to make a blind leap of faith, dangerously launching themselves onto the horse as he departs, or ask someone to hold the horse to prevent him leaving. In all these cases, the horse is demonstrating his opposition and it's potentially a recipe for disaster, so here are some other suggestions.

How do I do this?

❏ Preferably go through the saddling process in Exercise 56, and make sure your horse is not braced or tense before attempting to mount. Check your girth.

❏ Stand at your horse's shoulder and ask him for lateral flexion. Turn to face his tail and hold the inside rein (short enough to keep the flexion) and a handful of mane in the hand nearest him.

❏ Put your foot in the stirrup and hop round on the other leg so you are now facing the front, with your other hand over the waist of the saddle (don't hold the cantle – you will twist your saddle tree) (Figure 1).

❏ Check your horse is still soft and hop up and down a couple of times, putting just a little weight in the stirrup. If he becomes tense or tries to move or straighten, take your foot out of the stirrup and yield his hindquarters a turn or two, keeping the flexion. When he is still again, try putting a little weight in the stirrup again to gauge his reaction.

❏ Only when he stands still patiently should you hop right up and actually stand in the stirrup. Don't swing your leg over yet, but with both legs and body straight put your hip into the saddle and look for the balance point where you are across the saddle but with very little weight in the stirrup so you are not twisting your horse's back. You should be facing forwards at this point and the horse should be flexed around you standing still (Figure 2).

❏ If all is well and you don't detect any tension, rub the far side of his neck and make sure he has seen your hand out of the far side eye before swinging your leg over and gently sitting in the saddle. Keep the flexion until you are sure he is not going to walk off.

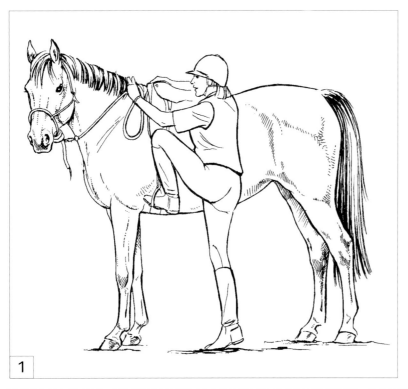

1

Remember

❑ He should maintain lateral flexion throughout the exercise because it tells you about his level of acceptance and enables you to control him if he reacts against you.

❑ Don't get on unless he lets you on!

❑ Take time to work on this with your horse. It will make mounting much safer.

Hint

If you need to work on your suppleness to get your foot in the stirrup, use stretch exercises on a gate, progressively working up the bars to improve your flexibility.

Benefits

❑ This exercise helps you to judge whether your horse is safe to get on.

❑ Mounting from the ground means you can bend the horse to stop him if he walks off, without risking him knocking a mounting block and hurting or frightening himself – essential with young or tense horses.

❑ It teaches your horse to stand still patiently.

❑ It means you can get on again if you (voluntarily or involuntarily) dismount while out riding.

❑ It helps keeps you supple and even-sided!

HORSEMAN'S TIPS

Use your groundskills to work on his mindset and you will find your horse becomes happy to let you on.

Problem solving

❑ Your horse won't give you soft flexion – practise Exercise 11.

❑ All seems fine until you put your foot in the stirrup, then he becomes tense and or moves his feet – remember, emotions run down to the feet and either cause them to stick or move (freeze or flight mode). Try to identify the cause and work on a suitable exercise on the ground – for example, cause him move his feet until he is more relaxed and listening (Exercises 16 and 56); work on his claustrophobia (Exercises 41 and 49); work on respect and left-brain responses (Exercises 5 and 6).

❑ He stands until you get in the saddle and then moves off – bend to a stop (Exercises 60 or 61).

2

Mount from a fence

In this exercise, you will learn how to cause your horse to come *sideways* towards the mounting block and stand patiently where you want him so that you can get on in your own time.

How do I do this?

You will need a secure fence or gate to sit on.

❑ Sit on the top rail and hold the reins in your left hand about 15 cm from your horse's head. In this example, you will be mounting from the near (left) side to start with (though practise from both sides until they are equally good – you never know when you might need to mount from the 'wrong' side).

❑ Ask him to come close to you and stand with you on his left side (Figure 1).

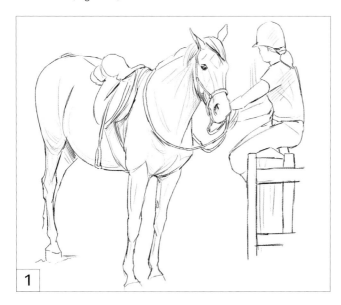

❑ Take your stick in your right hand and rub your horse's back with it to make sure he is not frightened (see Exercise 2).

❑ Using the stick so that you can reach over his hindquarters from where you are sitting, lightly and rhythmically tap the air above his right hip to encourage him to move his hindquarters away from the stick and towards you at the fence. To begin with he is unlikely to understand this cue, so start to reinforce it by gently tapping the top of his right hindquarter, with rhythm (Figure 2).

❑ Gradually increase the pressure level of the tapping by degrees, keeping the left side of his jaw towards your body to enable his hindquarters to swing towards you.

❑ When he makes the slightest move in your direction, stop immediately. Take all the pressure off and just rub him with the stick and give him some time to think about what happened.

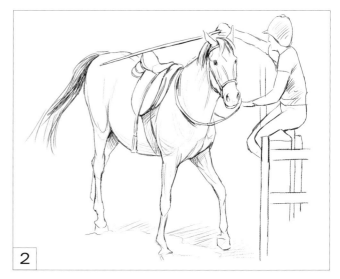

❑ Repeat until he comes to stand along side you by the fence (Figure 3).

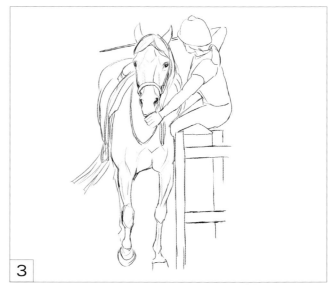

❑ Once your horse understands and comes easily to the fence, test that he will remain standing there while you put your foot in the stirrup – if he moves, go through the above procedure again as many times as necessary until he stands there quietly while you put weight in the stirrup.

❑ Before getting on, make sure you have stroked his neck on both sides so he has seen you out of both eyes and then have his head slightly turned towards the fence. Only when he is confident, relaxed and consistently stationary should you then swing your leg over and complete the mounting process (Figure 4). If he does move at the last minute, gently bend him towards the fence.

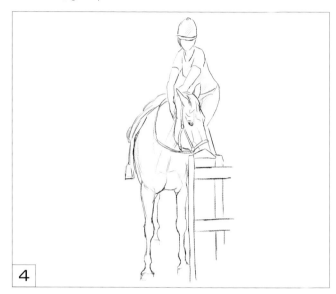

4

Problem solving
❑ He moves away from you and towards the stick, swinging his hindquarters in the opposite way to what you want – this is normal! Don't give up – just keep tapping with the same pressure on the right side of his hip (you may need to change the stick into the other hand for a while until he is coming back towards you again) (Figure 5).The fence is there to stop him going 360 degrees around you, so don't worry if it looks like it's going wrong. If he is moving his feet, the pressure is enough, just keep tapping until he makes the slightest move in the right direction, then reward.

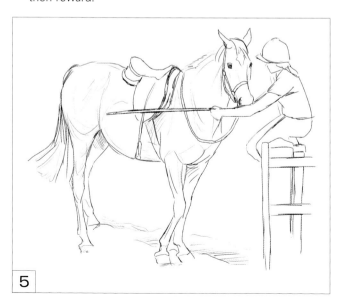

5

❑ He becomes defensive and tries to run away – the pressure is too much. You only need enough to cause him to move his feet, because at that point he is trying to find a way to get the stimulus to stop – you just have to reward the right way.
❑ He tries to swipe you off the fence – you may have put on too much pressure, or not taught your horse to respect your space (check Exercise 1).
❑ He doesn't move at all – increase the pressure of the tapping until it is firm enough that he can't ignore it but not enough to cause pain. If it still doesn't work, go back to your fundamental ground work until your horse understands to yield to direct and indirect feel.

Remember
❑ Take the pressure off when he tries – don't expect to do the whole exercise in one go. Build it up, one step at a time and give plenty of rest time as a positive reward.
❑ The pressure is more psychological than physical.
❑ Use your cue before you reinforce it.

Double check
You keep his head close to you, but don't hang on tight. You will need to allow the reins to slip a little as he comes along side so he can stand with the saddle next to you.

Benefits
❑ Teaching your horse to help you mount says a lot about the relationship you share.
❑ Once this is established you can go back to using a mounting block, as your horse will be less inclined to walk all the way around it.

HORSEMAN'S TIPS

When your horse becomes really good at this, you can start to build in a more subtle cue for this exercise, such as clicking your fingers above the saddle before you start to tap. Soon your horse will probably position himself for you to get on as soon as you climb on the fence.

Lateral flexion

Just as on the ground, how softly our horse can flex tells us a great deal about his acceptance levels, as suppleness and flexibility start in the mind.

So having established this on the ground, it is now time to see if the situation is any different when you are on top since it is a prerequisite to many of the following exercises.

How do I do this?

❏ With your horse standing still and keeping your energy low, pick up your reins in your left hand at the buckle and take it to your sternum.

❏ Run your right hand down the rein as far as it will go without dropping your shoulder or leaning forwards in the saddle. Drop your left hand down and forwards so you can feel some stretching of your left ribs.

❏ Close the fingers of your right hand slowly around the rein and very softly 'kiss' your horse on the flank with the calf of your right leg.

❏ If you have prepared well on the ground, your horse will know that the touch on the right flank means he should flex to the right.

❏ As he brings his head around, you simply take up the slack in the rein by lifting your right shoulder and hand up (not back) (Figure 1).

❏ If he doesn't bring his head around, lift your right hand to apply some pressure on the rein and wait for him to find the release. Don't pull his head around, just keep the pressure steady and in a moment or two he will probably look for release as by now he will be starting to understand that he just needs to yield from pressure.

❏ As soon as he tries, even slightly, release all pressure by loosening the rein back to the buckle, so rewarding your horse's try with comfort.

❏ Repeat until his response is reliable. As he understands the idea and learns where the comfort lies, you will not need to drop the rein, but be able to hold soft flexion for longer as he will stay softly within the rein length you allow him.

❏ Practise from both sides.

1

Benefits

❑ Being able to flex his neck is a prerequisite to being able to disengage his hindquarters and safely bend him to a stop.

❑ It is good measure of relaxation.

❑ It is good suppling exercise.

❑ It teaches your horse to follow your feel and respond softly to the rein.

Remember

❑ Lateral flexion should start at the poll, go through the neck and extend as a soft curve through the body (see Exercise 11). Allow his ribs to go to the outside by keeping your outside leg very soft.

❑ Do the exercise slowly, if you rush you will cause resistance.

❑ Don't take it, wait for him to give it.

Problem solving

❑ He is more braced now you are riding – hold the feel on the rein until he gives, then reward.

❑ He doesn't respond at all – tweak your fingers to put a little pulsing in the rein so it's hard for him to ignore it.

❑ He tries to turn his head the other way – open your hand out to the side like a direct rein (see 'Rein positions', page 16) to bring his head to the right and match the resistance he gives you – anchor your fist on your thigh if you need to and have your left hand on the pommel of the saddle for support if he is pulling you out of the saddle. Just hold, don't pull back. Don't give up while he is bracing or he will learn to do it again. Release instantly when he gives. Practise over and over again until his response is reliable.

❑ He moves his feet – that's acceptable as long as he is bending and turning, let him move if he needs to. Just stay passive with low energy and wait for him to stop and become soft in the rein before giving release. If your horse moves his feet a lot, practise this in an enclosed space to begin with, and wait until this becomes a positive reflex and he is less anxious before moving to an open space.

EXERCISE

60

Yield the hindquarters

Control of the hindquarters is paramount for control of the whole horse, whether by engaging for power, disengaging to reduce power, or adjusting position for bend, lateral work, lead changes, balance and so on. In this exercise, you will learn how to isolate the hindquarters and teach your horse to yield willingly from your seat and leg, step his hindquarters over and walk around his inside foreleg, which lifts and sets down in roughly the same spot. It is also known as turn on the forehand.

How do I do this?

Make sure you can do Exercises 5 and 59 first.

❑ Sitting on your horse in halt, pick up lateral flexion to the right and hold your hand in place just above the withers.
❑ The ridden aids are progressive just as on the ground, and you should always use them in order – focus, seat, leg then rein. If you offer pressure by degrees like this, your horse will soon tune in and start to follow your body language.
❑ Turn your head to the right (keeping your shoulders level).
❑ Turn your belly button right (this should give you the feeling of stepping your right hip slightly back in the saddle and bringing your right thigh closer to your horse).
❑ Turn your right toe out slightly to bring your calf muscle into contact with your horse's flank and squeeze gently.
❑ If he doesn't move from your leg, twist your wrist and lift slightly so that the rein comes closer to your horse's neck and your fingernails are pointing upwards. This is an indirect rein and just as you practised on the ground, it communicates with the hindquarters. The lifting action will help to lighten your horse's inside shoulder and stop him drifting forwards (Figure 1).

❑ Reward the try by taking the pressure off his flank and relax so he stops moving, but keep the flexion for a moment before releasing that too.

Reminders

❑ Make sure you keep lateral flexion throughout.
❑ Build up from a step or two to a full turn, and find the balance between quality and quantity.
❑ If you do this slowly, you will be able to make subtle corrections as you go.
❑ Practise from both sides (you may notice that your horse is more flexible on one side than the other).
❑ Don't allow your horse to make you use your leg strongly. Use a soft leg and support your request with your stick if necessary.

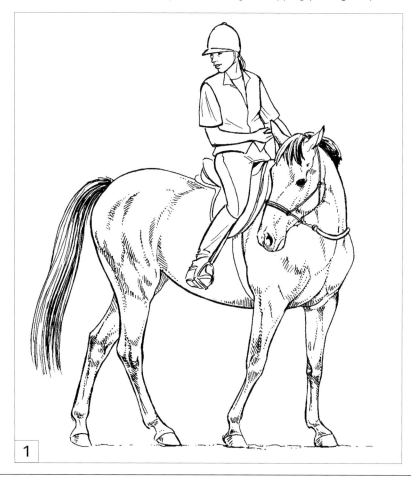

1

Benefits

❑ This is where all your preparation on the ground starts to pay off as your horse understands the transfer of commands to the saddle.

❑ Controlling the hindquarters is essential for safety and also for lateral movements, impulsion, straightness, transitions and canter leads.

❑ It is a great suppling exercise when it is performed slowly.

Problem solving

❑ Your horse walks forwards when you apply your leg – correct by lifting your inside rein. If using a halter, you can put some rhythm pulses down it if necessary (but not with a bit). He doesn't yet understand that one leg doesn't mean go faster, it means yield.

❑ Your horse doesn't yield his hindquarters from leg or indirect rein – draw your leg back a little or tap rhythmically behind your leg with a stick until he moves. Repeat until he doesn't wait for the stick.

❑ Everything becomes braced and he doesn't move – check that you don't have too much bend and are not pulling back on the rein. If he is 'jack-knifed', he will be unable to move his feet.

❑ Your horse moves too much – this is common in impulsive horses. Just relax but keep the flexion and wait until he stops turning – don't make him stop, let him find the stop. Repeat until he understands and accepts your leg command (such horses are great at training you not to use your leg – work on getting him to accept and to respond to your leg rather than react).

Moving on

❑ Feel which hind foot is on the ground just through your seat. Aim to apply your aids in rhythm with his footfall so that your indirect rein asks his outside hind to step over and your inside leg asks his inside hind to lift and step under.

❑ Test how much you rely on the rein – ask your horse to yield his hindquarters without using any rein at all.

HORSEMAN'S TIPS

We humans find it very difficult to use our focus, seat and legs before our hands, and to isolate our hands and legs to communicate specific footfall to the horse.

For the purposes of developing clarity on this exercise, try not to use your outside leg or rein.

Teach your horse what each rein and leg does in isolation and your communication will be more sophisticated when you put them back together.

EXERCISE
61

Emergency stop and dismount

This exercise involves the same procedure as Exercise 60, but merits mention because Exercise 60 assumes the horse is soft and calm and everything is ideal – but situations aren't always like that. If you need to get off in a hurry, this is a safe way to do it.

Let's take a scenario where your horse is travelling at a speed you have not asked for and want to reduce (this could be walk or gallop), or is behaving in any way that makes you feel unsafe to be on top.

HORSEMAN'S TIPS

Preparation, preparation, preparation!

Practise for a true emergency stop by making sure you can bend, disengage and dismount at a stand still before you walk, at a walk before you trot, and at a trot before you canter! Do this in an enclosed space before you go to an open space.

How do I do it?

❑ Run your hand down the rein on the side you are going to bend him and make sure the other rein is loose to allow him to bend.

❑ Draw your rein out to the side to help you get some bend if necessary and then make an indirect rein.

❑ If he is really pulling on you, put your other hand on the pommel of the saddle to support yourself (Figure 1).

❑ Then just as in Exercise 60, turn your head and belly button and use your inside leg behind the girth to cause him to disengage his hindquarters and start turning in a circle (Figure 2).

❑ The faster he is travelling, the bigger your circle will be to start with, just hold that shape using your inside leg to push the hindquarters out making the circle smaller and tighter so he slows down and finally stops (Figure 3). Don't let him become straight or he will get going again.

❑ If you want to get off, maintain the flexion with your inside hand holding the rein and mane, quit both stirrups and swing your outside leg over the cantle to dismount on the side the horse is bent to (Figure 4). Use your now free outside hand to give him an effective tap on the hindquarters so he yields it away and faces you (Figure 5).

Reminder

❑ In an emergency situation, you will need to use your rein first.

❑ Only use one rein to take the power away. Two reins will give your horse more power.

❑ The faster or more urgent the pace, the more important it is that you bend him, but the more difficult that will be. As your horse gets faster, he will want to stay straighter.

❑ Try not to grip with your hands and legs – this will make your horse go faster.

❑ Only use one leg to yield the hindquarters. Two legs will block the disengagement and make him go faster.

❑ Be effective – match your horse's resistance and add a bit more. You have to take control of this situation.

1

2

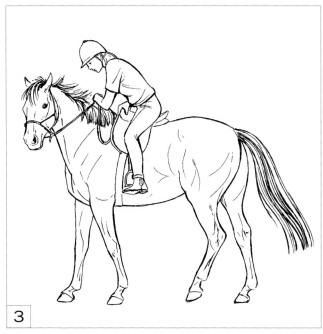

3

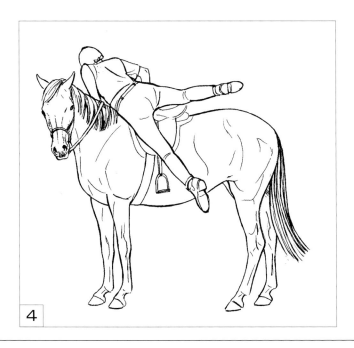

4

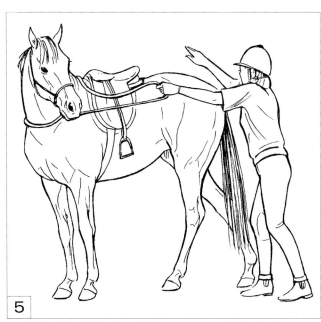

5

Yield the forequarters

Steering the shoulders is sometimes a problem and many riders have difficulty with horses dropping shoulders in or out of circles. In this exercise, you are going to learn how manoeuvre the forehand with lightness by following your energy focus and body signals more than your reins. In this example, you will begin in halt, keeping the hindquarters still and in Exercise 63 you will practise steering while going forward.

How do I do this?

❏ To turn to the right, pick up a little lateral flexion (Exercise 59) so the horse is bending and looking in the direction he will go.

❏ Look to your right and focus on something in the distance. Then turn your belly button to the right, which will bring your outside (left) thigh and hip more firmly against the saddle. Have the sensation of pushing him around away from your outside leg and hip. Your horse should feel this and yield away from the pressure.

❏ If he doesn't, exaggerate the feel by turning your toes in the direction you want to go (imagine you have a flashlight on each foot and you are illuminating the path you want to take), which will bring your outside left knee and lower leg into more contact with your horse. Don't put your outside leg back at this stage as it will encourage the hindquarters to move also.

❏ If he still doesn't step his forehand over (many horses won't understand this to start with), then give a direct rein with your right hand to indicate the turn and 'push' him towards it with your left hip and left leg (Figure 1).

❏ Reward one step and gradually build up as he understands that you will release the pressure when he moves.

If you practise this enough, you will find your horse starts to respond from your body and that you don't need to use the reins to get the shoulder to yield.

Hints

❏ Your horse needs to understand that one leg means yield, not go forward.

❏ Your inside leg should just hang softly by the girth and help maintain the bend.

❏ Try to turn your horse around his inside (right in this example) hind leg. This will be easy when he has true flexion in the direction of the turn.

1

2

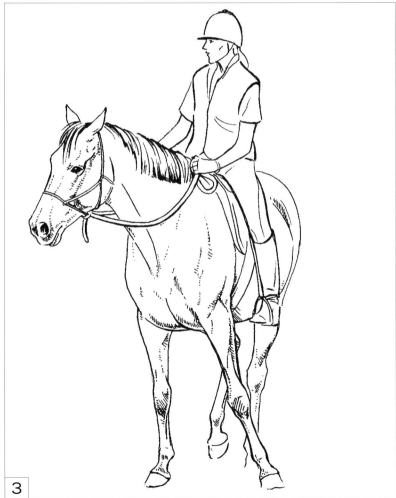

3

Benefits
- Lightening and turning your horse's forehand while loading the hindquarters sets the horse up for many activities that require power and elevation. This exercise helps achieve that and gives you control of the shoulders, which often cause problems in steering.
- Once your horse follows your natural aids, the reins can be used with lighter contact for flexion and individual foot placement.

Problem solving
- He steps forward – back him up (see Exercise 75) and try again. If the problem persists, you could try starting with a fence in front of him so he understands not to go forwards while learning to follow your feel.
- He moves his hindquarters rather than the forequarters – you probably have too much bend in his neck. Use your outside rein to adjust the bend and make sure your inside hand is not pulling.
- He just won't move from your seat and leg – rhythmically tap your stick on the outside shoulder until he steps over.

Moving on
Once your horse has the basic concept of this and is successfully making a turn on the haunches with lightness, you can refine your commands so that you start to communicate with individual feet, as you want them to move.

The direct rein controls the inside (right in Figure 2) foreleg, and your outside leg and supporting rein controls the outside (left) foreleg (Figure 3).

Thus when you want to start the turn, ask the inside leg to lift with the direct rein, so the inside shoulder is elevated and when it is the turn of the outside foreleg to come across, use the outside leg and supporting rein. Try to ask when the relevant leg is on the ground, or you will lose the benefit of this refinement. Release when the chosen leg is lifted – in this way you will learn to tune into your horse's rhythm and be able to control one step at a time (for more information, see 'Rein positions and responsibilities, page 16).

Double check
To test whether you are using your focus and body language more than your reins, try doing this without touching the reins at all and see if he follows your feel and body signals.

Follow focus around a figure of eight

Now you are going to test your preparation and see if you can ride a figure of eight in walk just using your focus and body dynamics on a loose rein (see diagram below).

How do I do this?
❑ Have your hands in a normal riding position but with the reins totally loose and the buckle just hooked with a little finger.
❑ Use your focus, seat and legs to guide your horse around a figure of eight. It will help if you imagine you have flashlights on the end of your toes and turn them to illuminate the path you want the horse to take.

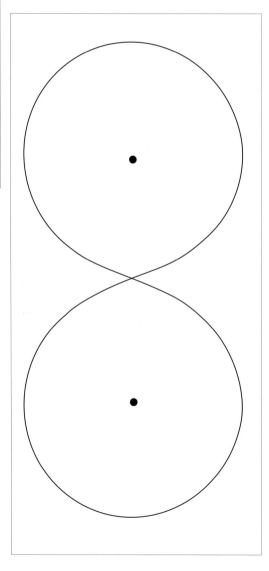

❑ If he doesn't follow your feel, use your direct rein to put him back on track but then return to the buckle. Don't rely on the rein.

Benefits
❑ This exercise is really good for helping you and your horse tune in to the power of focus and body dynamics.
❑ Once this is established, your steering problems will be over.

Remember
Focus, seat, legs then rein.

Problem solving
❑ Your horse doesn't follow your feel well enough – work on the previous exercises more to prepare. Be really consistent about how you increase your pressure in stages.
❑ Your horse just feels lost and goes faster – he may feel insecure without the contact on the rein and it indicates that you both may rely on the reins too much for guidance and balance. Pick up the inside rein and bend him to slow. Go back to long reins again when he walks and repeat as often as necessary until he can maintain gait without the contact. Walk him on a small circle to start with if it helps to settle him. If that doesn't work, or you feel nervous with long reins, ride with them how you would normally and gradually ease them out little by little as you both gain confidence – this could be over several sessions.

Moving on
❑ Try different patterns, including straight lines – try to steer just by using focus and body dynamics.
❑ Once you can do it at walk, try it at trot.

Supporting a turn

This exercise is very similar to Exercise 62, only now the emphasis is on using an outside or supporting rein to help the shoulders come across if your horse doesn't follow your focus, seat and leg instead of the direct rein to lead the nose.

How do I do this?

❑ In halt, pick up a little lateral flexion, just so your horse is bending and looking in the direction he will turn and is bent around your inside leg.

❑ Focus where you want to go and turn your belly button that way – this will bring your outside hip into more contact. Use your outside leg to ask him to yield across (don't draw your leg back – see Exercise 62).

❑ If he doesn't turn, instead of using your inside rein to guide his direction, pick up your outside (supporting) rein and touch it against his neck. Reinforce with your stick on his shoulder if necessary (Figure 1).

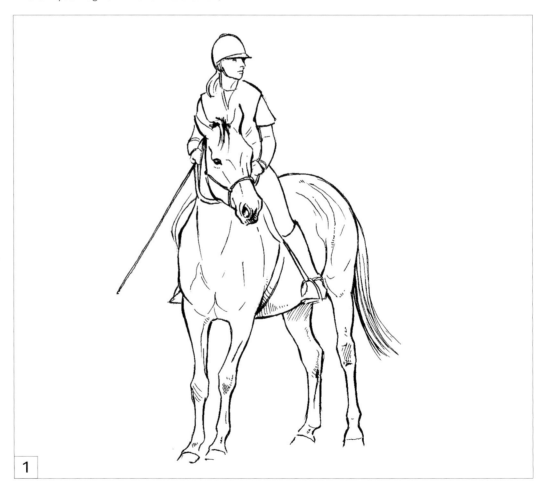

1

Problem solving

❏ He doesn't respond to the supporting rein
– add some rhythm pulses, either against his
neck or using your stick against his shoulder
to ask it to move over.

❏ He walks forwards – lift your inside rein a
little to prevent this.

❏ He bends his head towards the outside
rein – make sure you are not pulling back or
crossing the rein over his neck. The support
rein should push like a stick not pull. If
necessary, to make it very clear for him,
carry your stick horizontally between both
hands above his withers and as you bring the
supporting rein against his neck push your
outside hand forwards a little so the stick
starts to push on the air around his neck. If
your forequarter yield (Exercise 8) is working
well enough, your horse will recognize the
command and step across for you.

Remember

❏ Your inside hand should not do any steering,
keep it and your inside leg neutral, just
maintaining the flexion.

❏ Keep your focus strong, it will help your body
dynamics communicate what you want.

❏ He should make a turn on the haunches, not
walk forwards.

Benefits

❏ This exercise helps with steering the
shoulders and stops them dropping out on
a circle by making him more sensitive to the
outside rein.

❏ It is excellent for horses that push their
shoulder out through an outside rein.

❏ It helps to control shoulders for lateral work.

Moving on

❏ Do this without the inside rein holding the
flexion. (See Exercise 59 to see how you can
hold the flexion just with your inside leg.)

❏ Put this together with Exercise 62 and use
your focus, seat and legs to effect the turn
and use your reins in rhythm with his footfall
to refine the control of each step – direct
rein for inside fore; supporting rein for
outside fore.

HORSEMAN'S TIPS

It's all in the fundamentals!

Ride a figure of eight with supporting rein

This exercise combines what you have learned in Exercises 63 and 64 so that you can ride a figure of eight using your supporting (outside) rein instead of your direct (inside) rein to make corrections if your horse goes off course (see diagram below).

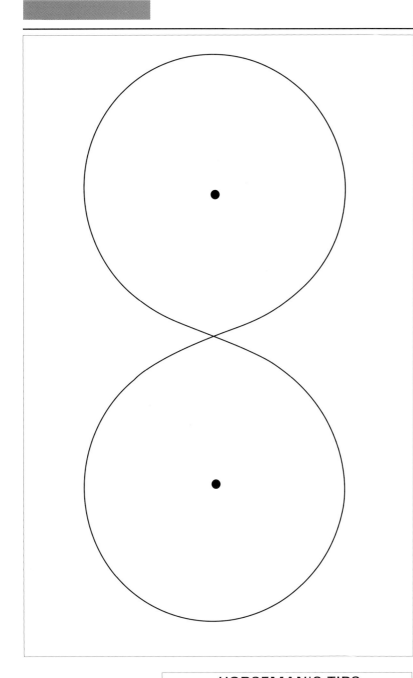

How do I do this?

Try riding the figure of eight on a loose rein, again using your focus, then your seat and then your legs to guide your horse where you want to go. You will need to use your outside hip and leg to push the turn. Your inside leg should hang softly by the girth to maintain the bend as you go round (see Exercise 59). If he doesn't follow your feel, use your supporting rein against his neck to reinforce your request.

Benefits

❑ This exercise refines your horse's response to your aids and the supporting (outside) rein.
❑ It improves your body dynamics and focus.
❑ It develops confidence in both you and your horse to be able to proceed without *needing* the reins.

Problem solving

❑ He ignores the rein against his neck and doesn't turn – you can tap his neck with your hand to encourage him to move away from it, but try to keep your body upright (not leaning forward) or carry your stick horizontally and tap his bubble with it as described in Exercise 64.
❑ He turns towards the outside rein – you are probably pulling back on it or crossing it over his neck, both of which will turn his head the wrong way. Think of trying to push him away with the rein.

Moving on

❑ See if your horse will follow your feel on different patterns. Try circles, straight lines, serpentines, around or between objects and so on.
❑ When it is working in walk try trot.

HORSEMAN'S TIPS

Make a plan and stick to it – don't let your horse out focus you!

Remember

You can use the stick to help him understand and help your body dynamics, then build to doing it without the stick.

Flex to the inside on a circle

We hear a lot about straightness in the German Scales of Training. And, of course, straightness is not the same as stiffness. A horse bent with his spine curved in the same arc as a circle is said to be 'straight' on the circle. This requires suppleness and flexibility (in mind and body), so this exercise exaggerates the flexion to increase suppleness and also tests your ability to control the placement of the shoulders and the hindquarters.

How do I do this?

❑ Ride a 15 metre circle at walk. Imagine the circle has several lanes painted on the ground, like a running track, and that you are riding in track two.

❑ Run your inside hand down the rein and pick up a lateral flexion. (Remember to create the bend from your inside leg.)

❑ Ask your horse to travel with his nose in track one while his body stays in track two (see diagram below).

❑ Make sure your outside rein allows this bend by offering your hand forwards and down. You should feel your outside ribs open and stretch, so allowing your horse's outside ribs to stretch.

❑ You will need to use your inside leg to keep his forequarters out in lane two and stop him turning in on the circle.

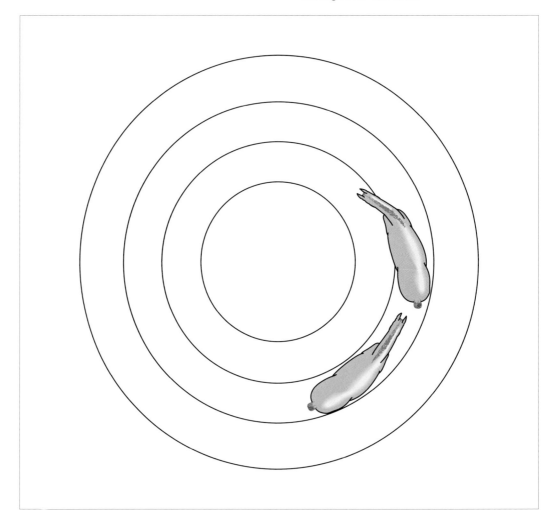

Problem solving

❑ Your horse steps across with his shoulder – work on forequarter yield (Exercise 62). You should be able to ride his shoulders independent of his nose. Make sure you are not pulling back with the inside rein or holding it too far from his neck. Just hold it in neutral, a little higher than your outside hand to encourage his inside shoulder to lift.

❑ He doesn't yield to your inside leg – don't squeeze harder and harder as it will probably cause him to get heavier. Use rhythm with your leg or stick as firmly as necessary to put his shoulder back in track two, then release.

❑ He swings his hindquarters out in an effort to stay straight – use your outside leg behind the girth to put his hindquarters back in track two. If this doesn't work, go back to Exercise 60 and get his hindquarters yield better.

Benefits

❑ This exercise is good for stretching and suppling – it shows up any stiffness.

❑ Being able to control the shoulders and hindquarters independent of the nose will be important when you come to lateral work.

Remember

❑ Your horse should have bend from his poll to his tail.

❑ Keep focusing where you want to go – it will help the horse keep moving forwards.

❑ If you lose the forwards, ask for less bend. Build up gradually and begin with only a few steps at a time

❑ Practise on both reins.

Moving on

❑ Build up to trot (rising will help keep him going forwards).

❑ Once this is going well, reverse the bend and flex to the outside for a few steps.

HORSEMAN'S TIPS

Do this with feel. Make sure you don't pull your horse's head from one side to the other and see-saw on the rein. The idea is to build suppleness and softness.

The better the relaxation, the better the flexion.

Circle with hindquarters out

This exercise builds on Exercises 60 and 66 and all the preparation you did on the ground. It will help your horse bring his inside hind underneath him more (see Exercises 18 and 19) and give you the ability to play around with the angle of the hindquarters for lateral movement.

HORSEMAN'S TIPS

Feel for his rhythm and try to ask with your inside leg when his inside hind is on the ground. This will give you a better step and using rhythm stops him becoming dull to your leg. If you are doing rising trot on the correct diagonal, you should use your leg when you are sitting as this is when the inside hind is on the ground.

How do I do this?

❑ As seen in Exercise 66, ride a 15 metre circle in walk with the idea of lanes like on a running track.
❑ Ride in lane two with some flexion to the inside and move your inside hip and inside leg back to ask your horse to put his hindquarters in track three for a few steps while his forequarters stay in lane two (see diagram below).
❑ Your outside rein will help support the shoulder and your horse should stay flexed to the inside throughout.
❑ Repeat until he really understands and is happy to step his hindquarters out from a light command from your seat and leg.

Benefit

If you can control the hindquarters, you can improve self-carriage, alter bend, perform lateral movements and make canter lead changes.

Reminder

❑ Like anything else, begin by asking for only a little and reward the try. Gradually build on the foundations you have laid.
❑ When he uses his hindquarters better, it will improve his posture, lifting the back and withers and lowering the head.

Problem solving

❑ He swings his hindquarters out too far, disengaging and facing the centre – use your outside leg behind the girth.
❑ He doesn't step his hindquarters over – work more on Exercise 60 or improve Exercise 5 on the ground.
❑ He falls in towards the centre of the circle – focus where you want to go! Use your inside leg on the girth more effectively (see Exercise 66) and open your outside rein to guide the direction. Make sure your inside hand is not lower than your outside hand, or pulling back. What you do with your shoulders will be mirrored by the horse. If it remains a problem, practise along a fence first – use Exercise 72 to help understand the idea.

There are only two ways to bend in lateral work:
❑ Towards the direction of travel – half pass, renvers and travers.
❑ Away from the direction of travel – shoulder in, leg yield.

This exercise develops the shape that bends away from the direction of travel; Exercise 70 works on developing bend towards the direction of travel.

Moving on

Build up to trot and canter.

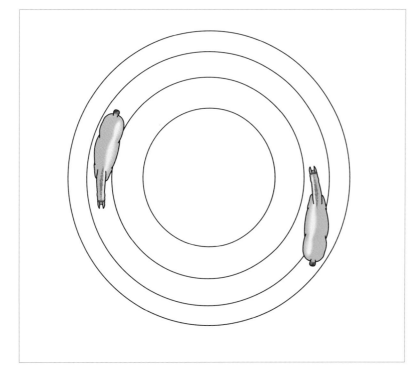

Sideways on a circle

Building on from the previous exercises, you will now ride a circle with imaginary tracks and ask your horse to move his hindquarters out so that he is travelling fully sideways – first in walk, then in trot.

HORSEMAN'S TIPS

Imagine the centre of the circle is quicksand – be effective and don't let him fall in there!

Set up

Put four cones at the edge of a 15 metre circle at equal distances.

How do I do this?

❑ Walk around the outside of the cones with a light contact on the reins, imagining you are in track one (see diagram below).

❑ As you approach a marker, feel down the inside rein and lift for flexion. At the marker cause your horse to put his hindquarters all the way out on the circle so that he is facing the centre while travelling sideways with his front feet still in track one.

❑ Stop at the next marker and stand still, giving your horse comfort on a loose rein for at least 30 seconds.

❑ Ride forwards, through the centre of the circle and rejoin the track on the other rein.

❑ When your horse is balanced and listening, pick the next marker and repeat the exercise until he starts to travel sideways willingly to get his break at the second marker.

Remember

❑ This is a leg yielding exercise – keep the bend around your inside leg.

❑ Keep your horse's front feet in track one at all times.

❑ If your horse is using his hindquarters correctly, he will not fall forward.

Benefits

❑ This exercise is great for developing balance and hindquarter control.

❑ It is good for suppling.

❑ The comfort breaks give your horse incentive to put more effort in.

Hint

As you lift for the flexion at the first marker, start to focus and turn your pelvis towards the centre of the circle. This will bring your inside hip and leg on and help the horse step his hindquarters over.

Problem solving

He can't keep his front feet in track one – he may be unbalanced at first. The more he brings his hindquarters underneath him, the less he will fall forwards (Exercise 18, also see problem solving Exercise 67).

Expand and contract a circle

Still using the idea of the running tracks, now you will practise changing lanes to make the circle larger and smaller (see diagram below). Practise in walk first and build up to trot and canter.

How do I do this?

❏ Ride the circle in lane one first.

❏ Making sure you have your horse bent around your inside leg, ask him to yield to the outer track to make the circle bigger.

❏ Try to do this by pushing with your inside leg and hip rather than steering with the reins, which should just have a light contact and be feeling for the bend. This is a leg yield shape. Watch that your outside leg is not blocking him.

❏ Once you are in the outer track, keep the bend to the inside and use your outside hip and leg behind the girth to ask the horse to yield back to the inner track. This is a half pass shape. Watch that your inside leg is not blocking him.

❏ At first only ask for a little, change one lane, and as he understands, you can change more lanes and expand and contract the circle more.

Remember

❏ Keep your focus and direct your belly button where you want to go – it will help your body dynamics.

❏ Practise on both reins.

Benefit

An easy way to introduce half-pass shape.

Problem solving

Expanding the circle from the leg works better than contracting it – not surprising, this is the first time half-pass shape has been introduced. Keep practising and also work on Exercises 70 and 72.

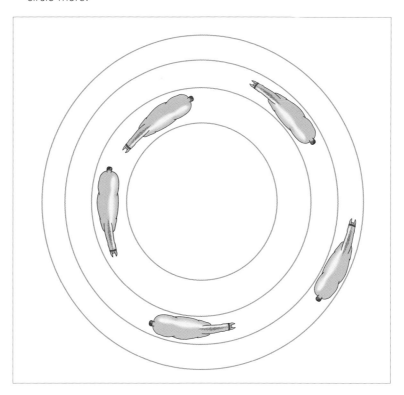

Hindquarters in on a circle

The last in the series on the circle with the track lanes, this exercise shows you how to have your horse bring his hindquarter in on the circle while maintaining the bend (see diagram below). This is a more advanced lateral movement that will eventually enable you to ride half pass, renvers, travers and canter lead changes.

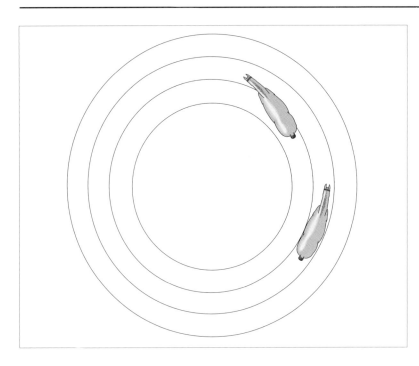

Remember

❑ These movements take time and practice – don't give up if it doesn't work straight away.

❑ Controlling the hindquarters is the secret to success! The better you get it on the ground, the better it will be when ridden.

❑ Practise until you can do this on both reins – start with a few steps and build up.

Problem solving

His whole body moves into track one – make sure your inside seatbone is not heavy. Lift your inside hand a little to lighten his inside shoulder, which should make it more possible to keep it on the track with your inside leg. Don't pull or he will become heavier in your hand – just lift and, if necessary, use some rhythm pulses down the rein (if using the halter – not with a bit). Use your outside leg to push the hindquarters over, tap with your stick to support your request if needed. Make sure your hips do what you want his hips to do.

How do I do this?

❑ Ride on your circle in track two with flexion to the inside.

❑ Keep your inside leg softly on the girth to maintain the bend.

❑ Keep focusing forwards and turn your belly button to the outside of the circle, which will step your outside hip back in the saddle and bring your outside leg back behind the girth to ask your horse to bring his hindquarters into lane one while his nose and forequarters stay in track two. This is the beginning of half pass.

❑ You may only get a step or two to start with, and that's fine.

❑ Reward and ride 'straight' in track two again. Then repeat.

Moving on

Yes you've guessed it – do it in trot and canter.

HORSEMAN'S TIPS

Having the ability to step the hindquarters over and bend in the direction of travel is a major key to flying lead changes.

Improving 'stop' on an impulsive horse

This exercise uses reverse psychology to encourage your horse to travel more than he ideally wants to so that he starts to actually look for a signal to stop.

Note

Balance is probably the most important factor in impulsion (see Balance and biomechanics, page 14). When a horse is impulsive, he is out of balance. This could originate either in his mind or body but as they are directly connected, it's a chicken and egg situation.

Most of the preceding exercises work on physical balance, asking the horse to use his hindquarters better and lighten his forehand so that he doesn't fall forwards or rush, thereby helping his emotions become more balanced. However, some horses remain inclined to be impulsive and don't listen to subtle cues from your seat so you have to rely more heavily on the reins than is ideal.

Set up

You will need nine markers – for example, cones or plastic bags tied with sand inside.

Mark out a square with one marker at each corner and one in the centre. The remaining markers are then placed at the half-way point of each line of the square (see diagram below).

The size of the square depends on how impulsive your horse is, as the bigger the open space the more he will want to travel.

You can do this in arena at walk and trot but its too tight for most horses to canter. I suggest you start in an arena and only progress to a bigger size and more open environment once your stop signal is working effectively.

How do I do this?

With the reins as loose as you feel comfortable with, walk or trot (later canter) around the outside of the square on the left rein and each time you pass a half-way marker turn left and ride across the centre of the square, past the marker that is in the middle of the square and out to the other side, turning left again when you meet the track. Ride round to the next half-way point and turn left. Keep turning left at every half-way marker.

Repeat this until you feel that your horse is getting the idea of the pattern. Ride it for long enough until he is feeling less energetic and more settled. The next time you go through the centre of the square ask him to stop at the centre marker by building your stop in stages. (Don't use any more stages than you need to.)

❑ Think stop and breathe out.
❑ Tuck your seatbones under you a little so you really centre and connect with your horse, but sit light.
❑ Imagine that you have suction cups on your seat bones that lift the horse's back up underneath you so he will glide to a stop without becoming hollow.
❑ Take a light feel on the inside rein but don't pull. Close your fingers and bend him gently to a standstill at the centre marker.

Rest there. If it took 10 minutes for him to feel like he wanted to stop, then rest for at least 10 minutes. Repeat this several times only stopping

< Approach

X

Stop at x

Markers

in the centre when he is ready, so he begins to understand where the comfort spot is.

Soon you will find that he is beginning to slow down every time he gets to the centre marker and if you give him lots of comfort every time he stops, you will find that, in time, you scarcely need to use your reins and will not need to turn him to stop.

Repeat this exercise every day for a week and then every other day for the next two weeks. By then, your horse should be listening to your slightest stop signal and you will find you can stop anywhere on the cue of your breath or seatbones.

Remember

Note – don't begin this exercise when you have limited time. You need to see the process through and it may take a while!

The point of this exercise is to create his desire to stop by making the right choice easy and the wrong choice more difficult.

You are trying to learn not to pull on two reins to stop at this stage, because using two reins to stop engages your horse's power. This is not what you want when he is impulsive, as it is often the cause of the problem in the first place.

Practise on both reins equally.

Hint

Putting your horse on a pattern with a relatively loose rein and letting him move his feet as much as he needs to – and beyond – can bring a him back to balance through the emotions, because it causes him to 'think' stop.

Benefits

❑ This can be a very powerful exercise and some horses become a lot less impulsive very quickly.
❑ It helps the rider and the horse learn an effective stop signal from the seat rather than the hands.
❑ Once your horse understands your cue to stop, you will not need the pattern and will be able to stop anywhere.

Problem solving

Your horse just gets faster – make the square smaller and more difficult. Bend him if you feel he will take off with you, keep him in the gait you want and work him on the pattern for longer before stopping.

Your horse catches on very fast and starts to dive towards the centre point – keep riding the pattern but vary which marker you chose to stop at.

HORSEMAN'S TIPS
Make sure he flexes around the turns so he stays balanced.

Sideways along a fence

This exercise helps you teach your horse to yield laterally from your leg by using a fence as a block in front.

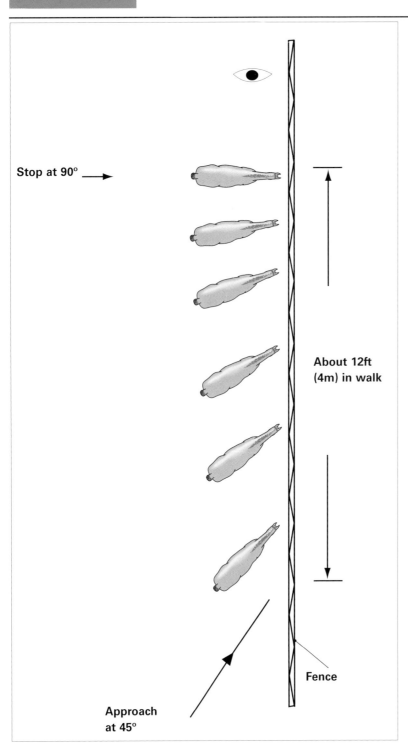

Stop at 90° →

About 12ft (4m) in walk

Fence

Approach at 45°

How do I do this?

Ride towards the fence at an angle of 45 degrees, and as you get there, ask your horse to swing his hindquarters to the inside by putting your outside leg back (see diagram left). As he reaches 90 degrees, ask the forequarters to travel along the fence line for a few steps also. Your supporting rein should be against his neck, with your inside rein open, giving him direction as to where you want to go. At all times keep your focus on a point at the end of the fence. This will help your body dynamics.

Reward him with comfort when he has travelled a little sideways and next time he will put more effort into it.

Remember

❑ Sideways is just moving the forequarters and the hindquarters at the same time.
❑ Beginning with walking towards the fence at an angle helps keep the momentum , just as you did on the ground in Exercise 36.
❑ He should yield away from your outside seat, leg and hand.

Benefits

❑ Using the fence to begin with is helpful for a horse that goes heavy on the forehand in lateral work or just gets faster when you apply your leg to ask for lateral yield.
❑ It helps the horse and rider understand the feel of lateral work.
❑ It is very useful for helping your horse to think and adjust his balance so that he doesn't fall forwards.
❑ It makes tasks such as opening and closing gates much easier.

Problem solving

❏ He goes backwards – he may feel claustrophobic or be afraid because he doesn't understand what you want. Make sure you are not pulling back on the reins, your inside leg is not clamped on and you are focusing and projecting your energy down the fence. You don't have to get full sideways straight away – reward if he travels at an angle and build up.

❏ He doesn't yield the hindquarters so that he is facing the fence – get it better on the ground (Exercise 35). Use your leg lightly, and support with some rhythm from your stick (only make contact if necessary).

Moving on

When you can do this well on both reins, start to do without the support from the fence – use a pole on the ground, and then a line. Reach a level where you can ride sideways without anything in front. (You will need a good back up signal for when his weight goes forward – Exercise 75.)

HORSEMAN'S TIPS

Give him somewhere to go – keep your inside leg off at this stage, until he understands or you may confuse him. Later on you will use it to create bend or in rhythm with his footfall for forwards impulsion – for example, half pass.

Playing with direction and bend

Once you have mastered Exercise 72, you can start to play with the direction your horse is bending while he travels – bending towards the direction of travel or away from it (see the diagram below). This is a combination of Exercises 69 and 72.

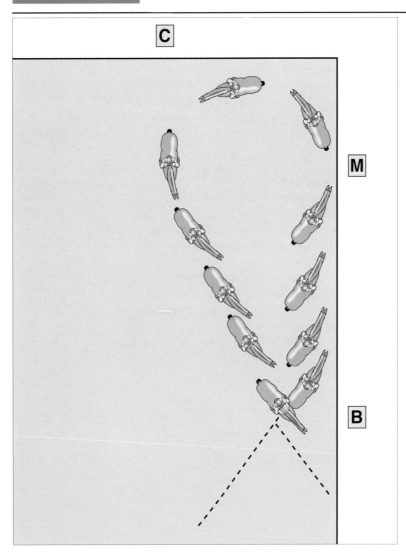

Travel like this for 7 to 10 metres and then ride forwards and start to make a 10 metre circle to the left. As he begins to look at the fence again, ask your horse to travel to his right approaching the fence again at an angle (travelling right but still bent to the left). Your left leg is still the inside leg but with your left hip will now be asking for the yield sideways. You may need to open your right rein to lead the direction, but be sure keep the flex with the left rein.

Try it on the other rein.

Remember
- ❏ Focus where you want to go – it will help your body give the correct signals.
- ❏ Give comfort at the end. He should already know how to go sideways before you tackle this so you won't need to reward until the end.
- ❏ Look for lightness – it shouldn't cost you or the horse anything.

Benefits
- ❏ The fence helps support him and can really help him learn to listen to your instructions.
- ❏ It is especially useful for horses that go faster when you put one leg on.

Problem solving
If you have prepared with the preceding exercises, this shouldn't be too difficult.

If you are having trouble with the different bends, try to sit lighter on the side that he is travelling towards, or you may block his direction (regardless of the bend).

Moving on
As your control improves, you will be able to have your horse travel on three tracks or four tracks by altering the angle.

HORSEMAN'S TIPS

This is a suppling exercise and as such is best done slowly.

How do I do this?
Use a fence to help you begin. Starting on the left rein as an example, approach the fence at a 45 degree angle. Use your left (inside) rein and leg to create a little flexion to the left, while your right hip, leg and rein ask your horse to yield so that he travels sideways down the fence at an angle, hindquarters in off the track, looking in the direction he is going (travelling to the left, bent to the left).

Sideways over something

Many horses become concerned with things under their feet. Here you will see if you can manoeuvre your horse over an obstacle using your skills in riding sideways to help build his confidence and ability to think.

How do I do this?

❏ Prepare for this exercise using Exercises 37 and 72.
❏ Ride your horse forwards over the middle of a pole and stop with the pole directly underneath him.
❏ Let him stand there for a moment.

❏ Ask him to step sideways with his front feet (not forwards) and then his hind feet, so he will travel down the pole in a zigzag pattern (see diagram below).
❏ When he understands, you can ask him to side pass over the pole so his front feet and back feet move together (see diagram below).

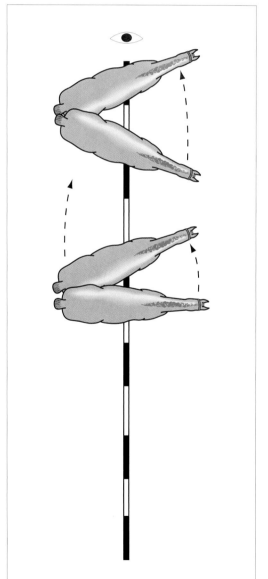

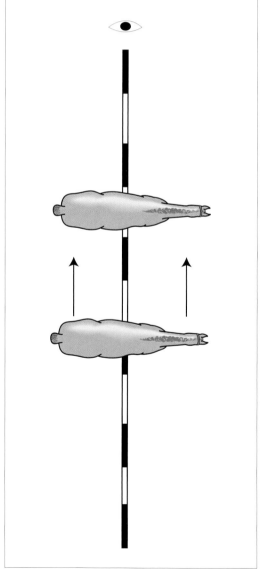

Remember

- ❏ Reward the try – there is no hurry, do one step at a time until he understands and is comfortable with what you are asking.
- ❏ Use your focus, seat and legs before you use your reins.
- ❏ Use a heavy pole.

Problem solving

- ❏ He can't stand with the pole underneath him – get this better on line first.
- ❏ He goes forwards or backwards but not sideways – isolate the element he doesn't understand and work on improving that before putting it back together as an exercise.
- ❏ Slow everything right down, give him time to get confident.

Benefits

- ❏ This exercise is excellent for horses that rush after jumps and for those that get worried about claustrophobic situations with a rider on board.
- ❏ It teaches th horse to think his way through a puzzle and to not rush out of it forwards or backwards.

Moving on

Change the obstacle – try using a log or a barrel on its side, elevate the pole, use a tarpaulin on the ground to simulate a ditch and so on. Use your imagination.

Rein back softly

Rein back is an important ingredient in training but is not a natural direction for a horse under normal circumstances, so they often have resistance to the idea. In this exercise, you will learn how to have your horse move softly back from your seat rather than by pulling back on the reins.

How do I do this?

❏ Have your horse stand in front of a fence on a loose rein.
❏ Sit up as you lift your reins at the buckle and run your hands down to pick up a contact (Figure 1).
❏ Hold it until he softens to your feel and gives you lightness (Figure 2). Release and relax.
❏ Practise this a number of times until he yields softly to a slight feel on the rein.

❏ Then focus on a point in the distance and imagine you had suction cups on your seatbones. Tuck your pelvis under you a little but sit light and imagine the suction cups lifting your horse's back and drawing him up underneath you.
❏ Wrap your legs around his body to create some energy and *don't pull* back. Just keep your hands in place – above his withers and in front of the pommel (Figure 3).
❏ Because the fence is there he cannot push forwards so he has to look for another way to find release. When he takes a step back, release immediately and reward. Gradually you can ask for more steps.
❏ Try to actually push your hands *forwards* as he steps back from the feel, so his neck lengthens rather than shortens (Figure 4).
❏ Repeat many times until he moves back from your seat and leg easily without resistance and then do it without the fence.

Problem solving

❏ He is heavy on the rein and doesn't get soft – this would indicate there is a hole in your preparation! Work more on exercises that develop softness through direct feel – for example, Exercise 5. The fence is there to help him not push through your rein and give him the idea of yielding from your seat. If he really leans, put some rhythmic pressure in the rein (only if you are riding in a halter) to teach him to get off your hand and release when he does, but don't forget focus, seat and legs before rein.
❏ He gets agitated and may go up instead of back – disengage his hindquarters to diffuse the situation. Try without the fence and make sure you are not putting too much pressure on him to do something he doesn't understand. Ask for less and reward more. Work on all the backup exercises including Exercise 14 so he understands the idea of backing while you are behind his driveline.

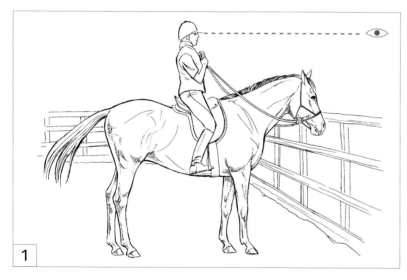

1

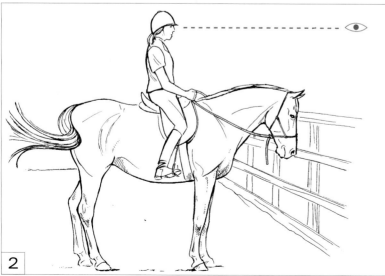

2

❑ He runs backwards – again, do it without the fence so he feels less crowded, but work on his claustrophobia issues to help him be more confidence.

Remember
❑ Focus forward - project your energy forwards and imagine it bouncing off your focus point and coming back to your horse's chest.
❑ Keep him straight by yielding his hindquarters if he goes off course.
❑ Don't ask his feet to move until he is soft on the rein.

Hint
It is very difficult not to pull back on the reins, so if you tuck your elbows against your hips you will find it keeps your hands from taking. When he moves, try to imagine that he is walking backwards away from his own forehead. As he steps, his neck will become longer, you will need to give with the reins to enable this (this feels very unnatural to us at first because we naturally tend to take).

Benefit
❑ Yielding backwards is a fundamental part of your horse's foundation.
❑ It causes him to shift his weight back to his hindquarters and engage more.
❑ Tuning him to respond to your seat will help with downward transitions, halt and half halt.

HORSEMAN'S TIPS

When he backs up without resistance he will carry himself better and back up in a two-time beat.

Some people worry that teaching a horse to back up will cause him to do it all the time, but this is not the case if you teach him to respond rather than react. A horse that runs back is defensive, so confidence is the issue, not the direction.

3

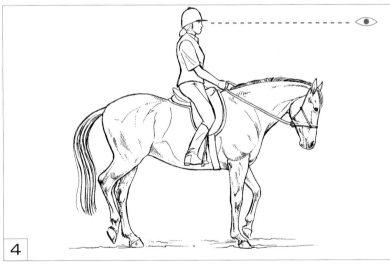

4

Back over a pole

Once you have learned to back up without resistance you can develop the idea to include backing over things.

How do I do this?

To help succeed in this your horse should already be familiar with this exercise on the ground (see Exercise 31).

Follow the same procedure as described there, making sure you can walk over the pole forwards and stop with it underneath first.

The best way to build it up is to start with just backing the front feet over and then rewarding. Once he becomes confident with this, you can come further forwards and back all of him over (Figure 1).

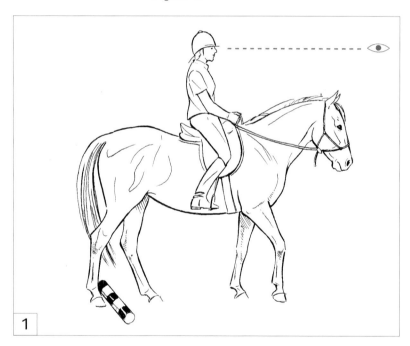

1

Remember

❑ Reward the try!
❑ Use a heavy pole.
❑ Focus ahead and imagine bouncing your energy back from a point in the distance towards your horse's chest.
❑ Keep the hindquarters straight.
❑ Some horses find this a claustrophobic experience.
❑ Do this slowly so he has time to balance.

Problem solving

❑ He swings his hindquarters away when the pole is behind – this is normal, he can't see behind him. Take more time and break it down to give him confidence and understanding of what you are asking.
❑ He braces and feels like he will rear – too much pressure and not enough preparation!

Benefits

❑ This exercise is good for testing and developing trust, confidence and control.
❑ It helps your horse be aware of where his feet are and improves his co-ordination and balance. It also helps him learn to think.

Moving on

You could use a bigger pole (no bigger than a telegraph pole) or back him up a hill or step.

HORSEMAN'S TIPS
Tie his tail up if it is long and he is in any danger of stepping on it!

Backwards and forwards

Here you will practise a series of transitions to improve your impulsion and control of footfall.

How do I do this?
- ❏ Ride along the centre line of the arena at walk.
- ❏ Stop and back up.
- ❏ Walk forwards, stop and back up.
- ❏ Walk forwards then trot.
- ❏ Stop and back up.
- ❏ Walk then trot, then stop at the end and back up.
- ❏ Once you have done this a few times and your horse is listening to you, waiting for the next command, you can start to become more particular about the numbers of steps he takes – for example, 10 walk, 5 back, 10 walk, 10 trot, 5 back and so on.
- ❏ It's a good idea to vary your plan, but once you have decided on a target try and stick to it. (See diagram.)

Benefits
- ❏ This exericise helps your horse to listen.
- ❏ It improves his ability to change his balance and use his hindquarters more.
- ❏ Setting targets helps you become aware of footfall.

Remember
- ❏ Use your seat and legs more than your reins.
- ❏ Stay straight

Moving on
- ❏ Once this is working well, you can alter the order of the gaits and miss some out – for example, trot to back up to trot, or walk to canter to walk.
- ❏ If you have really done your preparation and your horse is following your focus and stop and go signals from your seat and legs, you should be able to get to where you can do this without picking up the reins!

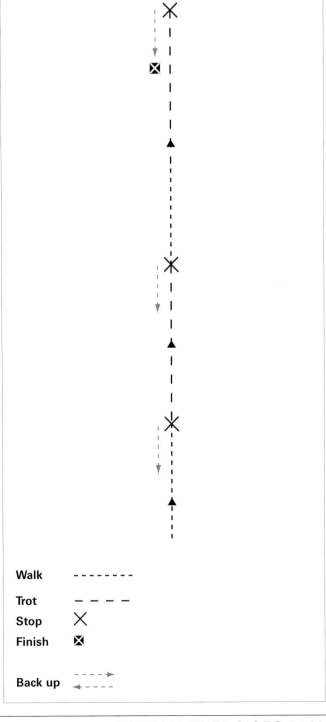

Walk	- - - - - - - -
Trot	– – – – –
Stop	✕
Finish	▨
Back up	- - - - -➤ ◄- - - - -

Manoeuvre through a maze

This exercise tests how accurately you can control your horse's footfall, while travelling in various combinations of direction.

Set up
You will need six straight line markers – preferably heavy jumping poles, arranged in the pattern shown below.

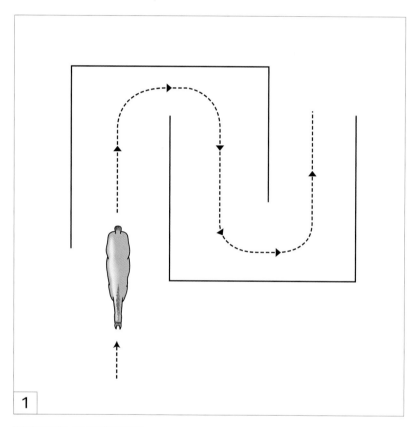

1

How do I do this?
- ❏ Start by making sure you can ride through the maze forwards, and your horse is confident to stop between the poles.
- ❏ Next ride into the maze and back out again.
- ❏ Then try backing into the maze and coming out forwards.
- ❏ Repeat until you can achieve that quite easily and your horse is comfortable with the idea.
- ❏ Next back through the maze, yielding the horse's hindquarters and forequarters around the corners.

- ❏ When you have that working well, try going sideways over the poles and negotiating the corners without stepping 'out' over the poles.
- ❏ Use your imagination to invent different ways to make it interesting but remember to make it progressive. The idea is not to confuse your horse, so if something is not clear, look for a way to break it down for him to make it easier to understand.

Benefits
- ❏ It tests your control.
- ❏ It tests your preparation.
- ❏ It helps your horse gain confidence under saddle in confined spaces.
- ❏ It tests and builds your communication and your horse's trust.
- ❏ It helps keep your training both progressive and interesting.

Remember
- ❏ Ride this from your seat – keep your rein and leg signals light.
- ❏ Keepyour focus.
- ❏ Don't rush – the slower you do this the less opposition you will cause and the more accurate you will be.
- ❏ Try to make the turns very accurate, one step at a time.
- ❏ Stop and rest inside the maze so he doesn't see it as an uncomfortable place to be.

Problem solving
- ❏ Your horse doesn't want to enter the maze backwards – give him incentive by giving comfort in the maze (much like Exercise 27).
- ❏ He won't steer in the maze but will outside it – remember horses stay straight for possible departure in claustrophobic situations. Work on his fear of confinement.

Hint
The narrower the space, the greater the challenge.Set it up so your horse can succeed.

EXERCISE 79

Developing an independent
seat from Mary Wanless

It is often said that riders should have an independent seat, and most people realize that this means sitting in such a way that the reins and stirrups are not needed for balance. This is not so difficult at walk, but in trot and canter it becomes much harder, and when the unexpected happens it is harder still.

How can we recognize an independent seat?

The acid test is to look at a rider and ask, 'If the horse were taken out from under her by magic, how would she land on the riding arena?' If she would land standing on her feet, with her knees bent and a shoulder/hip/heel straight vertical line, then she is riding independently and in balance. If she would land and then topple either back onto her backside, or forward onto her knees and nose, then she is not. It is also useful to ask, 'What would happen to the rider if we cut the reins, and/or removed her stirrups?' If she would topple backwards, or flounder in any other way, then her balance is dependent on her hands and/or feet. A huge

price is then paid by the horse in his restricted movement and carriage.

Few riders live up to the ideal of the independent seat, but even fewer would admit that they use the reins and stirrups for stability. Sadly, pushing into the stirrups and pulling on the reins is the default option for human beings on horses, and it puts the rider into a counter-balance that I call 'water-skiing'. She shoves her feet forward against the stirrups, and is towed along by the horse, which acts as her motorboat. Even experienced riders who want their horses 'on the bit' unwittingly end up pulling on the reins and fiddling with their hands, with the result that they too will often end up 'water-skiing'.

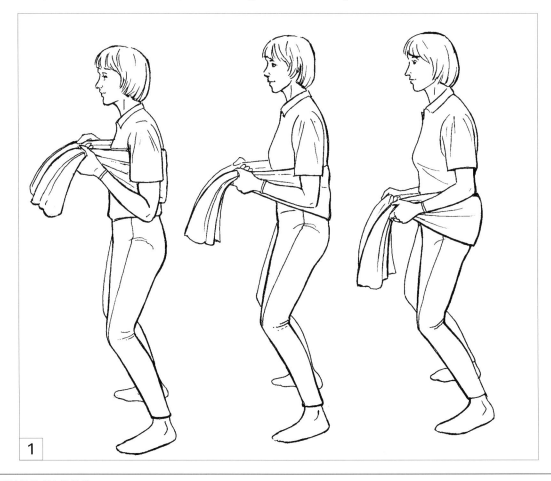

1

The rider can only have an independent seat if she sits with a straight vertical line joining her shoulder, hip and heel. The foot must just rest in the stirrup, but must not press down into it, as this straightens the rider's joints and pushes her backside up out of the saddle. She is then much more likely to 'water-ski'. Staying 'with' the horse is rather like bouncing along on a pogo stick, which means that the rider is using the muscles of her torso to match each bound that the horse makes. This is a far cry from being towed along by the horse, which draws instead on the strength of the rider's arms and legs.

How do I do this?

Stand sideways on to a full-length mirror in an 'on horse' position, and check that you have a shoulder/hip/heel straight vertical line. As you do this, believe what you see in your reflection, realizing that if you normally lean forward or back, you will not actually feel vertical even though you can see that you are.

Roll up a large bath towel, and put it round your back beneath your armpits (Figure 1). Be sure that your shoulders and elbows stay down, and push back against the bath towel at the same time as you pull on it. Do this for about half a minute before you move the towel down a few inches and repeat. Keep checking in the mirror that you are remaining vertical, and keep breathing deeply. When the towel reaches waist level, notice what happens to your abdominal muscles (Figure1). You will find that they have firmed up, just as they do when you clear your throat or giggle. When you have bought the towel down to the level of your

pelvis, stand quietly, breathe and notice how the muscles of your back and front are working (Figure 1). Do this often to increase both your awareness and your strength.

Benefits

Skilled riders maintain the muscle-use you have just discovered, but few realize that their muscles are so much firmer than the average. Sitting with a shoulder/hip/heel straight vertical line brings you much closer to finding an independent seat; but to keep this alignment as the horse moves requires extra tone and strength in the muscles of your back and front. This makes the torso much more stable, and able to stay 'with' the horse in each bound. This in turn makes it much easier for the rider not to resort to using her hands and feet in the quest for stability. Both her torso and limbs are then free to make the minute adjustments needed for transitions, turns, circles, lateral work and so on.

Hints

When you increase the tone in the muscles of your front and back you may find it difficult to breathe. Imagine a chemistry flask inside you, with a long neck going down to a round bowl that lies within your pelvis. Think of the air going all the way down the long neck and into the round bowl. If necessary, seek extra help from a singing or voice teacher as you learn to maintain diaphragmatic breathing.

Other ideas for stabilizing your body

❑ Stand in an on-horse position with one leg slightly ahead of the other, and put your hands out in front of you as if holding the reins. Push your knuckles against a wall, or against a partner's knuckles (Figure 2). Feel how this too changes the tone in your abdominal muscles, and realize that when you are riding, you can only push your hands forward consistently when you can maintain this abdominal tone. The converse is that when your stomach sucks in, your hand automatically pulls back.

❑ With your horse at halt, and sitting with a vertical shoulder/hip/heel line, have someone stand on a block so she can make a sustained push on your upper back or upper chest. Resist her pushes, noticing which muscles you use, and maintain this muscle-use as you ride.

❑ Use exercises with a gym ball to increase your core stability.

❑ Take a Pilates class.

❑ Buy a pogo stick, and practise until you can bounce in straight line as well as in circles to each direction!

2

Yield to feel on the bit

If you have worked through the exercises in this book, you will already be developing the feel, timing and balance necessary to achieve lightness, and you will have taught your horse to trust that there is always a way to solve a puzzle and find comfort.

The same principles are applied to feel through the reins to the bit in his mouth – the most sensitive area of all, yet all too commonly, the most abused.

How do I do this?

Contact is not the same as pressure. Contact to the horse's mouth completes a circuit of energy generated by the rider that travels to the horse's hindquarters, over his back and neck to his head and back to the rider's hands via the reins, in just the same way as a wire does on an electrical circuit. When the horse works correctly and is not leaning or resisting, this contact weighs no more than holding hands with someone you love.

❑ Make sure your lateral flexion is working well (see Exercise 59).

❑ Sitting on your horse at halt with his tail against a fence, lift your reins at the buckle and sit light and tall.

❑ Shorten your reins and, as you do so, softly close your calf muscles against his flank at the girth to help him lift his belly and back.

❑ Your reins should be short enough to feel his mouth. Don't pull back, just hold with steady pressure until he finds release and softens to your feel.

❑ This is very much like the yield you practised in Exercise 75, but you don't give the signal from your seat to back up and the fence is there to help him stand still.

❑ Release as soon as you feel him soften! Even if it is only a little.

❑ Run through the process again, each time starting with lifting the rein at the buckle because it gives him a signal that you are about to ask for something.

❑ Eventually (after many repetitions) he will take the cue from your legs closing under his belly to lift his back and withers and relax his neck and jaw to give soft feel in your hands.

❑ Gradually increase the length of time you hold the feel.

Remember

❑ If you show your horse how to find release, he will always look for it.

❑ If you try to make him become soft, you will always get the opposite.

Benefits

❑ This exercise helps your horse accept your light contact through the rein.

❑ Is a prerequisite to resistance-free selfcarriage and collection.

❑ You will not need to use tight nosebands to mask resistance.

Problem solving

❑ He leans on the bit – hold your feel very steady and wait. Make sure you have the same resistance as he has without pulling back, and let him find the solution to the puzzle. If the release just doesn't come, go back to lateral flexion (preferably in a halter) and teach him to yield to feel better (in the halter you can use rhythm pulses in the rein if he really leans on you).

❑ He walks forward through the feel on the rein – teaching him to yield doesn't mean there will never be any weight in the rein. If he pushes through it, you clearly have to do something. Imagine (or even place) a marker on the ground near his front foot, level with your hands. Your hands must not move from there. If he travels forward, try to keep your hands anchored level with that marker. This is passive resistance and different from pulling back. There may be a lot of pressure on the rein but it is of his making, not yours. Release as soon as he stops leaning.

❑ He softens but chews frantically on the bit – anxiety or discomfort can cause this (check his teeth). Hold the feel until he is soft and still in the mouth and then release. If it is a long-standing pattern, it may take a while to resolve but consistency will win the day.

Moving on

Once it is reliable at a halt, do it at walk, then trot, then canter.

Flat figure of eight

This exercise will test your control of shoulders and hindquarters by working on your steering along a straight line, and stopping or making transitions in a small space.

How do I do this?

❏ Place two poles at X, either side of the centre line about 1.2 metres apart (see diagram).
❏ Start at halt between the poles facing C and walk along the centre line then turn right.
❏ At B trot and at A turn down the centre line and stop between the poles.

❏ Rest.
❏ Repeat on the other rein.
❏ Progress to where you can proceed from X at trot and canter at the half-way marker on the long side (B or C depending which rein you are on), canter straight down the centre line and stop between the poles.
❏ Practise riding straight lines and straight transitions (both upward and downward) between poles.

Benefits

❏ You need a strong focus to stay straight without a fence for guidance.
❏ It helps your horse become brave about entering a confined area.
❏ It is very useful for horses who shy at dressage boards.

Hint

Play with speed within gaits.

Problem solving

❏ He doesn't want to enter the tight space between the poles – give him more incentive, make them wider and/or rest longer.
❏ He overshoots the centre line in canter – work on exercises that will improve his balance – for example, Exercises 69 and 77.

Moving on

You could make the poles closer together, or raise them so they form a corridor.

HORSEMAN'S TIPS

If your horse has a negative association with something, always look for ways to make it more positive.

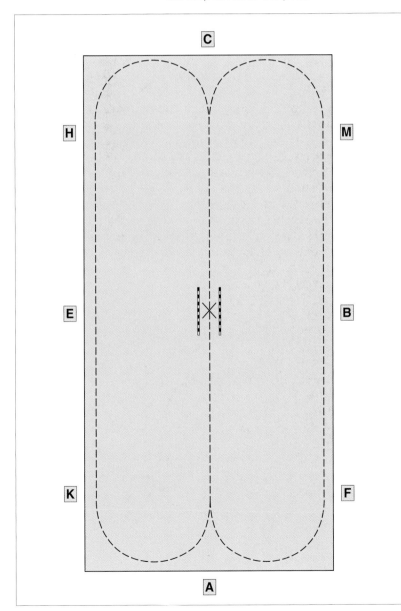

Play with balance on a see-saw

Many horses become concerned about unusual or hollow surfaces, such as bridges. This is especially so when they move, such as trailer floors. This exercise builds from Exercise 48 on the ground but this time you will ride your horse onto the see-saw and reach a level where he is not worried by the movement. Once he is confident, you can experiment with how posture affects balance.

Set up

You will need a sturdy 2 metre wooden planks at least 5 cm thick, braced at the back to make a very strong panel about 75 cm wide, placed on top of a length of half-round fence rail for the fulcrum or rocker.

How do I do this?

Make sure your horse is confident to stand on this without you on top first and isn't worried when the see-saw tips backwards and forwards (see Exercise 48). If he is not confident without you on board, then you are not ready to do the exercise ridden.

❑ Ride up to the see-saw and ask him to place one foot on it.
❑ The more he sniffs, chews or paws at it the better. Encourage his curiosity, he is learning.
❑ Ask for one foot at a time, rewarding the try by taking the pressure off each time.
❑ Use approach and retreat to let him know he can return to firm ground if he needs to.
❑ Keep your horse straight and in the middle of the panel.

❑ There will come a moment when his weight causes the see-saw to tip. Don't tense up, just let him adjust his balance and try to leave him to work it out.
❑ Reach a level where he can stand square with the pivot (fulcrum) directly underneath you. Then experiment with your balance, leaning forwards and then backwards and see how little it takes to tip the see-saw one way or the other – this is a good example of how your balance affects your horse when you are riding (Figures 1 and 2).

Problem solving

❑ He won't go near the see-saw – make sure Exercise 48 is working well first. If it already is but he is less confident with you on top, this just indicates there is more to do in gaining his trust under a rider. Make the exercise simpler by putting the panel on the floor without the fulcrum, or work on other surfaces such as tarpaulin, water and so on (see Exercise 44).

1

2

- ❏ He can't keep his balance – play around with the box used in Exercise 48 to help him.
- ❏ He gets off when it rocks – slow every thing down. Take one step at a time and work up to it.

Remember

Persevere and give your horse time to learn that his environment is not as scary as it seems.

Benefits

- ❏ This exercise helps your horse become confident with ramps and bridges or any unusual footing.
- ❏ It gives a clear experience of how posture affects balance.

Moving on

- ❏ Play with Exercise 80 while you are up there. If he starts to lift through his withers when you feel on the bit, you will see how this helps his balance point shift backwards as his front end lightens.
- ❏ Try to find the balance point where both ends of the see-saw are in the air!
- ❏ You could also try playing with your backup signals (see Exercise 75) to see how his balance changes.

Allowing your horse to jump
from Pat Burgess

When asking your horse to jump, it is important to allow him to jump by giving him the *freedom* to use himself naturally. All too often horses knock jumps because riders stay in balance in the air by using their hands for security (maintaining too strong a contact) rather than using their legs for security, and it is the horse who gets the 'pain and the blame'!

How do I do this?

To allow 100 per cent freedom with your hands, you need 100 per cent security in your legs.

The following two-part exercise will help you develop a more secure jumping lower leg consisting of 60 per cent gravity and 40 per cent grip for 100 per cent security.

Part 1

❑ Sit on your horse and put your stirrups to a comfortable length for show jumping (cross-country would be shorter).
❑ Check that your thighs are at about 45 degrees diagonally across your saddle flap.
❑ Put your stirrups on the balls of your feet.
❑ Push your feet to the insides of your stirrups.
❑ Turn your feet (like the hands of a clock) to 'five to one' – that unblocks your ankle joints.

❑ See that the stirrup leathers are vertical and your toes are up and your heels well down.
❑ Stand up in your stirrups and feel your body weight purchasing against the stirrups (by the law of gravity) sinking down through your hip joints, knee joints, ankle joints, through your stirrups and out of your heels to the ground.
❑ Now trot around the school (to practise the 60 per cent gravity security).
❑ Post (rise to the trot) a little and then stand in your stirrups keeping your body semi-vertical – to begin with you may need to hold the mane or the neck strap until you find your balance.
❑ All your joints should feel like shock absorbers with your weight sinking through your heels with your stirrup leathers vertical.
❑ Have someone on the ground to watch and help you get your position right.

1

Part 2

Having worked on your lower leg, you are now going to practise giving your horse the freedom to stretch in the air. You need to train your body to be able to free the hands and still keep the legs secure, so to begin with exaggerate the exercise to attain independent hands and legs.

- ❏ Sit vertically and lightly in the saddle on your seat bones (as if they are plugged into the saddle).
- ❏ Ask your helper to stand on your left side and to cup her right hand at the back of your heel to stop it swinging back. Next she should clench her left fist and dig her knuckles into your left hip joint at the top of your leg to make you aware of this folding point. (Repeat on the right to make sure both sides of your body are doing the same thing.)
- ❏ Now allow your weight to drop into your stirrups keeping the stirrup leather vertical and heels down. Fold from your hip joints, keep your back flat, your head up and slide your hands along the crest of your horse's neck as far as they will go, keeping your seat well back just above the saddle.
- ❏ Don't straighten your knee joints – this would open up the angle at the back of the knees and throw your body forward, thus unbalancing your horse.
- ❏ Practise sitting up, then folding and stretching, purchasing against the stirrups (secure legs – soft, free hands). Do this standing still first, then at walk and then at sitting trot.
- ❏ See that you stay with the saddle because your legs are tight (40 per cent of your security is grip).

Remember

- ❏ Your horse needs to stretch his neck muscles in the air in order to:
    - ❏ lift his front legs up
    - ❏ use his head and neck to balance
    - ❏ lift his hind legs up
    - ❏ absorb concussion on landing.
- ❏ You should feel a sinking grip through your knees into the top of your calves and down through your stirrups.
- ❏ Do not over grip with your thighs and knees (unless in an emergency) because it will make you pivot on your knee, your feet will go backwards and you will lose the 'gravity' through your feet
- ❏ Your legs must not go back, even once your horse has taken off (though you are using your legs behind the girth to create impulsion before take off).
- ❏ Your horse needs to stretch his neck muscles and ligaments to lift his front legs and his hind legs up.

Benefit

When you use your legs for security rather than using your hands, your horse will be able to stretch his neck and jump with freedom, balance and confidence.

When your stability comes from your legs not your hands, you can offer your horse guidance through light reins as and when necessary.

Improving canter departures

You will ride a half circle from the fence back to the fence, stop, turn and canter back the other way to your starting point (see diagram below).

x marks loaded hind leg

x marks loaded hind leg

Fence

Benefits
- ❏ The turn helps the canter departure on the correct lead by engaging the outside hind.
- ❏ The fence helps encourage the horse to stop with his hindquarters under him.
- ❏ The back up engages your horse and 'coils the spring' for a good departure and balanced canter.
- ❏ You can give him the stop cue from your seat and you don't pull on the reins.
- ❏ It is great for obtaining balanced impulsion.

Remember
- ❏ Focus where you want to go.
- ❏ Put energy into the departure not the turn, and the turn will start to flow on its own.

Problem solving
- ❏ He leaves on the wrong lead – he is probably not weighting the correct hind leg in the turn.
- ❏ You will need to use your outside leg behind the girth when you want to stimulate the outside hind to strike off on the correct lead.
- ❏ Don't look down at his inside foreleg to check the lead or you will unbalance him and may cause him to lead with the wrong leg.
- ❏ He becomes over excited – he needs to learn to control his emotions to have balanced impulsion. Pause between each element to slow his mind and therefore his feet until he starts to settle into the exercise. Stop on a good note and repeat for several days in a row until it's not a big deal any more.

How do I do this?
- ❏ Start with your horse's hindquarters on the fence, canter around in a half circle to the left towards the fence and stop.
- ❏ Back up a couple of steps and make a turn on the haunches to the left, which will put the horse's weight onto the left hind leg. This sets him up correctly for a canter departure on the right lead.
- ❏ Canter the half circle back to the original starting point.
- ❏ Stop and give comfort.
- ❏ Turn on the hindquarters to the right. This loads the right hind for a left canter lead.
- ❏ Repeat until your horse gives you an energetic canter departure off a light leg.

Moving on
- ❏ Reach a level where you can do this pattern without any intermediate steps of either walk or trot.
- ❏ Start making simple lead changes through walk or halt on different patterns – for example, serpentine or straight lines.
- ❏ Use an in breath as a cue to 'go', and an out breath as a cue to 'slow'.

One-handed riding

It's quite revealing when you try riding a set of school movements with your reins in one hand as it shows whether your communication comes mainly from your focus, seat and legs, or hands.

How do I do this?

❑ Put your reins in one hand by forming a bridge across your horse's withers and holding your hand with fingernails down. This will enable you to swivel your wrist a little.
❑ Keep your spare hand on your sternum (Figure 1).

❑ With a light contact, ride around the arena making circles and serpentines to check your ability to manoeuvre your horse.
❑ Ride straight lines, make transitions, turns on the forehand, turns on the haunches, leg yield, shoulder in and so on.
❑ Start riding the exercise in walk, and progress to trot and then canter.

Hint

Don't attempt with one hand what you can't yet do with two. This exercise is for testing rather than training.

Remember

Don't change hands mid-way through the exercise, but do make sure that you can do this with either hand.

Benefits

❑ It is a great test of your body dynamics because your hands cannot be too active.
❑ It is good for being able to do practical things on horseback, such as opening gates, leading other horses, or picking blackberries!

HORSEMAN'S TIPS

Some people actually find their horse goes better doing this because their hands are more still and they use their bodies more.

1

Ride and lead

Leading one horse off another is undoubtedly a useful skill to have in your toolbox but to do it safely and successfully requires good preparation. So in this exercise we will look at the ideal training needed for both horses and practise some manoeuvres in the arena to check your control before venturing further a field.

How do I do this?

First, make sure you can do the following exercises with the horse you are leading: all the fundamentals, 13, 14, 20, 25, 36, 41, 49 and 53.

And on the horse you are leading from: all the fundamentals, 14, 20, 41, 49, 51, 53, 57, 59, 60, 61, 62, 67, 69, 71, 72, 75 and 77.

This may look like an exhaustive list, but with these in place you will be able to deal safely with most situations. You will also need to make sure your ridden horse is totally confident with you carrying a stick and moving it about while you are riding.

If you are right handed, you will probably find it easiest to start with the led horse on your right side.

❑ With your horses side by side, put your reins and lead rope in your left hand and your stick in your right.

❑ Rub both horses with the stick to check they are not worried by it.

❑ Ask the led horse to walk forward by extending your left hand and exerting some forward feel on his halter. If he doesn't follow, move your stick along his back and rhythmically tap his rump to drive him forwards – just as in Exercise 20 (Figure 1). As he steps, you then ride forwards with him.

❑ At first, travel on a right rein, as this will make it easier to turn the led horse if he is on the inside.

❑ Once this is going well, change the rein and ride with him on the outside, being careful not to trap him too close to the fence or he may pull back or shoot past you.

❑ At a point along the fence, ask both horses to stop and back up. If this doesn't work, you can reinforce your request by putting your stick along side their necks between them and moving it up and down – as in Exercise 14, Figure 3.

❑ When they are happily travelling along side each other, you can hold the lead rope in your right hand and stick in the left, but when you want something, you may need to change hands so you can use the stick for control.

❑ Practise until you can make transitions and turns and keep the horses together.

1

Problem solving

❏ The led horse pulls back – good job you have a 3.5 metre line! Don't try to pull him back towards you. It will make him pull away more. Allow a little drift on the rope, and go with him if you can. The horses may be feeling threatened by each other. Try walking around him, riding at his hindquarters to have him turn and face you, then ask him to come along side you by tapping the air above his hindquarters to move him up to the feel (you may need the string on your stick to reach). Make sure your preparation is good. If he is not yielding to your feel, go back and work on Exercises 3 and 4.

❏ The led horse rushes past – bend your horse away from him (as much as a turn on the haunches) and disengage the led horse. Practise turns that have him on the inside and use your stick in front of the driveline to stop him getting ahead or turning across you (see Exercise 25).

❏ The horses try to bite or kick each other – this is common, even among friends! They may feel more claustrophobic in close proximity and become defensive. One may be threatening the other not to come too close. Allow them to be further apart, and put your stick between them to discourage them if it is still a problem but recognize that there may be signals going on between the horses that you cannot detect, so give them the benefit of the doubt and don't get annoyed if they don't do this well to begin with.

Remember

❏ Don't pull the led horse forwards, you should drive him forwards.

❏ Use your body dynamics clearly to steer the horse you are riding as you will only have one hand on the reins.

❏ Make sure you can do this from both sides.

❏ Keep the led horse's head about level with your hands.

Moving on

❏ Add some obstacles, go sideways and so on.

❏ When it is all going well, try sitting still in the middle and circling the led horse around you while yours waits patiently as the rope goes over his head and over his hindquarters. (This may seem extreme but is exactly the kind of hazard that can happen out riding – the better you prepare for the unthinkable, the safer you will be.)

HORSEMAN'S TIPS
Preparation, preparation, preparation!

SPECIFIC ISSUES

THE EXERCISES

This chapter will address the common issues that horses and riders have. It is presented in the context of what has already been said. It is not designed as a stand-alone or 'quick fix' chapter as the point is that these problems only exist because of a break down in communication or understanding between horse and human.

Studies have shown that a desperately high percentage of the horses sent to slaughter are sent there for behavioural reasons (up to 66 per cent in some cases).

If the exercises have been followed in the preceding chapters, it is highly likely that most of these specific problems will disappear as the horseman will have learned to look for ways to approach the subject from a different perspective, resulting in a dramatic reduction in confusion and conflict behaviours.

However, some more detailed help would be useful in some circumstances, so some commonly encountered situations are addressed here, with reference to other places in the book that these issues can be dealt with and together they give you some clues about how to re-train your horse's behaviour with regard to:

❏ Going forwards off a light leg
❏ Opening a gate
❏ Accepting clippers
❏ Tying up without pulling back
❏ Eating grass at inappropriate times
❏ Picking up feet/accepting the farrier
❏ Spooking and shying
❏ 'Reefing' and running away
❏ Pulling on the bit
❏ Napping and planting
❏ Bucking and rearing
❏ Biting or sour attitude
❏ Avoiding being caught
❏ Loading in a trailer
❏ Scrambling/falling in a trailer

Going forwards from a light leg

There can be all sorts of reasons why a horse is not willing to go forward – medical conditions, discomfort, lack of balance, lack of motivation, naturally not very energetic or being hampered by the rider. Let's assume you have checked that the cause is not medical.

What happens?

The biggest problem with horses that don't respond to the leg is that we often end up squeezing harder or even kicking more with our legs, but this actually makes the problem worse. Imagine someone on your back giving you a bear hug – would you feel you could move? The harder and more constantly you kick, the more you actually desensitize your horse and he becomes less responsive to lightness. Eventually, this results in what behavioural scientists call 'learned helplessness' and you may have to use your legs or spurs for every stride to maintain movement.

If you want your horse to be responsive to your legs, you need to use them sparingly, but effectively, and leave him alone when he is doing what you want. You also need to make sure you are not holding him back at the same time with your reins.

How do I do this?

- ❏ By offering lightness and reinforcing it with pressure until you achieve the response you are looking for, then giving instant reward.
- ❏ Put two cones as markers in the arena on the centre line about 20 metres apart. You are going to ride from one to the other
- ❏ Start beside one, facing the other, and focus strongly beyond it.
- ❏ Lift your energy and project your 'belly button power' where you want to go.
- ❏ Squeeze gently but clearly with your legs.
- ❏ If he doesn't move, make a firm sharp tap inwards towards the girth so your calf muscles 'spank' him.
- ❏ Give him a smart tap with your stick just behind your leg to make sure he does move!
- ❏ As he is moving, keep your leg off him. If he slows, go through the whole process again, even if you are convinced he won't respond to the lighter pressure – he certainly won't if you don't offer it!

- ❏ Ride to the other cone using the most energetic gait you can and stop and relax for 30 seconds.
- ❏ Turn around and go through the process repeatedly until he is more responsive to your lightest cue.

Remember

- ❏ You are making the right choice easy and the wrong choice difficult.
- ❏ Keep focusing your energy, one day that's all you will need.
- ❏ Make sure you are not holding him back on the reins, especially as you use stronger pressure to get him to move. Many people get nervous and don't realize they are pulling back at the same time.

Hints

Doing this as an exercise using the cones is just to give you and you horse the idea. But you should go through these stages whenever or wherever you ask him to respond to your leg. If you take the pressure off when he does respond, you will quickly find he becomes more sensitive because it is to his advantage.

Reminders

- ❏ Your horse can feel a fly on his flank!
- ❏ It is true that some horses are lazier than others, but all will choose comfort over discomfort given the option.
- ❏ Spurs were designed to be used lightly and with finesse to create elevation and extreme precision for advanced movements in highly schooled horses. If used inappropriately as a substitute for good training, they cause pain, resistance and conflict behaviours. They should only be worn by experts, who have great feel and timing.

Opening a gate

Opening a gate is a practical skill that we don't tend to work on ahead of actually needing to do it for real. It can be difficult, especially if you are out on a ride, and the horse has his energy up and is going forwards. Stopping to fiddle with a gate can be hard enough, but going through quietly, holding it for others and patiently closing it again is often just too much for some horses. So taking some time to work on your technique and to teach your horse to be calm and patient will really help.

How do I do this?

It's best if you can keep one hand on the gate at all times so it doesn't swing away or into your horse. In order to do this, the method of opening depends on whether the gate opens towards or away from you. Each requires a completely different technique (see diagram).

A gate that opens away from you:
❏ Stand next to it with your horse's tail at the hinge end.
❏ Have your reins in your outside hand, undo the latch and push the gate open with the hand nearest to it.
❏ You will use a combination of yielding the forequarters and riding sideways and will go through the gap facing forwards.
❏ Then yield the hindquarters to manoeuvre around the gate and push it closed again.

A gate that opens towards you:
❏ Stand next to it with your horse's nose towards the hinge end.
❏ Have your reins in your outside hand, undo the latch and pull the gate open with the hand nearest to it as you move sideways away from it.
❏ Then yield the hindquarters around and go through the gap backwards.
❏ Then ride sideways to pull the gate closed.

Benefits
❏ It's just plain useful!
❏ Someone who can open gates while mounted will always be a popular riding companion!

Problem solving
❏ Your horse drifts away from or won't push the gate – you are probably leaning over and have too much weight on your inside seat bone and leg effectively pushing him away. Make sure you keep the pressure coming from hip and leg furthest from the gate.
❏ Your horse rushes through the gateway – work on Exercise 41. Practise stopping and waiting in the gateway, making it a place of comfort (see Exercise 55). Also try backing him through it (see Exercise 78).

Hint
You can simulate a gate by using a rope looped between two jump wings.

SUGGESTED EXERCISES
1–11, 41, 60, 62, 64, 72, 78 and 85.

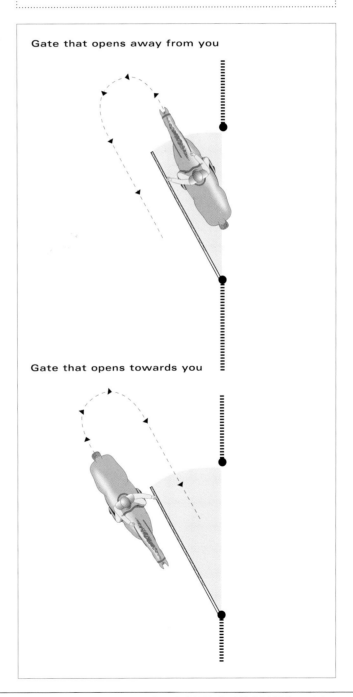

Gate that opens away from you

Gate that opens towards you

Accepting clippers

Horses' fear of clippers is commonly encountered, but rarely unfixable given enough patience and understanding of how horses tick.

How do I do this?

You will need to fully understand the principles of progressive desensitization and approach and retreat, and also know how to control your horse's footfall to keep him and yourself safe. I recommend you spend time on the suggested exercises before attempting to work with the clippers. Ideally do this in the summer when you are not in a hurry to use them!

Follow the instructions for Exercise 2 with your rope, stick, a plastic bag, then with an electric toothbrush switched off and then switched on. Only when he can accept these items should you approach with the clippers and run through the whole process again – first with them off and at a distance to begin with when you first switch them on.

Remember

❑ Your horse is emotional and will need to be able to move his feet, so don't try to do this with him tied up.
❑ Remain calm and passive – never become angry or raise your voice.
❑ Don't be too direct, approach and retreat – take pressure off more than putting it on.
❑ Breathe! If you hold your breath, your whole body will be tighter. Relax, smile and be casual and you will be amazed how much it helps him.
❑ Take care and take time.

Hints

❑ If you can't get hold of wireless clippers, try an electric toothbrush.
❑ If you can't get near him, walk away with him leading behind you until he feels less threatened or even curious. Then walk in an arc in front of him, allowing him to turn and face his fear. Gradually getting closer as he can accept you (see Exercise 51 for more information on how to approach this).
❑ If he rushes backwards, allow drift on the rope until he finds his threshold of tolerance.
❑ If he kicks or strikes, tape the toothbrush to your stick and rub him with that to give you a safety zone.

HORSEMAN'S TIPS

Don't drug him or twitch him. Put the process before the goal and take time to obtain his consent – it will take less time in the future.

SUGGESTED EXERCISES

1–11, 16, 35 and 41.

Tying up without pulling back

A horse that pulls back when tied up is a danger to himself and to others. But it can be difficult to prevent given the panicky nature of horses, and even more difficult to change if it has become an ingrained pattern.

Note

There are different types of 'fly-backs' (as they are sometimes known):

❏ Those who do it in a 'right-brained' way and instinctively panic to escape.

❏ Those who do it in a 'left-brained' way and are no longer worried, but do it deliberately having learned that it is a strategy that works for them – this is the horse who calmly snatches at the string loop and wanders off.

Various methods work with varying degrees of disaster or success. Here are some options that are commonly tried:

❏ Tie to something solid and let the horse struggle until he gives up – can work, but also can kill or injure (not recommended).

❏ Tie to string – can work, but can teach him to pull back and break free (should always be used while travelling).

❏ Tie to a slip ring – allows the horse to travel backwards while it applies resistance but not solid force, though it will release if he pulls hard enough.

❏ Tie with an elastic or rubber 'bungee' cord – these have been known to break, and the recoiling hook to cause frightening damage.

❏ Never tie up – not always practical and avoids the problem rather than solving it.

How do I handle this?

If you can address the cause and response by building his confidence in his surroundings so that he is less likely to panic and teach him to yield from pressure on the back of his head, you have a good chance that he will tie up normally and in an emergency just might stop and think.

Personally, when possible, I prefer to use a combination of these preparation techniques and a slip ring. This is just because, with all the preparation in the world, in any horse that values his life, the flight response is never far below the surface.

SUGGESTED EXERCISES

1–11 (especially 2 and 3), 13, 20, 41, 47, 49, 52 and 53.

Eating grass at inappropriate times

Most of us have at some point been towed to a juicy clump of grass by a horse or pony who seems oblivious to the 'water skier' behind them! And when they get there, it can be a struggle to get their heads up to stop munching.

The horse is clearly demonstrating the power of motivation, and that he is prepared to push through pressure when he has a goal in mind.

How do I do this?

You may well find that as you work through the exercises in this book the problem disappears as your understanding of pressure and release improves. But it's hard to even get started if he is not listening, so here is a technique that will help you get him to stop eating and pay attention to you.

When your horse drops his head to eat, lift the lead rope using rhythmic pressure in the following way:

❏ Move up and down without any feel on the halter (indirect pressure). This is really just a visual cue. Lift the rope softly like this two or three times.
❏ Increase the pressure in the same rhythm so he can feel the clip bump the halter under his chin, but still only lightly.
❏ If he doesn't respond (which he probably won't), make the pressure quite strong, so that the clip and knot under the halter bumps his jaw firmly. If he stops chewing for a moment release (reward the try), and as he starts again go through the whole process once more.
❏ If he doesn't lift his head, use a very strong upward bump that he cannot ignore.

He will probably lift his head quite smartly and then drop it again and carry on eating. Just repeat the process from the beginning being careful to use the lightest pressures first, and within three or four attempts you will probably find he has lost his appetite!

Remember

❏ If you want lightness, you have to offer it.
❏ Never try to pull his head up, you will teach him to become heavier.
❏ Be consistent when he is persistent.
❏ Don't try to prevent him eating by hanging on to his head – let him learn the consequences of his actions. This will help him make the right choice.

Benefits

❏ Your horse will learn that there are times for eating and times for paying attention.
❏ You won't have to struggle any more – the visual cue will be all you need.

HORSEMAN'S TIPS

Only be as firm as you need to be effective.

SUGGESTED EXERCISES

1–11, 13, 14 and 16.

Picking up feet/accepting the farrier

Horses have a natural opposition to picking up their feet for us because they are then unable to run away, and some also find it hard to balance on three legs.

The more we try to make them lift their feet, the more they are likely to want to prevent us and protect themselves.

However, all horses need their feet looking after, so teaching him that he has nothing to be defensive about is essential for preparation for you and the farrier.

How do I do this?

Without having him tied up and with your rope over the arm nearest him, run your hand down his foreleg and feel for his chesnut.

This is a sensitive area that you can use as a 'lift' button. Begin by tapping it gently, then squeeze, and then pinch if you need to. Release the moment he lifts his foot for you and be ready to receive it with the other hand. If he puts it down again, repeat as many times as necessary. For the back feet do the same but on the point of the hock.

Once he picks his foot up for you, rub his leg and gently reassure him. Don't hold his foot up, put it back down so he receives comfort for the behaviour that you want. As he learns the idea, you will be able to hold for longer periods of time.

If he snatches or kicks out, don't get angry, just disengage his hindquarters and cause him to move his feet around purposefully for a while. Then offer him the chance to stand still. Repeat the process of asking for the foot and moving him around if he is not willing to give it to you (this is why he is not tied up). Soon he will realize that it is preferable to stand still.

If he is really trying to kick you, you need to spend more time on Exercise 2. Then using your stick and string, apply the technique in Exercise 47 to teach him to lift his feet from the feel of the string to give him more confidence while keeping yourself out of kicking or striking range.

Hint

Don't use force – reach the stage where your horse will offer you his foot. Be as polite as you would like him to be.

Remember

❏ When they lack confidence, horses' natural instincts are 'hard wired' to do the opposite of what we want.

❏ Take time – if you don't rush it, you will get there quicker!

❏ It is not your farrier's job to train your horse to pick up his feet politely; equally he should not undo any trust you have managed to build with your horse.

Note

If your horse and farrier don't have a good working relationship, do your preparation so that your horse stands still and lifts his feet for you. Then ask your farrier to work on the issue with you and your horse, and pay him for his time. Make the focus about trust and acceptance rather than getting a shoe on or a trim done and stop on a good note. Repeat the session if necessary. It may seem a little costly, but will be far less expensive to you and your horse in the long run.

Most farriers are very professional and happy oblige with this – they know a confident, well-trained horse is in their interests too. If your farrier is not prepared to do help you with this, you should change to one who will.

HORSEMAN'S TIPS

If you suspect a pain or balance issue (horse leans or collapses on you), try Exercise 48, and have him checked by a suitably qualified professional.

SUGGESTED EXERCISES

1–11, 47 and 48.

Spooking and shying

Spooking and shying are indicative of confidence levels, and also of adrenaline levels, which can be related to high spirits or to stress.

SUGGESTED EXERCISES

1–11, 14, 16, 20, 21, 27, 31, 37, 41, 42, 44, 45, 48, 49, 51 and 53.

Why does my horse spook?

A horse may ignore an object one day or jump at it the next depending on how he feels, what he's been eating, how much energy he has, what the weather is like and so on.

But also remember that there are other triggers.

Negative associations with things, such as dressage markers or jumps, can arise in certain settings that under different circumstances would not cause problems. Sometimes it is tension from the rider or the occasion that can cause this (very common at competitions). It may not be the markers themselves he is afraid of but what happens to him in the arena. If he then receives some form of punishment for his behaviour (often brought about when we believe he is not actually frightened of the object), then this all adds fuel to the fire of negative association.

Some horses, confused and stressed by their training, may show their lack of confidence in apparently unrelated situations and exhibit 'displacement behaviours'. These 'fearful' dramas can be the indicator of a deeper level of concern.

Sometimes the reason is simply that horses cannot see something clearly. Just because it is clear to our eyes, doesn't mean they can see it well, especially if we restrict the movement of their head so they cannot adjust their focus. Holding them tighter or punishing them for this can quickly make their world seem hostile and a spiral of fear can result, creating a problem where there previously wasn't one.

What can I do about it?

The obvious starting point is to help him become confident with the kinds of things he might find scary, and the list of suggested exercises will help you with that, but you may also find that the more you work through the exercises in this book, the less spooky he becomes in general as his confidence grows when his world becomes more predictable.

When he does spook at something, confrontation is not the answer – try to address the cause.

First, give him the benefit of the doubt if he is worried. He may not know that the plastic bag in the hedge or the hole in the road are not potentially lethal. Scepticism is natural for a horse. If he is exhibiting some fear of an object or place, offer him the chance to rest there, use approach and retreat and allow him to move his feet if he needs to. When he tries to take a step closer, reward, stroke his neck or scratch his withers and help him relax.

Try to keep him facing his fear by gentle but firm guidance, but don't hang on to the reins and kick or you will create far more opposition. Gradually build up to where he is close to the object and you can feel him relax as he realizes the object will not eat him! If it takes all of your allotted riding time, so be it – it's time well spent.

Avoidance techniques, such as turning his head away from the object in an effort to ride past it, may or may not be successful at the time, but do nothing to help him gain confidence by learning he has nothing to fear.

As I've mentioned before, when we are tense, our horses detect it. Perhaps we smell different or have a spiky green aura around us. Who knows? Certainly they can pick up on our mood and this can make them more edgy than usual. So if you are nervous, your horse will be more likely to develop these tendencies.

It is also worth mentioning that some sparkiness is not always a bad thing as long as it is manageable. To achieve an exuberant performance out of a horse, you will probably need some adrenaline. If he is too relaxed, he may appear 'flat'.

To me, the difference between the confident horse with a little edge and the stressed, confused or unconfident horse is his ability to come off the 'high' and back down to earth. The confident horse has more control over his emotions and is able to hold himself together in the heat of the moment. The extra adrenaline can actually enhance his performance, whereas under pressure the unconfident horse's performance is adversely affected.

'Reefing' and running away

Horses who set their neck, turn and 'reef' (pull) the rope out of your hand on a regular basis can be tricky to retrain.

Why?

As with most situations, the issue originates from lack of confidence, but some horses start to use it as an exit strategy at the slightest request from the handler and it can be as dangerous as it is frustrating.

Voting with the feet like this clearly indicates that your horse doesn't appreciate something that is happening to him but to work on how to rectify that through the exercises in this book does require the horse to still be on the end of the rope!

Since you can't use your strength against him, and stronger equipment and restraint will probably add to the cause not address it, you need to find ways to change his mind, by making the right choice easy and the wrong choice more difficult.

How do I do this?

Start in an enclosed space that has secure fencing (but not a stable) – preferably a space without corners.

Try not to let him become straight or turn away from you, keep lateral flexion all the time you are working with him. Develop your hindquarters disengagement (Exercise 6) to a level that you only have to look at his back end and he turns to face you.

If he does turn to run, don't pull him back. Try to move forwards and to his side to obtain some leverage. The further behind him you are, the less chance you have of stopping him. The more you try to pull him back, the more he will leave.

If he is really determined, just let him go, and then make him move his feet (see Exercise 95) but don't be aggressive about it. You don't need to chase him, just keep him moving. Offer him the chance to stop and if he is ready to be caught, go back to what you were doing. Repeat as many times as necessary until he works out the consequences of his actions.

Once you can control his feet a bit more and have created some positive reflexes and soft yields, start working through the book doing as many exercises as you can to build confidence and control as he learns to yield from pressure. Once your horse sees you as a valuable resource that he wants to be with the problem will be resolved.

Remember

❑ Take care that you never make him feel wrong or criticized. You will just make him want to leave even more.

❑ Give him lots of comfort and be careful about how you apply pressure.
❑ Don't let him train you not to ask for anything, just think how to make it seem like his idea!

Hint

Just before he takes off, his body will stiffen and flexion will be lost. Watch out for the signs – you won't be given much warning!

HORSEMAN'S TIPS

Commonly (though not exclusively) horses originally bred for draft work are particular masters of this trick. They are no less sensitive than other horses, but sometimes don't show it in ways we easily recognize – appearing quiet, even shut down (see 'Reading horses', page 14). Because they are big and strong, people often dominate them at an early age with an attitude of 'show him who's boss before he works out how strong he is'. Unfortunately, this can cause them to be extremely unconfident with the result that they become over defensive and use their stocky conformation and pulling power to their advantage.

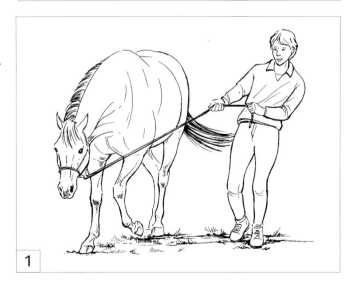

1

SUGGESTED EXERCISES

1–11 (except 7 and 8 to start with) with particular emphasis on 1, 2, 3, 6, 9 and 11.

Pulling on the bit

No horse is born with a hard mouth. Indeed, it is one of the most sensitive areas of the body, and yet people often complain that their horses 'pull' and are difficult to stop and sadly resort to stronger and stronger equipment for more effective 'brakes'.

Note

A horse cannot pull against himself!

He has to have an accomplice applying an equal and opposite force.

There may be a number of reasons why your horse doesn't respond to a light signal down the reins – emotion, pain, lack of balance, lack of understanding, too much energy and so on will all contribute to him becoming heavier in your hand, but the harder you pull the reins the worse it will become.

The more you use both reins to pull him to stop, the more you will be engaging the hindquarters, thus giving more power to the engine. The more you pull back, the more he will lean forwards – it is just simple physics, and you will quickly arrive at a situation that is very uncomfortable for you and your horse.

The human habit of gripping with the hands is a fundamental problem. We think that if we create enough discomfort by pulling, the horse will slow down, and of course sometimes he does, but if we continue to hold the reins tightly giving no release, he can only try to find ways to resist, giving rise to many health issues and chronic stress behaviours, not to mention many accidents. Remember that when they become emotional, horses need to move their feet more and while they are sensitive enough to feel a fly on their flank, they can also push through extreme pressure if necessary. This becomes a vicious circle and is what happens when a horse runs away with you despite your desperate attempts to stop him. Once the adrenaline kicks in, you have a potential disaster on your hands.

Balance needs to be restored in the mind and the body of both the horse and rider before communication can resume and many ways to achieve this are covered in the suggested exercises.

Remember

There may be many contributory factors that cause the horse not to stop when you ask, but one thing is for certain – *pulling* takes two!

SUGGESTED EXERCISES
1–11, 14, 16, 17, 18, 59–62, 71, 77, 79 and 80.

Napping and planting

When a horse plants his feet and refuses to go forward, he either doesn't want to go towards something or he doesn't want to go away from something.

Why?

The origin is usually a lack of confidence – in himself or the rider or both. In the case of horses that plant while schooling, it is usually because the pressure/reward balance is wrong so he is de-motivated (rather like when we are over worked and under paid, it doesn't take long before we feel resentment and stop trying).

Kicking and shoving and trying to make him to go forwards tends to make him dig his toes in even more and pushing harder at that point will result in a buck or rear, often followed by a spin and speedy exit. It doesn't take many repetitions for this to become an ingrained pattern, which takes less and less to trigger it. Unfortunately, if a horse is concerned about something and runs into heaps of pressure from you, it just adds to the negative associations he already has and so the whole situation becomes a vicious circle.

If your horse is 'napping' more often than not, the problem is resolved by taking a lead from another horse. This tells us that horses gain confidence from their own kind more than us but also shows that they are natural followers who respond to good leadership. A mare can get her foal to follow her anywhere, even swim across a river if necessary, so what you need to do is work on the relationship so your horse sees you as someone he can trust and value as a problem-solving resource. Once this happens, he will have less anxiety about leaving his home and companions and being with you.

How do I do this?

Make sure you can do the suggested exercises, because they all teach you how to communicate with your horse to develop his confidence in himself and in you.

In the process, you may well find that the problem just disappears, but if you do have a 'sticky' moment, the key is to 'unstick' his feet. Bend him and disengage his hindquarters for a few turns and then offer him the option of going forwards by allowing with your hands and squeezing with your legs. If he doesn't take it, disengage again and then offer forwards. Reward the try by taking the pressure off as soon as he steps forward.

Don't be too ambitious – confidence comes in thresholds. He may find some confidence to go forwards a few steps and then stick again. Just repeat the process. Making it easier to walk that to baulk.

Remember

- ❑ The key is control of footfall, but set it up so you don't have a head-on battle.
- ❑ Being effective doesn't mean being confrontational. Just make yourself more compelling than what your horse was focusing on before.
- ❑ Don't be too straight line in your thinking. Try to see it as a symptom of a bigger picture and address the cause.
- ❑ There is no shame in getting off and sorting things out on the ground. Your ground skills are for communication!
- ❑ Accentuate the pleasure of going out for a ride by giving the horse some grazing time while out riding and so on.
- ❑ Think laterally and you will help him gain courage and even curiosity.

SUGGESTED EXERCISES

1–11, 14, 16, 17, 20, 41, 48, 55, 59, 60, 61, 74 and 78.

EXERCISE 97

Bucking and rearing

Horses can buck or rear out of exuberance or because of resistance to something, or a combination of both.

Note

In order to rear or buck, your horse must plant his feet; if his feet are planted, his mind is stuck. So you can look at the 'problem' in two ways – eliminate the cause and unstick his feet.

The causes of resistance can be discomfort, claustrophobia, fear, pressure, loss of balance, confusion, lack of confidence or stress. If the horse succeeds in ridding itself of the cause of the problem by his actions, he is likely to repeat them because the strategy works for him. Sometimes the original cause may no longer be present – for example, pain – but fear of pain may be still be a trigger.

Many horses experience these causes but do not buck or rear, so experience, character, environment and management differences also play a big part in tolerance levels of individuals.

If your horse is prone to bucking or rearing:
❑ First have him checked by a suitably qualified professional for possible causes, such as a vet, physiotherapist, dentist, body worker, farrier, saddler.
❑ Then try changing his diet – cut out feeds and balancers that contain any grain.
❑ Look at whether his lifestyle is causing him any stress.
❑ When you have done all that, start working on the exercises in this book, paying particular attention to suggested exercises.

Hints

❑ Work on exercises that encourage all the feet to move fluidly. Look for the stuck spots.
❑ When a horse is flexed he will be less likely to buck or rear.
❑ Remove the bucks before you get on by making sure you have cantered and jumped on line with the saddle on before you mount – a horse will hide a buck at walk and trot, but they usually show up at canter or jump.
❑ His acceptance and lack of resistance is indicated by his willingness to flex.
❑ Resistant mind equals resistant body.

SUGGESTED EXERCISES

1–11, 16, 20, 22, 30, 31, 35, 41, 44, 55, 56, 57, 59, 60, 61, 66, 67 and 96.

Biting or sour attitude

If your horse tries to bite you or seems generally grumpy, he is trying to tell you something. For example, he may be in pain, he may be fearful and feel the need to defend himself, he may not rate you above him in the pecking order, or may feel resentful of something you or someone else has done, or a combination of any of these. Horses are not born with a sour attitude, but the training and lifestyle we impose on them can create this.

What do I handle this?

Obviously, have him checked for discomfort and illness as a first course of action and if that doesn't reveal anything, look at whether his needs are being met in terms of equine company and play time, freedom of movement and expression, interest and variety, suitable diet, adequate turn out, work–reward balance and so on. Once you start looking at life from your horse's point of view, you will be well on the way to exposing the root cause and then you can make appropriate changes to improve the situation.

Meanwhile, you may need to protect yourself from being bitten!

❏ Try and keep him out of biting range – that is, out of your bubble. If he does try to take a chunk out of you, defend your space with your arm or elbow used rhythmically on the edge of your bubble (see Exercise 1). It is surprising how often people inadvertently ask for trouble by allowing horses who bite into their personal space.
❏ If he does bite you, try not to become angry and retaliate. A spiral of violence can ensue and may well have been the cause in the first place. You will only succeed in making him defensive or more offensive.
❏ Move his feet around, disengage him, establish some relative dominance without being violent and maintain clear boundaries. Make the wrong thing difficult and reward the behaviour you want.
❏ Being firm, fair, clear and 100 per cent consistent with your horse will usually improve matters no end.

HORSEMAN'S TIPS

Biting often starts as playfulness when horses are young, and if not addressed appropriately, can result in resentful 'sparring', which can escalate into an aggressive spiral.

SUGGESTED EXERCISES

1–11, 13, 14, 15, 16, 17, 26, 27, 35, 41, 42, 50 and 52.

Avoiding being caught

If your horse doesn't want to be caught, you need to ask yourself why. If all you ever did with him was catch him, give him a good feed and a bit of love and then turn him out again, it is most unlikely you would have a catching problem. Now this may not be practical, but it simply illustrates that your horse needs motivation to want to be with you.

Note

You may find that he is happy to come in if it's pouring with rain, or when other horses have been caught and he is suddenly alone, or that he will only come at feed time and so on. He is motivated, and being caught is then something he wants.

So how can you motivate him to want to be with you at any time?

Take a look at the effort–reward balance in the time you spend together and work through the exercises in this book to help change the relationship to a more positive one.

Before you can do that, you have catch him in the first place. So this exercise will show you how to get him to choose to be caught.

It's all about changing his mind by controlling his footfall, applying and releasing pressure at the right time.

How do I do this?

Think of a shoal of fish darting and turning. One fish may be following another, then alongside, then in front, they change direction yet stay connected and fluid in their movement.

This is the simplest way in which I can describe what you need to do with your horse.

If he moves away when you approach, keep approaching. This pressure will cause him to move away more. Keep the pressure on (no more than necessary – you may be just walking after him). If he turns across, you turn to stay parallel with him – so reducing the pressure on him. If he stops, turns or looks at you, turn away instantly to take the pressure off by stopping and dropping your energy or turning away (see diagram below). If he walks towards you, walk away, but not so fast that you lose the connection, allow him to gain on you if he will – let him catch you!

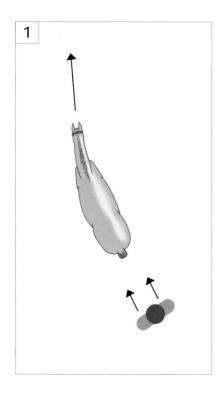

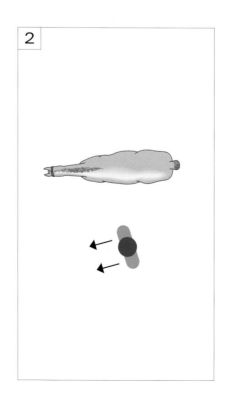

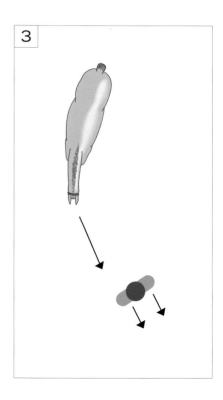

If he stops and looks but doesn't come towards you, stop and wait a while and then approach him quietly, with low energy but without looking creepy! Breathe, smile and approach him from an angle or walk in a ziz-zag pattern towards his shoulder rather than face to face.

If he leaves again, repeat the process from the start.

This may take many repetitions. Be patient!

You are exhibiting your ability to move his feet and through doing this your horse will start to see you differently.

When he finally allows you close enough to touch, don't grab him – scratch him or stroke him, make it a pleasure. Show him the halter, and if he takes off again, you have not created enough desire in him to be with you. Repeat the process.

Note

The only time you take pressure off is when he stops leaving. Reward the right thing only. At any other time you need to keep him moving!

HORSEMAN'S TIPS

Horses are gregarious herd animals that rely on numbers for safety. The herd must be bonded to keep it together. The more an individual is isolated and pushed out the more he wants to 'join-up' and return to the group and the stronger that bond becomes.

Remember

❏ Horses vote with their feet!
❏ The more anxious we are to catch him, the more we tend to resort to stealth – our predatory nature makes us want to capture our prey.
❏ Horses are extremely sensitive to intention. Our body language shows what we intend in ways that are sometimes too subtle for us to read, but not for our horses.
❏ Show your horse that leaving has consequences – that is, pressure, either mental or physical – and that comfort is only to be found with you.
❏ The smaller the paddock, the more concentrated this experience will be. It will still work in a big area but will take longer and you will have to travel a lot more. So get him into a smaller space if you possibly can before trying this.
❏ Try to think of it as a game of chess rather than a game of chase. There is no need to chase him around at speed. The more 'left brained' the whole experience, the better, safer and more positive it will be.

SUGGESTED EXERCISES

1–11, 16, 17, 19, 20, 60, 62, 77 and 84.

Loading in a trailer

Given a horse's strength, panicky nature and instinct to fight his way out of a trap, the only loading that is safe is loading that the horse consents to.

Why is loading a problem?

Loading in a trailer is a trust test. Does he trust that he will come out alive?

To a horse a trailer is a potential death trap – if you have ever travelled in the back of a trailer, you will probably agree. It's horrible!

On the whole, lorries give a better ride and many horses are less worried by them, but in both cases you can run into huge opposition from a horse that doesn't want to load.

How do I do this?

Apart from the many methods used to load without the horse's consent, there are also many ways that can help him decide that it's not such a bad choice after all.

It's a huge subject. It could fill a whole book on its own, so here I can only make some broad suggestions of techniques to try, and the more you build a relationship based on trust and communication, the easier it will become.

Look for the obvious, non-confrontational approaches first. For example, can you make the trailer more appealing somehow? – open it right up without the partition, let him walk right though, stop a while inside and then let him out, feed him in there and so on. Help him feel more confident.

Sometimes it may only take a small change to make a big difference to the horse, and certainly the more time you put aside to practise, the better – because you will be in less of a rush to get the job done. Horses don't work to timescales, but they are intensely aware of our intention. The more we want something, the more suspicious they become. So the first course of action is make sure you don't have an agenda when you work on trailer loading – for example, don't leave it until you need to go somewhere!

If your horse is simply too sceptical to consider the trailer, even when it's opened up, you will have to help him start to see the trailer in a different way. Not as a death trap but as a place where he finds relative comfort.

Remember, comfort means doing nothing. So get him doing something active outside the trailer and give him the option to stand still and rest near it (and ultimately, in it).

You can teach him to seek the trailer (see Exercise 55) by giving him a job to do – for example, walk or trot in small circles over the ramp for a few circuits till he would like to stop (Figure 1). Then offer him the trailer as a stopping place. Do nothing if he stops there, or tries in any way to investigate the trailer – this is the curiosity you want. He might sniff it, or

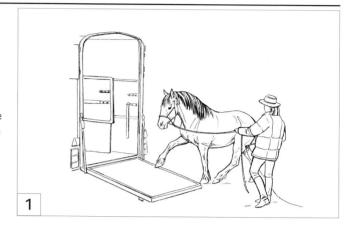

1

paw at the ramp and this is great. Leave him alone while he is trying.

When he stops trying, go back to the job – he only gets to rest when he has made a try.

For safety, I prefer the loading technique where you remain outside the trailer standing beside the ramp and send the horse in by creating some rhythmic pressure behind his driveline. However, it demands excellent timing and you may find you can lead him in satisfactorily but not send him in. This is fine to begin with but try to get to where you can stay outside so you don't need an assistant to do up the breeching bar. It is a much more sound gauge of your horse's confidence if he can lead the way in to the trailer and much more practical if you are loading alone.

So when he is showing an interest in the trailer, stand at the side of the ramp next to the body of the trailer and give him a clear feel on the lead rope by extending your arm into the trailer and asking him to step forward (Figure 2). If he doesn't, support your request with degrees of pressure using the technique you learned in Exercise 4 (Figure 3) – lift your stick above his rump, tap is rump lightly with rhythm, then firmly with rhythm. It doesn't need to be hard, just firm enough that he can't ignore you. Keep tapping until he makes a try, then release (Figure 4). Be happy to accept one step at a time.

He may become agitated and pull back, allow some drift on the rope travelling with him if necessary but keep the feel on it until he comes forwards again (see Exercise 3) (Figure 5). Gradually, he will learn what is required. It takes patience and practice to get your feel, timing and balance between pressure and release.

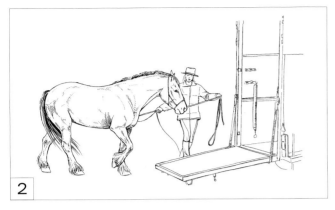

2

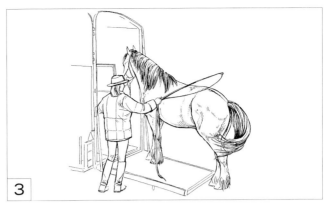

3

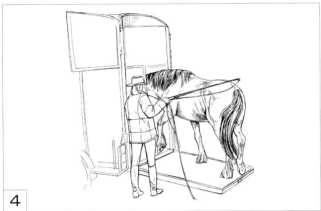

4

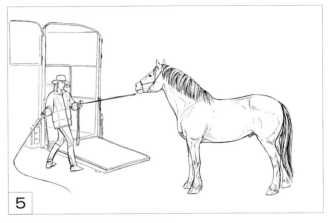

5

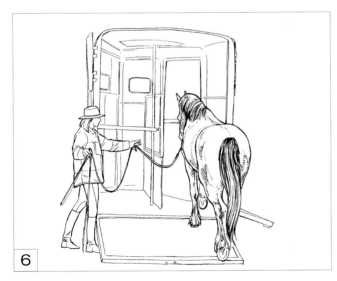

6

If your horse will go in but then backs out again, allow this (or you will just reinforce his sense that it is not safe to be in there). It is very tempting to try to stop him coming out because it seems counter productive to let him out, but it is actually not. Remember that confidence comes in thresholds – if he is rushing out, it tells you he is not yet confident to stay in, and because of this is not ready for the breaching bar. If you put that bar across when he is still thinking about coming out, he may well panic when he feels it blocking his exit.

So, let him come out, but remind him that the consequence is that there is pressure outside. After a while, you will notice that he will start to be more attracted to the trailer, eventually loading himself when you point inside it!

Don't even attempt to do up the breeching bar until:

❑ He walks in confidently and is happy to stay there.
❑ You can ask him to come half-way out and then send him back in again several times.
❑ If he starts to come out, you only have to tap the root of his tail lightly and he goes back in again.
❑ Once he is confident with the breeching bar up behind him for a few moments, undo it and let him out. Repeat many times, increasing the length of time his is inside, adding the ramp and short journeys to your progressive training.

Note
❑ Bars are far preferable to webbing straps and should be lower than the point of the horse's buttock.
❑ Never tie him up before the bar is up, as he may pull back and then panic.

SUGGESTED EXERCISES

1–11, 16, 20, 27, 30, 36, 37, 41, 42, 46, 48, 49 and 55.

HORSEMAN'S TIPS

Accidents can happen – because of the horse's inherent nature, something can trigger a prey animal reaction and result in a wreck no matter how well prepared you are. However, the better he can control his emotions, the more likely he is to think instead of panic; so the more exercises you can work through, the better prepared you will both be before tackling the trailer loading.

Scrambling or falling in a trailer

Scrambling in a trailer is a horrible experience, for both horse and human. Sometimes it happens as a one off, and sometimes it becomes a pattern that in extreme cases can happen as soon as the vehicle starts to move.

Often it is not clear what causes it and it is the source of much debate, as is how to handle it.

Note

The width and headroom, floor surface, driving technique and travelling position all need thinking about in an attempt to improve the experience and reduce stress caused to the horse. As horses are deeply claustrophobic, the smaller the space available, the more stressful the experience and may be partly why many horses seem to prefer lorries to trailers. If the footing is slippery, you can add rubber matting, sand, or wood shavings and this will also help reduce the amount of vibration transmitted through the floorboards.

Some horses seem to lose their balance possibly because they can't get their feet far enough apart. For example, it seems to be more common problem going around a left-hand bend when the horse is on the right of the trailer, suggesting he can't spread his legs to the right for support, and others stand very stiffly and won't move their feet around inside the trailer to find their balance.

More research and information is needed and you should have him checked by your vet before trying to travel him again. If he is given a clean bill of health, there are techniques you can try which are sometimes successful.

What can I do about it?

Help him get over his claustrophobia by working on lots of variations of Exercises 41 and 42.

Work on Exercise 48 to help your horse reach the point where he can stand all four feet on the box and move around on top of it without losing his balance or becoming emotional. Reach a level where you can ask him to hang a front leg or hind leg off the box so he is standing on three legs without worrying.

Work on the see-saw also in Exercise 48, again it helps his balance, emotional and physical.

You may find that if you take the partition out of the trailer, he can position himself for better balance, or try travelling him facing backwards or even loose (check with the trailer manufacturer that it will be correctly balanced for this).

Research indicates that horses travel better when facing backwards or loose and are more relaxed and have lower heart rates. Many seem to travel well at an angle too, Indeed, if travelled loose, they will usually choose an angled position that helps them keep their balance.

One advantage of travelling without the partition is that if a horse does go down he can get up more easily, but this is only suitable for horses travelling alone.

If you have to travel with another horse, try to use a partition that doesn't go right to the floor, so he can space his legs out to be balanced – though if you know he is prone to this, I would not recommend you travel with another horse as you have double trouble if he goes down.

SUGGESTED EXERCISES
1–11, 27, 30, 41, 42, 43, 48 and 49.

Index